I0759576

KATHERINE MANSFIELD

KATHERINE MANSFIELD

A Hidden Life

GERRI KIMBER

REAKTION BOOKS

For John Wood

Published by
REAKTION BOOKS LTD
2–4 Sebastian Street
London EC1V 0HE, UK
www.reaktionbooks.co.uk

First published 2025

EU GPSR Authorised Representative
Logos Europe, 9 rue Nicolas Poussin, 17000, La Rochelle, France
email: contact@logoseurope.eu

Printed and bound in Great Britain by Bell & Bain, Glasgow

A catalogue record for this book is available from the British Library

ISBN 978 1 83639 162 3

CONTENTS

Publicity portrait of Mansfield, 1921.

Note on the Text

Knowing what to call Katherine Mansfield in a biography is always a problem. Born Kathleen Mansfield Beauchamp, even when still at school she had already started to reject that name. Calling her first Kathleen and then Katherine later on would be confusing. I have therefore opted for Mansfield throughout.

Mansfield frequently uses style ellipses in both her personal writing and her short stories. Where these occur, the stops (which vary in number) are double-spaced thus: . . . To avoid any confusion, all omission ellipses are therefore placed in square brackets [. . .]. The use of underlines in Mansfield's personal writing reflects the text as she wrote it.

Unless otherwise indicated, all references to Mansfield's works are to the editions listed at the start of the References and abbreviated as indicated. All letters, diary and notebook entries (not just Mansfield's) are quoted verbatim, without the use of the editorial '[*sic*]'. Frequently used library references are also listed in the endmatter.

Introduction

The long weekend that Katherine Mansfield spent at Garsington Manor, the home of Philip and Lady Ottoline Morrell near Oxford, from 13 to 17 July 1916, was a hectic one, with numerous literary and artistic visitors. One such visitor was the writer Lytton Strachey, who wrote the following letter to his Bloomsbury Group friend Virginia Woolf on 17 July:

> There were 16 souls here for the week-end that's just over: from Friday onwards the door seemed to open every two hours and new arrivals appeared in batches of five or seven. [. . .]
>
> Among the rout was 'Katherine Mansfield' – if that's her real name – I could never quite make sure. Have you ever heard of her? Or read any of her productions? She wrote some rather – in fact distinctly – bright storyettes in a wretched little thing called the Signature, which you may have seen, under the name of Matilda Berry. She was decidedly an interesting creature, I thought – very amusing and sufficiently mysterious. She spoke with great enthusiasm about the Voyage Out, and said she wanted to make your acquaintance more than anyone else's. So I said I thought it might be managed. Was I rash? I really believe you'll find her entertaining. But just now she's in the recesses of Cornwall, so it must be later on, if at all. I may add that she has an ugly impassive mask of a face – cut in wood, with brown hair and brown eyes very far apart; and a sharp and slightly vulgarly-fanciful intellect sitting behind it.[1]

This was the first time Mansfield was discussed by Bloomsbury proper, and it wasn't altogether a flattering portrait. She, of course, was enacting her normal levels of dissembling and pretending, while deciding which of these new acquaintances would be worth cultivating. And she may well have spoken enthusiastically about Woolf's first novel, *The Voyage Out*, but the truth was she hadn't actually read it. After her visit, she took Ottoline Morrell's copy home with her, returning it a month later. In that sense, Strachey's portrait of Mansfield as amusing, mysterious and sharp is perceptively accurate.

A little over a year later, with Bloomsbury gossipmongers divided over whether they liked her or not, Mansfield dined at Virginia and Leonard Woolf's house in Richmond. Virginia happened to have started keeping a regular diary and the entry for 11 October 1917 thus records:

> The dinner last night went off: the delicate things were discussed. We could both wish that one's first impression of K.M. was not that she stinks like a – well civet cat that had taken to street walking. In truth, I'm a little shocked by her commonness at first sight; lines so hard & cheap. However, when this diminishes, she is so intelligent & inscrutable that she repays friendship.[2]

Mansfield was indeed rather fond of an expensive French perfume called 'Genêt Fleurie' – 'Flowering Broom' – but scent was not approved of in the rarefied air of Bloomsbury, and she could not have known that a little spray of perfume would so upset the delicate olfactory balance of the woman who would famously become her literary sparring partner. Mansfield shortened her hems as soon as she was able. She wore brightly coloured clothes and scarlet stockings, and cut her hair in a bob when other women were still only vaguely thinking about it. She was risqué, she was modern, she was entertaining. But more than any of that, she had a supreme gift for storytelling that has rarely been equalled – and indeed it was a gift that started at an early age. Between the ages of fifteen and eighteen, she and her two elder sisters had been educated at Queen's College in London. Many years later, she recalled one of her first lessons at the school:

> [A teacher asked] any young lady in the room to hold up her hand if she had been chased by a wild bull & as nobody else did

> I held up mine (though of course I hadn't). Ah, he said, I am afraid you do not count. You are a little savage from New Zealand – which was really a trifle exacting – for it must be the rarest thing to be chased by a wild bull up & down Harley Street, Wimpole Street, Welbeck Street, Queen Anne, round & round Cavendish Square.[3]

The essence of Mansfield is encapsulated in this quotation: the fabricator, dissembler – and born entertainer. As Leonard Woolf recalled, many years after her death,

> By nature, I think, she was gay, cynical, amoral, ribald, witty. When we first knew her she was extraordinarily amusing. I don't think anyone has ever made me laugh more than she did in those days. She would sit very upright on the edge of a chair or sofa and tell at immense length a kind of saga, of her experiences as an actress [. . .] [T]he extraordinary funniness of the story was increased by the flashes of her astringent wit. I think that in some abstruse way [John Middleton] Murry corrupted and perverted and destroyed Katherine both as a person and a writer [. . .] Her gifts were those of an intense realist, with a superb sense of ironic humour and fundamental cynicism.[4]

This, then, in brief, is the person who is the subject of this biography: a feisty, charismatic, highly intelligent young woman who lived life to the full, who, as we shall see, experimented with all sorts of ways of living and who paid bitterly for her mistakes later in her life. But above all else, her main *raison d'être* was always her writing; nothing else was truly important.

Katherine Mansfield is that rare thing – a writer exclusively associated with the short story. Anthea Trodd pointed out that at the time she was writing, 'the brevity and relative marginality of this still, in English, fairly new form, offered her a refuge analogous to that of children's fiction.'[5] For many readers and critics, the perception was that Mansfield *was* almost writing children's fiction, since most of her stories are deceptively easy to read, although her themes are entirely adult in both form and content. Yet this notional superficiality of her stories, together with the premise that the short story is perceived to be a lesser form than the novel, meant that for many years Mansfield was viewed as a minor writer, though 'marginal' would be a more appropriate term. The development of her own particular free indirect discourse form of writing culminated in her position as an early exponent of the Modernist short story. Indeed, critic Peter Childs goes so far as to state that she became 'the most important Modernist author who wrote only short stories'.[6] Her themes incorporate violence, war, death, childbirth and relationships – especially in marriage – together with feminist and sexual issues. Her stories develop over the course of time into 'slices of life' – glimpses into the lives of individuals and families, captured at a certain moment, frozen in time like a painting or a photograph. On the whole, a single 'main' event is revealed and developed, and no case is presented for or against the characters' actions or their life; they simply 'are'. Above all, Mansfield developed a mastery of the art of being brief: there is nothing superfluous in her stories.

Mansfield, ever the innovator and seeker after new experiences, was fascinated with the then-new medium of the cinema. Her narrative art reflects this interest in the deliberate cinematic impression of so many of the stories; it is as if the narrator has a moving camera, panning across, and then focusing in, something that provides so many of the stories with their unique 'pictorial' quality. Indeed, in the last weeks of her life she even spoke about having been a camera in her quotidian observations: 'I've been a selective camera,' she said, but now she wanted 'to widen [. . .] the scope of my camera'.[7] One technique – *in medias res* – which acts as a marker for these particular stories is the way they begin, cutting straight through to the action from the very first line, as if a stage or film direction is being given, with the use of temporal constructions implying a prior knowledge of the event being described. A famous example is the beginning of 'The Garden Party': 'And after all, the weather was ideal.'[8] In that 'And after all', the reader is left to fill in the gap – the endless conversations and concerns about whether the weather would be fine for the Sheridan family's garden party. The theatrical/cinematic tone is also enhanced in some of the longer stories by their division into episodes or 'scenes': 'Prelude', 'At the Bay' and 'The Daughters of the Late Colonel' are each divided into twelve 'scenes'.

In free indirect discourse, we are never told which thoughts belong to which character: instead, the narrative moves between a more conventional narrator and a character's conscious thoughts. The result is an intimate method of storytelling, where, for certain moments, we *become* the character on the page. This use of free indirect discourse would become a hallmark of Mansfield's narrative technique, together with the episodic nature of certain stories and their theatrical quality; as Mansfield remarked in a letter discussing one of her most famous stories, 'Prelude': 'What form is it? you ask. [. . .] As far I know its more or less my own invention.'[9] Some years later, she referred to it as 'the Prelude method – it just unfolds and opens.'[10]

Mansfield's use of Joycean 'epiphanies', or, to use her own words, the 'blazing moment', is another prominent technique in her narrative art, exemplified in the title of one of her most famous stories, 'Bliss', although the sense of 'bliss' in this story underlies more uncomfortable feelings of self-discovery. Mansfield herself uses the word 'blissful' in the following letter, talking of the epiphanic moment:

> God forbid that another should ever live the life I have known here and yet there are moments you know, old Boy, when after a dark day there comes a sunset – such a glowing gorgeous marvellous sky that one forgets all – in the beauty of it – these are the moments when I am really writing – Whatever happens I have had these blissful, perfect moments and they are worth living for.[11]

Mansfield's narrative technique is characterized by a focus on the inner lives of her characters, a willingness to experiment with form and structure, and a deep engagement with the complexities of human experience. Her symbolism is constant, echoing recurrent themes. Mansfield challenges her reader to look beyond mere appearances, to confront superficiality, to despise cruelty, to deny false values, to revert to the notions and viewpoints of children, and, through this reversal, to overthrow the rules of society and to recreate laws governing life that are more spontaneous and less bigoted. While never offering a direct theoretical manifesto, her stories nonetheless reinforce her status as possibly the twentieth century's most gifted short-story writer.

Katherine Mansfield has not been short of biographers since her death in 1923, but this latest biography offers a new focus, where the complicated bond between Mansfield and her husband, John Middleton

Murry, is fully revealed for the first time, demonstrating how it was far from the loving relationship superficially portrayed in most of their letters, when Mansfield tended to obscure what she was actually feeling. As time went by, and their literary fame grew, both she and Murry became more acutely aware of posterity and publication – as evidenced in Murry's bowdlerized early editions of Mansfield's letters. In addition, there was another complication in their relationship – the covert, long-term bond between Mansfield and the editor of the *New Age*, A. R. Orage, which truly came to define her life – both artistic and personal – and her death.

In transcribing Mansfield's letters for publication, I had already come to a deep-seated understanding of the amount of dissembling in her missives to Murry: outwardly loving, she remained inwardly tormented by the fact that there never was a couple less suited to each other than they were, as Leonard Woolf so astutely recognized. At no point in their relationship did Murry ever *truly* step up to the mark. But one man nearly always did – Orage. Sadly, Orage famously never kept letters. We only have one from Mansfield to him still in existence, plus the short draft of another. Nevertheless, my suspicions were confirmed when I made contact with Orage scholar John Wood, who had written extensive notes on the subject but never published them, and who so generously allowed me to make use of his research for this biography.

What we uncovered together was a deep-seated relationship, both sexual and intellectual, which supported Mansfield throughout her adult life, and which left regrets on both sides – especially the realization that, because of their personal circumstances, neither of them was able to fully explore that relationship. But if any proof were needed of Orage's significance for Mansfield, one need only look to the last year of her life, and especially those precious few weeks spent together at George Gurdjieff's Institute for the Harmonious Development of Man in Fontainebleau-Avon.

While this biography examines Mansfield's work and life, it also traces that relationship with Orage, from its earliest beginnings, through frustrations and outward aloofness, to various rapprochements and covert liaisons, finally wending its complicated and thwarted route to its ultimate conclusion, in a way that has never been revealed before. Along the way, it uncovers other friendships and relationships barely acknowledged by other biographers, which all influenced Mansfield's personal and creative life. Those famously difficult and complex years between 1909 and 1911, nearly all evidence of which Mansfield so systematically destroyed, were, in fact, even more complicated – and wretched – than has previously been suggested. And her early relationship with Murry was far from the blissful coming together of two literary rising stars that he portrayed in all his writings about his dead wife. Friends and acquaintances of course knew the truth – or at least some of it, for Mansfield was a world-class champion at hiding details of her private life from those around her. But they knew enough to be certain that, after her death, the saintly Mansfield portrayed in the non-stop stream of sycophantically edited books by Murry bore little resemblance to the personality they had known. Such Machiavellian dealings led to Murry becoming widely vilified for his approach, which thereafter tainted his reputation – as well as Mansfield's – until after his death in 1957.

In particular, in the aftermath of Mansfield's death in January 1923 Murry started printing several pieces of Mansfield's work in every issue of his newly founded magazine, the *Adelphi*, beginning with the very first one in June 1923, and this editorial policy continued for two years. The amount of space given over to the Mansfield publicity machine became ever greater, until even her closest friends and admirers turned away in disgust. As Frank Lea, Murry's biographer, remarked, Mansfield 'became the presiding genius of the paper – till even the friendly Bennett was forced to remonstrate, while with the unfriendly it became an article of faith that Murry was "exploiting his wife's reputation"'.[12] And as book after book started appearing – of her so-called 'journal', her letters, her unpublished and incomplete stories, her 'scrapbook' (there never was such a thing), her reviews – the remonstrations became ever more vociferous. As Jenny McDonnell notes, 'Sylvia Lynd described [Murry's] generation of a Mansfield industry as "boiling Katherine's bones to make soup", while Lawrence claimed he "made capital out of her death"'.[13]

Murry most certainly had an agenda in promoting Mansfield's work, with himself as the sole guardian of her literary legacy. Nowhere is this more clearly seen than in his dealings with the young American student Ruth Mantz, who in the late 1920s wrote to Murry, seeking his permission to write a full biography of Mansfield's life. From his initial offer of help, Murry was soon installed as co-author, and straitjacketed Mantz's attempts to write the biography she intended. Thus Murry was able to end that first biography from 1933, *The Life of Katherine Mansfield*, in 1912 – at the beginning of Mansfield's relationship with him – directing the reader for all further information on her life to the published volumes of her so-called journal and letters, severely edited, of course, by himself. Murry's other main goal was to wipe virtually all evidence of Orage from Mansfield's personal life, and in that aim he was supremely successful.

Subsequent biographies were forced to make use of Murry's editions of Mansfield's works, and especially her personal writing – letters and notebook entries – unless the authors were able to see the original manuscript material for themselves (not an easy task, given that it was – and still is – spread over several continents). This biography is the first to draw on the most recent, fully annotated editions of her works, both fiction and non-fiction, as well as new transcriptions of her letters. These nine volumes have brought to life a fresh, vibrant and more complicated Mansfield than has previously seen the light of day.[14] And, in uncovering the true extent of Orage's influence on Mansfield – and not just in 1910–11 – it will be impossible for future biographers to ignore what was possibly the most significant relationship of her entire life.

1

Childhood, 1888–1908

Kathleen Mansfield Beauchamp (1888–1923), only later to become known as Katherine Mansfield, was born into a formidable colonial clan of high-spirited adventurers, known affectionately in the family as 'Pa-men', for whom adversity was a welcome challenge and who were determined to make good. The lives of the various Beauchamp 'Pa-men' ancestors, who originated from Highgate in North London and were celebrated for their larger-than-life personalities and pioneering spirit, would captivate Mansfield's imagination both as a child and an adult. Her great-grandparents were John Beauchamp (1781–1852), the last in the line of family silversmiths, celebrated as the 'poet of Hornsey Lane' because of his love of poetry, and Ann Stone (1796–1859). They had seven sons: Horatio, Arthur, Cradock, Samuel, Ralph, Frederick and Henry Herron, all of whom emigrated to Australia with varying degrees of success. Indeed, Great-Uncle Henry Herron would go on to play a significant role in Mansfield's early life, as we shall see.

Two of the sons, Cradock and Arthur, made the journey from Australia to New Zealand in 1861–2, where their father's sister, Jane Beauchamp, had bought several parcels of land in Wellington in 1839. They sold their aunt's bequests, however, preferring what they considered to be the safety of a tiny corner in the north of New Zealand's South Island, near the little town of Picton. Wellington was considered too much of a risk, having been largely demolished by three recent major earthquakes, in 1840, 1848 and 1855. Cradock set up home on 80 hectares (200 ac) of bush at Anakiwa on Queen Charlotte Sound with his wife Harriet, where a young Mansfield, together with her siblings, would spend frequent holidays.

Arthur Beauchamp (1827–1910), John Beauchamp's sixth son and Mansfield's grandfather, was the most celebrated of all the 'Pa-men'. His restless nature and inability to settle anywhere for long prompted many family stories, some apocryphal. It was said that his chickens were so used to being transported to new locations that, at the merest sight of a move, they would lie on their backs with their feet in the air, ready to be trussed up. Arthur, a witty and engaging individual, had married his young bride, Mary Elizabeth Stanley (1836–1917), in 1854, while still in Australia. (Harold, Mansfield's father, was their first surviving child, and he would go on to become the eldest of eight siblings.) He set himself up as a general merchant and auctioneer, and soon prospered.

Arthur's restlessness, however, soon got the better of him, and his long-suffering wife and family endured numerous moves around New Zealand, finally returning once more to Picton in 1907, where he died in 1910 at the age of 82. (This restlessness would be inherited by his granddaughter, Mansfield, who resembled him far more than she ever did her own father.) Arthur's wife, Mary, lived another seven years,

Harold Beauchamp, *c.* 1910.

dying in 1917. Mansfield's father, Harold Beauchamp (1858–1938), was the antithesis of his itinerant father, Arthur, and yet, in his own way, he was no less colourful a character. Solid, dependable, but with a strong ambitious streak, at the height of his career he was one of the richest businessmen in New Zealand, chairman of the Bank of New Zealand and eventually knighted for his services to the nation's commerce in 1923. Harold revered his mother and understood that his father's nomadic traits had made her life challenging. He therefore determined that the women in his own family would be offered every security and advantage that money could provide, and Mansfield certainly became a beneficiary of this approach. In addition, Harold's enjoyment of music and poetry (he was a proficient singer and pianist), inherited from his Beauchamp ancestors, would also run in the blood of his children, and especially his third daughter, born Kathleen Mansfield Beauchamp. However, if Harold could have chosen one of his grandfather John Beauchamp's sons as a father, it would undoubtedly have been Henry Herron Beauchamp (after whom he named his precious only son, Leslie, accidentally misspelling Herron on the birth certificate, so that Leslie's middle name was, in fact, 'Heron'). Henry's work ethic and success in Australia meant that within twenty years he was able to return to England a wealthy man. Harold only met his uncle for the first time aged seventeen in 1875, Henry having travelled to New Zealand to visit his brothers Cradock and Arthur. Uncle and nephew immediately hit it off, engendering a warm relationship that lasted until Henry's death in 1907.

Harold's early life was based in Picton, where his father Arthur had settled in 1861. He left school at fourteen, and immediately started working for his father in the family's auctioneering business. In 1876 Arthur eventually moved his family to Wellington, where he set up yet another auctioneering company: Beauchamp, Campbell & Company. Harold left his father's business on 7 May 1877 in order to join W. W. Bannatyne & Company, an established firm of Wellington importers, where he would work his way up to become a partner and ultimately a director. When he joined the firm, Wellington had been the capital of New Zealand for a mere twelve years. In the rapidly developing economic climate, the rather run-down Bannatyne's soon started to thrive, and Harold became indispensable.

Early on at Bannatyne's, Harold had met – and become infatuated with – fourteen-year-old Annie Dyer, the sister of Joseph Dyer, a clerk at the company. His mind firmly set, Harold waited patiently for six years before marrying her on 18 February 1884 at St Paul's Cathedral in Wellington. Annie, always frail following a severe bout of rheumatic fever in her childhood that had weakened her heart, also came from a close family. Her mother, Margaret Isabella Dyer – Mansfield's beloved 'Grandma', who features in numerous stories – would take over the running of Harold's household for thirteen years. Having brought up nine children of her own, yet still only in her late forties, she became instrumental in the care of Harold's own brood. Annie's younger sister, Isabella Dyer, known to the Beauchamps as Aunt Belle, would also move in with Harold and Annie after their marriage, alongside her mother, as would another sister, Edith (known as Kitty), for a short time. It was Belle who accompanied the family to London and looked after Mansfield and her two sisters during their time at Queen's College in Harley Street. Belle brought vitality and a liveliness to the household that Annie could not, due to her delicate health. In Annie's place, she partnered Harold at tennis and cards, sang while Harold played the piano and generally helped to entertain guests.

Annie's older sister, Agnes, married Frederick Valentine Waters, known as Uncle Val; with their two sons, Barrie and Eric, they were frequent visitors to the Beauchamp household, together with their spaniel. When Harold eventually moved his family to the small settlement of Karori in 1893, the Waters family moved as well, renting a smaller house nearby. The childhood of the Beauchamp and Waters children would be a close-knit one, as Mansfield would later depict in her Burnell stories. In 1897 Annie's brother Frank would marry the daughter of the then New Zealand prime minister, Richard Seddon, thus firmly allying Harold to New Zealand's great and powerful.

Wellington at the time of Mansfield's birth in 1888 was a small town by today's standards, with a population of around 28,000, and marked by a massive disparity in the lives of the rich and poor. Some parts of the town resembled medieval London in that there was no drainage or sewers, slops were thrown outside and some streets 'resembled a charnel house with masses of bones and animal matter lying around'.[1] Even worse, some tenants took in hospital laundry in order to make a living and used poultices and dressings were simply left lying in the streets. Whatever the immigrants had brought with them by way of household goods, clothes and so on were all sold to pay steep rents and buy food, and when these were gone, homelessness was a real and ever-present fear.

Annie Burnell Beauchamp, *c.* 1908.

Nevertheless, the upwardly mobile Harold Beauchamp and his family would know a different and more prosperous life from his own itinerant and unstable childhood. Following their marriage, Harold and Annie, together with her mother and two sisters, rented various properties in Thorndon, and then moved to a house Harold had had built in the Wellington suburb of Wadestown. Their first child, Vera Margaret, was born there on 22 October 1885, followed by Charlotte Mary (known as Chaddie or Marie) on 9 July 1887. But, as Harold recorded, 'finding the wind at Wadestown intolerable, I acquired the lease of a section, No. 11 Tinakori Road, and erected a house on it.'[2] Tinakori Road, in

Thorndon, was an excellent location in several respects for both Harold and his growing young family, who took up residence at the beginning of 1888. It was near to the harbour and his work at Bannatyne's, and St Paul's Cathedral was a short walk away for Sunday services, as were the burgeoning Botanic Gardens further up the Tinakori Road. Thorndon itself was a 'mixed' area of the well-to-do and the very poor. A pedestrian suspension bridge crossed a steep gully leading to the large and gracious houses on Hobson Street, while below, in narrow lanes such as Little George Street, were the poorest neighbourhoods (later depicted in detail in the story 'The Garden Party' (1921)).

Here it was then, in Thorndon, that Mansfield spent the first five years of her life, born upstairs in the back bedroom on the right, at 11 (now 25) Tinakori Road, on 14 October 1888, a Sunday morning. She was just six months old when, having developed jaundice, she was taken to Anakiwa by her grandmother, together with her two older sisters, Vera and Chaddie, to stay with Great-Uncle Cradock and his wife, Harriet. As she grew up, the 'middle' misfit of five siblings, Mansfield would develop a sense of solitariness and isolation that would stay with her all her life, and which, early on, mutated into irrational fears – mainly of the dark and of the wind – turning into nightmares that also haunted her as an adult.

Another child was born in the house on 11 October 1890, almost exactly two years after Mansfield's own birth: Gwendoline Burnell Beauchamp. Cholera would kill Gwendoline just three months later, on 9 January 1891 (curiously the same day and month as Mansfield's own death). Harold's brother Charles died of typhoid in Wellington in 1892 and just a year later his sister Florence, aged 31, would die of the same disease. There is a poignant photograph of Grandma Dyer holding the dead baby Gwendoline (a mawkish Victorian custom), with the windows of a large doll's house visible in the top left-hand corner, which Mansfield would later go on to immortalize in one of her most celebrated stories, 'The Doll's House' (1921). Ironically, Gwendoline would end up the only one of Harold and Annie's six children to be buried in New Zealand. Her small grave can still be seen in its original location in Wellington's Bolton Street cemetery (numerous other graves having been controversially moved – or destroyed – to make way for a motorway). Poor Annie could scarcely have recovered from the death of Gwendoline when she fell pregnant again just a few months later; Jeanne Worthington Beauchamp was born on 20 May 1892, also at 11 Tinakori

Road. From this time onwards, however, family sources reveal that Annie's famous aloofness (exemplified by Linda Burnell in 'Prelude' and 'At the Bay') really came to the fore. She was worn out from child-bearing and the loss of a baby, and so the role of mother was handed over to her own mother, as were the housekeeping and the cooking.

Following the recent deaths of so many family members from infectious disease, Harold Beauchamp took the bold step of moving his young family away from Wellington, thus hoping to prevent any further deaths.[3] He took a five-year lease on a large house with a 5.5-hectare (14 ac) garden (more of a 'farmlet', as he himself noted) called Chesney Wold, named after the estate of Sir Leicester Dedlock and Honoria, Lady Dedlock, in Charles Dickens's novel *Bleak House*. The house at 372 Karori Road was 5 kilometres (3 mi.) from Wellington, in the small settlement of Karori, surrounded by what was then mainly open country. In the large gardens of Chesney Wold were trees and flowerbeds, surrounded by paddocks, an orchard and various stables and farm buildings. In front of it, a circular drive that did its best to look grand swept around a shrubbery and a lawn, in the middle of which grew a solitary aloe (made famous in the story 'Prelude' (1917)). It was hard to imagine a more perfect setting for raising children, and Mansfield spent five of the most formative years of her childhood there, until the age of ten. Years later, as a professional writer, she would draw on her rich memories

Mansfield, 1898.

of her Karori childhood to fashion some of the most memorable stories ever written by a New Zealand author, using innovative, experimental techniques that we now associate with literary Modernism.

As noted earlier, Mansfield was often a lonely child. As the middle of five children, she never 'belonged' to the older set of Vera and Chaddie, yet was too young to play with the 'babies', Jeanne and the newly arrived son, Leslie Heron (known to the family as Chummie or 'Boy'), who had been born on 21 February 1894 in the civilized surroundings of Nurse Patrick's private hospital in Upper Featherston Terrace in Thorndon, less than a year after the family's move to Karori. Mansfield, then prone to chubbiness (the Nathan boys who had lived next door to 11 Tinakori Road used to shout 'fatty' at her over the fence), developed a fearsome temper as well as an idiosyncratic sense of humour, both traits inherited from her father. It did not help matters that in 1896 Mansfield had to start wearing steel-rimmed spectacles. Here was yet another reason for her to be singled out – to be different. No biographer has ever been able to ascertain why they were deemed necessary at this time; her capacity to note the smallest details of everyone and everything are not the normal traits of a myopic child. Nevertheless, she soon outgrew them and never wore glasses from her teenage years onwards.

In early 1898 (Mansfield had not yet turned ten), with the lease on Chesney Wold expiring later that year, Harold made the decision to

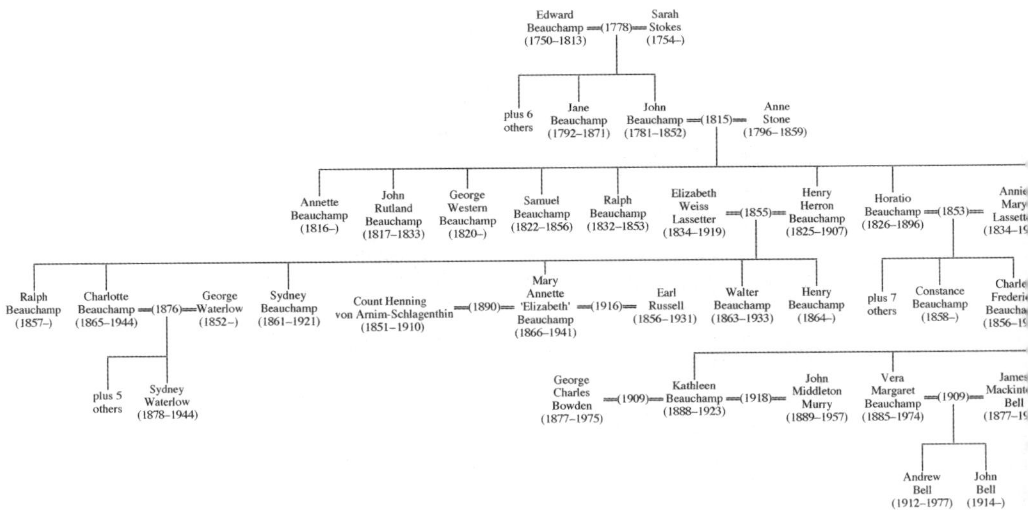

Beauchamp family tree.

move his family back to town, purchasing a fourteen-room, two-storey mansion at 75 Tinakori Road, with formal gardens and a tennis court, and a stone's throw from the prime minister's residence further up the same road. The three girls were now moved from the little school in Karori (later made famous in 'The Doll's House' (1921)) and enrolled at Wellington Girls' High School, just a short walk from no. 75. These arrangements completed, in March 1898 Harold and Annie Beauchamp made the second of their trips 'home' to England, for both business and pleasure, leaving the children in the care of Annie's mother, Grandma Dyer, and her sister Aunt Belle, together with the handyman, Pat Sheehan, and Alice, the kitchen maid. In the parents' absence, while they were still at sea, the organization, packing and move to no. 75 was undertaken in late April 1898.

Thorndon, as noted earlier, was indeed a very 'mixed' area of Wellington, with extremes of poverty and wealth living side by side. Mansfield's sensitivity, even as a child, to those less fortunate than herself is manifest in countless of her stories, and particularly in her New Zealand stories 'The Doll's House' and 'The Garden Party'. All the children were forbidden to enter Little George Street (Saunders Lane in 'The Garden Party'), which the house overlooked on its western side, an ugly little street of poor workers' cottages, always prone to flooding (something that never affected no. 75, of course, built high up on the hill).

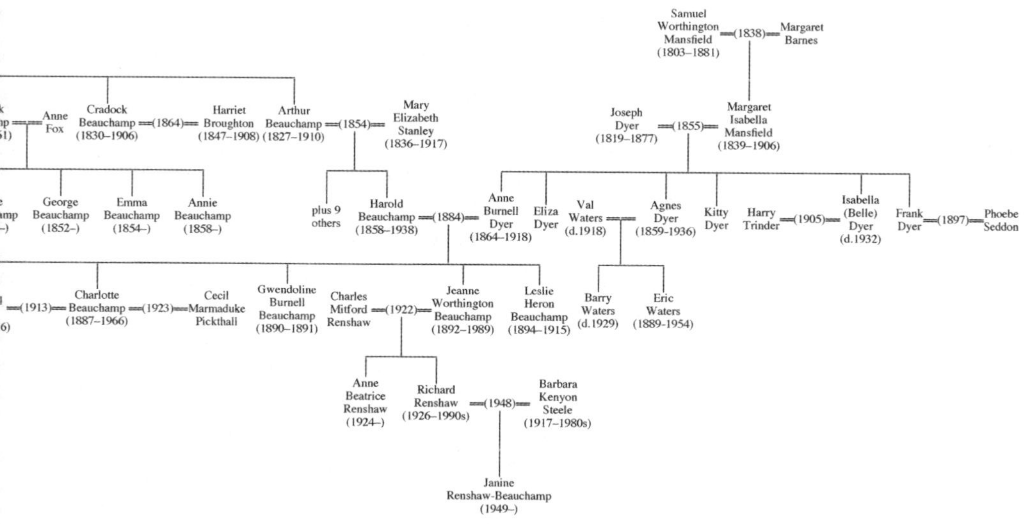

Beauchamp family, 1898. Mansfield is in the back row, second from right.

Harold and Annie finally arrived back in New Zealand in November and were quick to take up their old life, but with more panache and style, as befitted his role as a prominent Wellington businessman and hers as a charming – if frail – society hostess. Harold's *Reminiscences* for these years reveals not only a man devoted to his growing family, but an important businessman, friend to politicians and judges, whose star was rising higher and higher, on the boards of numerous companies, chairman of the Wellington Harbour Board and a Justice of the Peace. In December he would be appointed a director of the Bank of New Zealand. The Beauchamps were clearly now in the upper echelons of a small but still very class-conscious young country.

In September 1898, two months before her parents returned from England, there occurred a landmark moment in Mansfield's life when her first short story was published in the Wellington Girls' High School magazine, the *High School Reporter*. She was just nine years old. Coincidentally, in the same month, her father's cousin, Mary Beauchamp (Henry Herron's daughter), had published her first hugely successful book, *Elizabeth and Her German Garden* (a copy was brought home for the children by their parents), and became known thereafter as Elizabeth von Arnim. Mansfield's story 'Enna Blake' is set in England

– perhaps not a surprising choice, given her parents' recent voyage. The nine-year-old Mansfield tries to imagine the countryside in England, assuming that ferns (one of the national symbols of New Zealand, where they grow prolifically) are a main feature of the flora:

> The next day was very fine. Mrs Brown proposed that they should go ferning. So soon after breakfast they started. 'It seems just the day for enjoying one's self,' said Lucy, as they climbed the hill. 'Yes,' Enna answered, 'today is much nicer here than in London.' At about twelve o'clock the two girls sat on a log and ate their dinners. 'I think it would be very nice to get some moss,' Enna said; so off they trudged. The girls spent a very happy day, and got a great many nice ferns and some beautiful moss. And that night Enna said she thought it was the nicest day she had ever spent in the country.[4]

At the end of the published story, an editorial comment by one of the senior girls notes that the story 'shows promise of great merit', thus becoming in itself the first published critique of Mansfield's fiction. In conversation with biographer Ruth Mantz in the 1930s, Vera 'remembered Kathleen's excitement that night over her printed "story"'.[5]

From 1899 to 1902 Harold leased 'The Glen', a little seaside cottage nestled into the hillside on the landward side of the Muritai Road in Eastbourne, near Days Bay, on the opposite side of the harbour to Wellington itself, only accessible at that time by ferry. The native bush ran almost down to the sandy beach and the sea; it was a perfect summer retreat, and it was here that the Beauchamp children spent their summer holidays, looking out over paddocks and sand dunes, mostly looked after by Grandma Dyer and brought so vividly to life in Mansfield's story 'At the Bay' (1921).

During 1899, Mansfield continued to attend Wellington Girls' High with her elder sisters. Her second story, 'A Happy Christmas Eve', published in the *High School Reporter* in 1899, concerns the plight of the poor from the point of view of a little rich girl, once more showing how the young Mansfield was mindful of such disparities in society:

> 'As you break up today, I am going to take you with me to town, to get the presents for our tree.' For the Courteneys were going to have a tree for the poor children that year. [. . .]

> Such a funny crowd it was that came that night, ragged and dirty, but having a look of curiosity on their faces. When they had all come, the study door was thrown open and the Christmas tree was seen in all its splendour. I wish I could have let you see the delight on the faces of the children. Really it was a sight to behold. The tree was loaded with sweets, fruits and presents and there was a present for everyone besides the sweets. Then there were games, supper at which the children ate very heartily, more games, and then they went home.[6]

The father in the story is called 'Harry', and the largesse of the rich family towards the poor tantalizingly presages elements of 'The Garden Party'. Notwithstanding these early publications and their 'promise of great merit', when Mansfield announced to visitors that she wanted to be a writer when she grew up her announcement was dismissed out of hand.

In June 1900 Wellington Girls' High School was no longer considered quite socially elevated enough for his daughters, so Harold moved

Pupils at Miss Swainson's School, Wellington, including Mansfield (second row, fifth from right) and Maata Mahupuku (front row, second from left).

all the children, including young Leslie, to Wellington's most prestigious private girls' school, 'Miss Swainson's'. Located at 20 Fitzherbert Terrace, just a short walk from no. 75, it was the best that Wellington had to offer in terms of girls' private education at that time and included a little junior school for boys. Mansfield soon became a class rebel, to the consternation of the headmistress, Mrs Henry Smith, who ruled the school with a rod of iron and expected absolute obedience and discipline. She certainly met her match in Mansfield, who became the leader of a group of girls who formed a secret club with literary aspirations, and who produced a little magazine called *The School.*

Among Mansfield's fellow pupils was a young Māori girl called Maata Mahupuku (also known as Martha Grace). She was a strikingly good-looking young girl with a Māori father and an English mother, the granddaughter of Wiremu Mahupuku, chief of the sub-tribe of Ngati Kahungunu, which technically made her a princess. She was rich (being the sole heiress of her uncle's considerable fortune) and glamorous, and although two years younger than Mansfield, the latter instantly became besotted with her, the obsession continuing long after adolescence in that all-encompassing way that was to be such a feature of Mansfield's life. Another acquaintance made at this time, Edith (Edie) Bendall, although older, would also become a close friend during 1907 and 1908. Her drawing in Mansfield's childhood autograph book, dated 1901, attests to their already burgeoning friendship.

One sometimes gets the sense that Mansfield had started writing before she started walking. Her veins coursed with words that demanded an expressive outlet from an early age. When she was just eleven years old, 'His Little Friend' was published in 1900 in the *New Zealand Graphic and Ladies' Journal*, her first professional story.[7] It is another mawkish tale of a little wretch of a boy called Bobbie, who is befriended by a kind, elderly man called John Long before Bobbie shortly thereafter succumbs to a severe cold and dies, arms outstretched towards heaven, with the words 'Yes, I'se tumin' (yes, I'm coming). Nevertheless, glimmers of future talent and techniques pervade the story. Mansfield, from an early age it seems, understood the power of idiolects and reported speech, especially for children: '"Oh, please sir", he said, "mother's ill, and we hasent got nofing to eat"'. Her sentimentality, a trait she recognized had to be reined in in her adult work, and which some critics condemned her for, is given full throttle in all her youthful work, as here: 'John's love for Bobbie increased every day, and by denying himself comforts to give little gifts to him he won the child's affection.' Even with this first publication, Mansfield was playing with her 'professional' name – she was not just 'Kathleen Beauchamp', but instead the rather grander and more adult-sounding 'Kathleen M. Beauchamp'.

A more lasting legacy, and one that would have ramifications for the rest of Mansfield's life, was meeting the Trowell family in 1901 through her piano teacher, Robert Parker, who was a close friend of the father, Thomas Trowell, having conducted him in numerous concerts. Mr Trowell was a music teacher who had emigrated from England in 1882. His family consisted of his wife, Kate, his twin sons, Thomas Arnold and Garnet Carrington, and his ten-year-old daughter, Muriel Dorothy, known as Dolly. (Another son, Lindley, had died tragically from pericarditis in 1894, aged just eight, and was buried in Karori cemetery.) The red-headed twins – who, having been born on 25 June 1887, were a year older than Mansfield – were musically very gifted, especially Tom, the more dominant twin, who played the cello, though shy Garnet was also highly proficient on the violin. In time several subscription funds would be set up, to which Harold personally donated the then considerable sum of £25, in order to pay for the boys' musical education in Europe. Together with benefit concerts and other fundraisers, the grand total of £802 was raised. It is clear that Harold and Annie's musical family were soon caught up in Wellington's excitement over the talented twins and thus began a relationship that was to prove one of the most important of Mansfield's adolescent life. Immediately, of course, Mansfield had to start learning the cello with Mr Trowell. Harold was delighted, and an instrument was purchased without delay. Her musical talents now developed rapidly; she practised hard and was soon a proficient cello player, eventually playing a repertoire not dissimilar to young Tom's.

By the end of 1902 Harold's three eldest daughters had been at Miss Swainson's for over two years. Perhaps motivated by the talk of sending the Trowell boys to Europe, Harold conceived the bold plan of sending his girls 'home' to London to be educated. Since he was now a wealthy man, this considerable expense could be easily met and there was no better way to show Wellington society how far his star had risen. Mansfield and her sisters were thrilled. Queen's College, at 45 Harley Street (which took both boarders and day pupils), was chosen on the recommendation of Annie's cousin Joseph Frank Payne, a London physician, whose own three daughters were all happily

Tom and Garnet Trowell before leaving New Zealand, August 1903, with their sister, Dolly.

enrolled there. For Mansfield especially, the next three years would decide the course of the rest of her life.

The extended Beauchamp family – a party of nine – made the outward journey to England, leaving Wellington on 29 January 1903, with Harold the proud patriarch of his good-looking and distinguished brood. In an expansive gesture, he had taken the entire passenger accommodation of the SS *Niwaru* to accommodate himself and Annie, their five children and his two in-laws: Aunt Belle, who would remain in England to chaperone the girls, and Sydney Dyer, Belle and Annie's brother. On the final stop before England – Las Palmas, in the Canary Islands – the Beauchamps, together with the captain, took a ride around the island in two carriages, stopping for lunch in a hotel, where a photographer took a rather grand photograph of the entire party, with Captain W. P. Fishwick centre stage and Aunt Belle with a conspicuous rose adorning her chest. Mansfield stands slightly apart on the left at the back, those unbecoming wire-rimmed spectacles now a thing of the past, looking every inch the young lady with her straw boater (a relic of her

Beauchamp family at Las Palmas, 1903. Mansfield at left, back row.

Miss Swainson's school uniform) and with a slightly wistful expression on her face.

As well as enjoying the sights and sounds of London, the family visited their Beauchamp relatives and Harold's favourite uncle, Henry Herron, and his wife, Louey, at their home, 'The Retreat' in Bexley, Kent. Uncle Henry's children – Harold's first cousins – had all done well for themselves. Mary, as we saw earlier, had transformed herself into Elizabeth von Arnim by marrying a German count and had become a hugely successful, best-selling author. Charlotte (Chaddie) had married a stationer, George Waterlow (it was her son, Sydney Waterlow, a civil servant in the Foreign Office, who hankered after a more artistic life and hung around the fringes of Bloomsbury, and who would propose unsuccessfully to the then Virginia Stephen – later Woolf – in November 1911).[8] Sydney had become a successful doctor, and Henry (also known as de Monk in some biographies) in 1903 was a music teacher at the London Academy of Music and an accomplished cellist and singer. It was this last cousin who Harold chose as the girls' official guardian for their stay in England, a popular choice with his daughters, who thereafter referred to Henry as 'Guardy'. He would go on to become a professor of singing at the Royal Academy of Music, in post from 1907 to 1937, having a distinguished career conducting the choir as well as many opera productions. And so Mansfield and her two older sisters became boarders at Queen's College in Harley Street on 29 April, with Aunt Belle close at hand, eventually assisting their housemistress when a member of the boarding staff retired.

At the time, Queen's College was an unusual, avant-garde educational institution. School-age girls normally took a four-year course of study, although the college was celebrated for its provision of free evening classes, taken by women who were beyond school age; they were known as 'Non-Compounders', the boarders being 'Compounders' (from which Mansfield's original title of 'Non-Compounders' for her celebrated story 'The Daughters of the Late Colonel' (1920) is derived). Lectures were given, university-style, with no registers or class-marks, and the girls were treated as young adults; they were free to wander in and out of classes, or not go at all. The staff list boasted some renowned scholars in 1903, including the notable historian John Adam Cramb

Mansfield, standing, and her sisters at 'The Retreat', Bexley.

(1861–1913), literature expert William Hall Griffin (1857–1907) and Richard Gregory (1864–1952), the school's professor of astronomy.

However, it was Walter Rippmann (1869–1947) – who changed his name by deed poll to the less Germanic Ripman in 1917 – who, of all the teachers at the school, would have the greatest influence on Mansfield. He became professor of German at Queen's College in 1896, aged just 27, and stayed for nearly twenty years. Mansfield would become one of Rippmann's favoured students, invited to his bohemian home at 72 Ladbroke Grove, which he shared with a journalist and an artist, and which was decorated in an Art Nouveau style, including with Japanese prints, which were then hugely popular. There he would give 'rose teas', with rose petals scattered in the hearth, under the soft rose glow of his Art Nouveau lamps. It is probably not an exaggeration to state that in introducing the impressionable Mansfield to the works of Oscar Wilde, Walter Pater and other writers of the *fin-de-siècle* and Decadent movements (especially Arthur Symons, Ernest Dowson, Paul Verlaine and Nietzsche), Rippmann would alter the course of her reading – and writing – life.

Professor Walter Rippmann, *c.* 1910.

It was also in her first year at Queen's College that one of Mansfield's close school friends, Vere Bartrick-Baker (also known as Mimi), lent Mansfield the original *Lippincott's Monthly Magazine* serialization of Wilde's *The Picture of Dorian Gray*. Mansfield was entranced and soon obtained a copy of the book itself, which became almost a sacred tome for her during the next few years. She filled her notebooks with quotations from it and tried to imitate the wit in aphorisms of her own. For some time thereafter, Mansfield would refer to herself as the 'White Gardenia', referencing one of the preferred flowers of Wilde himself.

Life at Queen's College suited Mansfield. For the first time in her life she experienced emotional and intellectual freedom, and relished it. Not long after arriving at the school, she met a fellow student who would go on to become her life-long friend and companion, and witness to many of the most notable events in her life: Ida Constance Baker (soon after known as L. M. – Lesley Moore – the name given to her by Mansfield because her own was deemed too dull). Initially, it was Mansfield's oldest sister Vera who was the object of Ida's affection: 'I used to find her lying on the floor outside my room, waiting to ask if she could help me undress.'[9] But Mansfield must also have felt some sort of connection to Ida, the tall, shy, fair-haired young girl with the size nine feet, who showed them around, or perhaps she just wanted to spite her eldest sister and steal her admirer. Whatever the intention, a few weeks later, while walking in Regent's Park, Mansfield asked Ida simply, 'Shall we be friends?'[10] And thus began a relationship that dominated and defined Ida's entire life, and which would support Mansfield until her own untimely death. Not everyone thought the friendship a wholesome one, however. Mansfield was seen as dominating Ida, telling her what to do, and treating her in a dismissive fashion at moments when she had no need of her (a trait that would continue for the entire duration of their friendship). Hour after hour was spent in Mansfield's room, where Ida started the habit of photographing her adored friend, a hobby she continued throughout Mansfield's life.

There were many college activities Mansfield enjoyed participating in, including the debating society, croquet, tennis, swimming at the Marylebone baths and theatre and concert visits. Particularly appealing was the *Queen's College Magazine* (in which Professor Rippmann took a special interest). Between 1903 and 1906 Mansfield had five stories published in various issues, and she became its editor for a short time. The second of these stories – and the most outstanding – was 'Die

Mansfield with cello, Queen's College, *c.* 1903.

Einsame' ('The Lonely One'), published in March 1904. Its German-language title was taken straight from cousin Elizabeth von Arnim's latest best-seller, *The Adventures of Elizabeth in Rügen*, which had been published just a few weeks before, and in which 'Die Einsame' was the name of a resort on the beautiful Rügen Island, famous for its sandy beaches, chalk cliffs and lagoons. More importantly, the German title also hints at Mansfield's obsession with Walter Rippmann and her desire to be liked by him, while the contents, replete with Decadent, Symbolist and *fin-de-siècle* motifs, reveal just how much she had absorbed from Rippmann's suggested extra-curricular reading, as well as her memories (perhaps subconscious) of the pine-forests and flower-laden landscapes in Mrs Molesworth's *Christmas-Tree Land* (1884), a favourite childhood book:

> All alone she was. All alone with her soul. She lived on the top of a solitary hill. Her house was small and bare, and alone, too.
>
> All day long she spent in the forest, with the trees and the flowers and the birds. She seemed like a creature of the forest herself, sometimes.
>
> [...]
>
> In the forest, in the forest, silence had cast a spell over all things. She plucked a great bouquet of daffodils and snowdrops, and tenderly held them to her, and tenderly kissed their fresh spring faces.[11]

The repetitive phrases add to the hauntingly poetic, lyrical, almost mythical quality of the prose. And who better to write about isolation and loneliness than Mansfield, that difficult and complex adolescent, whose frequent preference for her own company, together with her notorious 'moods', marked her out as different? Alienation and loneliness were to become themes that Mansfield would pick up time and again in her mature stories. There is another theme here, too – death – prevalent in Mansfield's adolescent and early adult stories, in which the anonymous protagonist, part wood nymph, part sea nymph, in the end almost seems to have her wishes fulfilled in going to her death:

> Now the water was creeping, higher to her waist, and now it was at her throat. She could barely stand. 'Take me,' she cried piteously, and looking up she saw – the boat and the figure had gone.
>
> [...]
>
> Then a great wave came, and there was silence.[12]

As well as her writing, Mansfield's main preoccupation during these three London years was, of course, music and, by extension, Tom Trowell, with whom she had been besotted since their first meeting in Wellington. For Christmas 1905, Mansfield sent Tom a beautifully decorative edition of *The Story of Tristan and Iseult*, signed 'To Tom from Kass'. She and her sisters saw the Trowell twins intermittently during these three years, as they occasionally came to London from Brussels, where they were studying. Ever eager to impress Tom, Mansfield practised diligently on her expensive new cello, with lessons taken both at Queen's College with Professor Hahn and at the London Academy with her guardian, Henry Beauchamp. Tom's photograph stared up at her every day from her school dressing table, and many long letters were sent to Brussels – and a few, far briefer ones, returned, all sadly now lost.

Towards the end of March 1906, Aunt Belle took the girls abroad as a special treat, starting in Paris and then moving on to Brussels, to hear Tom Trowell perform in a concert. Tom, now officially using his middle name, Arnold (to distinguish himself from his father, also called Thomas), was to give a solo recital at the Salle de la Grande Harmonie on 27 March, paid for with £25 from the twins' New Zealand trust fund. Aunt Belle had already taken the girls to Germany – to Bollendorf – in 1904, to see them, but this visit was so much more exciting. The recital was an enormous success, garnering some excellent reviews in the European press, and would have done nothing to quell Mansfield's ardour for Tom as she basked vicariously in his triumph. The twins were physically alluring, too, fuelling her passion even more, with their red hair, huge black hats and immensely long, continental cigarettes. Their bohemian ways entranced her; she wanted to be a bohemian too, and Tom taught her how to smoke, fuelling a life-long addiction that not even severe tuberculosis in later life could weaken.

Mansfield's absorption in music, and the recent contact with Tom, now gave her the fanciful idea of becoming a professional musician (which for women in those days had a similar social stigma to putting your daughter on the stage). When Harold and Annie arrived from Wellington in mid-April 1906 to spend a few months in London before taking the girls back to New Zealand at the end of the school year, she must have broached the subject, but her father soon put a stop to any such fanciful notions. It was one thing to give your daughters the benefit of music lessons to enhance their marital prospects, but quite another to think of them making a career out of it. During the Easter break of 1906, the entire Beauchamp family was to be found installed in the luxurious surroundings of Fripp's Hotel, 30 Manchester Street (less than a ten-minute walk from the college), from where Mansfield wrote in despair to her cousin Sylvia Payne on 24 April 1906:

> A great change has come into my life since I saw you last. Father is greatly opposed to my wish to be a professional 'cellist or to take up the 'cello to any great extent – so my hope for a musical career is absolutely gone – It was a fearful disappointment – I could not tell you what I have felt like – and do now when I think of it – but I suppose it is no earthly use warring with the Inevitable – so in the future I shall give all my time to writing.

And then, echoing words that surely must have come from Harold himself, she notes, 'There are great opportunities for a girl in New Zealand – she has so much time and quiet – and we have an ideal little "cottage by the sea" where I mean to spend a good deal of my time. Do you love solitude as I do – especially if I am in a writing mood.' The whole letter is fascinating for what it reveals about Mansfield at this time. A little further on, she talks in a very 'modern' fashion about her attitudes to women and matrimony (which would be replicated in a passage in the unfinished novel *Juliet* (1906), which she had just started writing), as well as some of her thoughts on books she has recently read:

> I am so keen upon all women having a definite future – are not you? The idea of sitting still and waiting for a husband is absolutely revolting – and it really is the attitude of a great many girls. [. . .] I picked up a small collection of poems entitled 'The Silver Net' by Louis Vintras – and I liked some of them immensely. The atmosphere is so intense. He seems to me to belong to that school which flourished just a few years ago – but which now has not a single representative – a kind of impressionist literature school – Don't think that I even approve of them – but they interest me – Dowson – Sherard – School.[13]

Of course, the Decadent writers Ernest Dowson and Robert Sherard (the latter, Wilde's first biographer) had been introduced to Mansfield by Rippmann, but even so, for a seventeen-year-old girl, the comments demonstrate a mature grasp of some of the then-current social and literary trends.

Tom and his twin Garnet finally arrived in London in May, having completed their studies in Brussels and elsewhere on the continent. Tom visited Mansfield at Queen's College, and of course his presence now made the idea of having to return to New Zealand so much more painful. Mansfield was told of how the Trowells' musician friend, Rudolf Bottermund – handsome, though easily excitable and temperamental, and whom she had only recently met on her trip to Brussels – had committed suicide by shooting himself; she was profoundly affected by the news. Rudolf, it was suggested, had been a homosexual, and this was the reason he had taken his life. This was her first personal experience of the death of someone her own age and, what was more, someone close to Tom. It left her bewildered and unsettled.

Mansfield's first attempt at a novel, *Juliet*, was begun on '18.V.06.', just a couple of weeks after her decision to devote 'all of my time to writing'.[14] Given that this period represented the height of her infatuation with Tom Trowell, it was only natural that the male protagonist should be based on him. Tom's arrival in London did not quite play out to Mansfield's romantic plans, however. Her fluctuating teenage emotions made her an unattractive prospect for the overwhelmed young musician, who started to cool down the 'relationship' – such as it was. Nevertheless, the emotional turbulence stimulated by the presence of the Trowells, together with her own burgeoning sexuality, would all subsequently be poured into *Juliet*, which she carried on writing intermittently until January 1907, just a few weeks after her arrival back in Wellington, when it would be abandoned.

Mansfield is renowned for putting a good deal of her own experiences into her fiction. From her early teens onwards, she made a conscious effort to record what was happening to her, initially in diary entries or letters, and subsequently transposed into her creative endeavours. As Ian Gordon affirms,

> Katherine Mansfield to a degree almost unparalleled in English fiction put her own experiences into her stories. She wrote of nothing that did not directly happen to her, even when she appeared to be at her most imaginative and fanciful. Her stories, read in their order of composition, gain force and significance, and are illuminated at all points by the events of her own history. Her whole work read in this manner emerges as a kind of *recherche du temps perdu*, a remembrance of things past.[15]

Of course, allowance must be made for artistic licence. No claim is being made that everything Mansfield wrote in her fiction – or indeed even in her notebooks and diary entries – actually happened. But if the reader wants to understand Mansfield the small child growing up in Karori, for example, no amount of biographical research can compete with her own portrait of Kezia in the Burnell stories.

Mansfield's two unfinished novels, *Juliet* and *Maata* (1913), exemplify her use of 'autobiografiction', a term first coined in 1906 in an essay of the same name by the Edwardian writer Stephen Reynolds (1881–1919).[16] For Reynolds, his invention of the portmanteau word was an attempt to describe 'autobiographical fiction', that is, 'fiction with a good deal of the writer's life in it, or for those lapses from fact which occur in most autobiographies'.[17] More recently, Max Saunders's ground-breaking study *Self Impression: Life-Writing, Autobiografiction, and the Forms of Modern Literature* discusses 'how modern writers in the late nineteenth and early twentieth centuries found new ways to combine life-writing with fiction'. He offers a caveat, however, since 'reading something as "autobiographical" [...] is different from reading it as "autobiography"; its autobiographical dimension can be covert, unconscious, or implicit'.[18] Mansfield remains one of the most important exponents of Modernist autobiografiction. Indeed, in a letter to Sarah Gertrude Millin written in March 1922, less than a year before her death, Mansfield explored in depth her personal fictionalizing of the self:

> always my thoughts and feelings go back to New Zealand – rediscovering it, finding beauty in it, re-living it. Its about my Aunt Fan who lived up the road I really want to write, and the man who sold goldfinches, and about a wet night on the wharf, and Tarana Street in the Spring. [...] I think the only way to live as a writer is to draw upon one's real familiar life – to find the treasure in that [...]. Our secret life, the life we return to over and over again, the 'do you remember' life is always the past. And the curious thing is that if we describe this which seems to us so intensely personal, other people take it to themselves and understand it as if it were their own.[19]

In addition, the techniques Mansfield would go on to develop in her pitch-perfect later stories, utilizing inner consciousness as a technique for revelation of character, arose from an instinctive sense, honed very early on in her writing career.

The plot of *Juliet* (such as it is) involves a young woman eager to move from Wellington to London, especially after David, the musician with whom she is infatuated, travels there to study. Once in the metropolis, she becomes close to Pearl, a fellow student at a women's hostel, with whom David falls in love, while Juliet herself is seduced by his friend, Rudolph (the Trowells' friend, whom Mansfield had met in Brussels and who had recently committed suicide). Following a pregnancy and her refusal to consider returning home, Juliet lives in some degree of squalor (with the suggestion of an abortion), and a relationship is hinted at with another man called Walter. She is desperately ill when found by David and taken to live with him and Pearl, where she subsequently dies.

There are clearly elements of autobiografiction, as Mansfield describes the Beauchamp family (now Juliet's family) in some detail, and in particular her own teenage personality:

> Juliet was the odd man out of the family – the ugly duckling. She had lived in a world of her own, created her own people, read anything and everything which came to hand, was possessed with a violent temper, and completely lacked placidity. She was dominated by her moods which swept through her and in number were legion. [. . .] She criticised everybody and everything with which she came into contact, and wrapped herself in a fierce white reserve. [. . .] She had no defined paths ahead, no goal to reach and she felt compelled to vent her energy upon somebody, and that somebody was her family.[20]

At a musical evening, she meets 'David', in essence Tom Trowell. In what would become a familiar trope in her writing, utilizing windows to denote an unstable, liminal state, both characters 'crossed over to the wide opened window and both leant out'.[21] David, a talented musician, then travels to London, leaving Juliet isolated. Subsequently we find her on some windswept hill, presumably in New Zealand, buffeted by the wind: 'vague thoughts swept through her – of the Future, of her leaving this little island and going so far away, of all that she knew and loved, all that she wished to be.'[22]

The remaining extant sections all take place in London, with Juliet at school for a couple of paragraphs, and then, suddenly, she is grown up, living with Pearl (Vere), in love with David (Tom), but pursued by David's friend Rudolph. *Fin-de-siècle* exotic symbology is everywhere, from Juliet's favourite kimono to Pearl's throwaway comment, 'I should like to take opium this afternoon,' to an overtly sexual conversation between the two women:

> 'It's sure to be something physical. Why don't you sleep better Juliet? Are you – you're not . . . repenting?'
>
> 'Good Heavens, no. The truth is, my dear girl, well I hardly like to own it to myself even, you understand. Bernard Shaw would be gratified.'
>
> 'You feel sexual.'
>
> 'Horribly. And in need of a physical shock or violence – perhaps a good smacking would be beneficial.'[23]

David and Pearl go on to marry, and Rudolph, who had gone abroad, only much later learns of Juliet's death, at which point he composes 'a charming little morceau "Souvenir de Juliet"'.[24] The tone of the narrative throughout veers from heavily romantic to sharply cynical. There is also a notable and uncanny prescience in the writing, anticipating as it does the turmoil of Mansfield's own experience in the year after she returned to England in 1908, rejected by Tom Trowell, and her subsequent pregnancy by his brother Garnet, his rejection of her and her stillbirth in Bavaria, much of which forms the content of her other unfinished novel, *Maata*, from 1913.

While her New Zealand roots were imprinted in her brain, to resurface time and again in her mature fiction, Mansfield's three years in London had effectively cut the physical ties between her and her parents' stuffy, middle-class, colonial world. She wanted none of it. If there was a choice to be made between Art Nouveau interior decor and purple sofas in Ladbroke Grove, or a grand house in Wellington, with its incumbent dull round of parties and the same old faces, the choice was an overwhelmingly easy one. In a parting shot to schoolfriend Eileen Palliser, Mansfield announced her battle plan: 'When I get to New Zealand, I'll make myself so objectionable that they'll have to send me away.'[25] And, true to her word, that was exactly what she did.

And so the Beauchamp family (minus Aunt Belle, who in 1905 had successfully bagged an English shipbroker husband, William Henry Trinder) once more regrouped for the long voyage home, boarding the passenger ship SS *Corinthic* at Gravesend on 18 October, just four days after Mansfield's eighteenth birthday. On board the ship was an English cricket team, put together by the Marylebone Cricket Club (the MCC, the home of English cricket) and composed of little-known amateurs on their way to a financially disastrous tour of New Zealand; the players were, however, the only silver lining to Mansfield's dark cloud. Her escalating teenage sexual impulses quickly developed into a crush on one particular member of the cricket team, whom she called 'Adonis' because of his devastating good looks; elsewhere she also referred to him as 'R'. Possibly this was Ronny H. Fox (who had actually been born in Dunedin in New Zealand but who had moved to England as a young boy), or Percy R. May, both of whom were very handsome, and whom she photographed a number of times on the voyage home. Her diary entries at this time reveal her quickening sexual impulses for her cricketing 'Adonis'.

The *Corinthic* arrived in New Zealand on 6 December 1906, at the height of an Antipodean summer. Harold must have believed that once his rebellious daughter was home he would have her more firmly under his control, but in this he was mistaken. One poignant result of Mansfield's moodiness and self-absorption in her misery at being back in New Zealand was that she did not visit her beloved Grandma Dyer during the whole of December. Grandma Dyer herself remarked on this fact but showed no resentment. When the old lady died on New Year's Eve, just three weeks after the family's return, Mansfield's guilt was palpable.

Letters from Mansfield at this time to her closest friend, Ida – at least one a week – became the vehicle for outpourings of her frustration, misery and occasional periods of elation. (Frustratingly, many years later Mansfield forced Ida to destroy these letters, every single one of which had been painstakingly kept by her adoring friend.) Music, of course, was a solace. Letters to Tom were sent, and the proximity of the Trowell parents and young Dolly, still in Wellington, brought her news of the twins' life in London, which, although welcome, only reinforced the misery of her own life in what she perceived to be the provincial backwater of Wellington. Millie Parker, the daughter of a Wellington pharmacist and niece of Robert Parker, Mansfield's former piano teacher, became a good friend at this time through her connection with Mr Trowell (her family lived next door to the Trowells in Buller Street). Millie (piano), Mansfield (cello) and Mr Trowell (violin) made up a trio and played together every week. Even after the Trowells moved to London in September 1907 to be with the twins, the two young women continued to play together.

The Beauchamp family could now count themselves as one of the most prominent families in Wellington society, and Harold decided this called for an even bigger house to better reflect his newfound importance. Accordingly, in May 1907 the family moved a stone's throw away, still in Thorndon, to a much grander dwelling at 47 Fitzherbert Terrace; this new house had its own ballroom, croquet lawn, extensive gardens and grand pillared entrance, but without the encroaching slum areas that had dogged the views from no. 75 ('The Garden Party' house). It even had its own smoking room, which Mansfield used frequently.

There was an old friend whom Mansfield now sought out after her return from England: Maata. On 10 April 1907 she sent her a birthday telegram: 'Birthday greetings to my sweetest Carlotta K.'[26] The two friends, having exchanged diaries during a meeting in London, were now in close contact. Mansfield was making as much use as she could of a cottage right by the sea in Days Bay, leased by Harold for the enjoyment of his daughters. It offered an escape from her family and, under the pretext of needing peace and quiet to write, Mansfield was able to see Maata alone. From the evidence that still exists by way of diaries and notebook entries, it is clear that an affair of a sexual nature was now underway between the two young women.

Mansfield seems to have been sexually attracted to both women and men during this period of her life. She was clearly still passionately devoted to Tom Trowell, but given that he was several thousand miles away in London, and the fact that it was difficult for a single young lady at that time to be alone with a man without attracting attention (which Mansfield was wont to do anyway at dances and parties, to the annoyance and embarrassment of her parents), she was now able to explore other, more covert, sexual feelings. Maata's good looks made it easy for Mansfield to find her more than attractive, and she was not discouraged in her approaches. Being Mansfield, however, her life at this time was complicated by the fact that she was also soon conducting an affair with Edie Bendall, 27 years old and therefore nine years her senior, while all the time harbouring feelings for Tom – and Maata. It became a complex few months, increased her moodiness and made her almost impossible to live with at home. Edie and Mansfield would meet on Saturday afternoons, mostly in Days Bay. It seems that Harold's largesse in acquiring the little seaside holiday cottage for the amusement of his three elder daughters in fact became the illicit playground for Mansfield's sexual experimentation. Her notebooks at this time are a record of her emotional – and sexual – experiences, both past and present; whether embellished or not, they clearly indicate something beyond basic friendship.

A long passage, with its heading of 'Sunday night', was written in early June 1907 – winter in New Zealand. Anyone wanting to understand the turmoil of Mansfield's inner life at this time could do no better than to examine this strange, almost hallucinatory passage of writing. Both she and Edie are clearly at Days Bay, spending the night together. It is still the middle of the night when she begins writing; Edie is asleep as Mansfield records her feelings in her notebook. Some sort of powerful sexual episode has occurred, much anticipated by Mansfield, which makes her reject any previous heterosexual feelings for Tom Trowell (here Caesar) and the English cricketer (Adonis): 'I feel more powerfully all those so termed sexual impulses with her than I have with any men.' But there is a sense that these unleashed sexual feelings can no longer be contained: 'but now I feel that if she is denied me I must – the soul of me goes into the streets and craves love of the casual stranger, begs & prays for a little of the precious poison. I am half mad with love.' There is more than a hint that these feelings – and their physical manifestation – are not new and have happened on numerous previous occasions: 'And this is really my last experience of the kind – my last – I cannot bear it any longer. It really kills my soul, each time I feel it more deeply, because each time the wound is stabbed afresh and the knife probes new flesh and reawakens tortures in the old.' A passage of striking prose then follows, highly stylized, and redolent with *fin-de-siècle* and Decadent motifs: 'And so is Life, and so, above all, is Love – a vague transitory fleeting thing, & Pessimism gaunt & terrible stares me in the face, & I cling to old illusions.' She believes that what she is experiencing is real love and that any concept of heterosexual love that she may have had in the past – for Caesar, for Adonis – was never reciprocated: 'Never pure spontaneous affectionate impulse'. In her passion for Edie, however, 'I am child, woman, and more than half man.' This understanding leads her to reflect on the tragedy of such feelings, which, by their nature, can come to nothing (in the formal world in which she lives), and as a result of which she perceives nothing but tragedy ahead: 'my life is a Rosary of Fierce Combats for Two, each bound together with the powerful magnetic chain of Sex.' In addition, she can no longer continually love without any reciprocated feelings in the loved one: 'I cannot continue my hard course of loving and being unloved – of giving loves only to find them flung back at me, faded, worm eaten,' and then defiantly, she proclaims, 'I snap my fingers at Fate. I will not dance to the Music of the Marionettes. Damn it all!'[27]

A dream-like, hallucinatory passage then follows, in which fence posts outside turn into 'hideous forms of Chinamen', before she is once again enfolded in the embrace of her lover. In the closing lines, she invokes Oscar Wilde (who else?), whom she believes was a fellow traveller on her chosen path: 'O Oscar! Am I peculiarly susceptible to sexual impulse? I must be I suppose, but I rejoice.'[28] The passage closes with her expectation of more nights such as these to come. For Mansfield, who lived in an era where only heterosexuality was acceptable, Wilde's example offered her some sort of validation for her lesbian tendencies at this time, as well as helping to alleviate the guilt and anxiety brought on by such feelings. In later life, when she no longer had need of such validation, Wilde's importance to her diminished accordingly. In the restricted moral environment of colonial Wellington at the turn of the twentieth century, homosexuality was considered a deviation so horrendous that, as Guy Scholefield would later tell Mansfield's first biographer, Ruth Elvish Mantz, the word 'mental' was used to describe such behaviour, even by the courts.

It is clear to even the most inexperienced of psychologists that, at this time, Mansfield was a sexually experimental, hormone-driven, boundary-challenging young woman, moody and quixotic, to the frustration of her immediate family; she must have been a constant source of anxiety (to her parents) and annoyance (to her siblings). Nevertheless, a few days later, all her thoughts were turned once more towards Tom (Caesar) Trowell. Mr Trowell, Mansfield's cello teacher, his wife and their daughter Dolly were invited to Fitzherbert Terrace for an evening of music, where undoubtedly the talk would have been of the twins' – and especially Tom's – successes in London. Mansfield plied the family with bunches of camellias when they left: 'I became terribly unhappy, almost wept in the street, and yet Music enveloped me – again – caught me, held me, thank Heaven. I could have died. I should be dead but for that, I know.

I sent Mr T. a beautiful book – something that I truly treasure.'[29] All her thoughts and emotions were now turned once more to Tom – her first love:

> Everything about him seems to be made plain – now. I think of him in any every situation, and feel that I understand him too. He must always be everything to me – the one man whom I can call Master and Lover too, and though I know I shall have many fascinating connections in my Life none will be like this – so lasting, so deep, so everything – because he poured into my virgin soul the Life essence of Music – – Never an hour passes free from his influence.[30]

All the while, however, her bisexuality was troubling her: 'I love him – but I wonder, with all my soul – And here is the kernel of the whole matter – the Oscar-like thread.'[31] Now her thoughts were turning towards a literary, rather than a musical career:

> I want to practically celebrate this day by beginning to write a book. In my brain, as I walk each day, as I dress, as I speak, or even before playing my 'cello, a thousand delicate images float and are gone. I want to write a book – that is unreal yet wholly possible because out of the question – that raises in the hearts of the readers' emotions, sensations too vivid not to take effect, which causes a thousand delicate tears, a thousand sweet chimes of laughter. I shall never attempt anything approaching the histrionic, and it must be ultra modern. I am sitting right over the fire as I write, dreaming, my face hot with the coals. Far away a steamer is calling, calling, and – God God – my restless soul.[32]

This early literary manifesto reveals how, even at age eighteen, Mansfield was interested in writing modern fiction – what she calls here 'ultra modern' – where effect is the key, not the excesses of plot. But nothing like this could be written until that steamer took her away from colonial New Zealand, with its middle-class sterility and strictures.

The two younger Beauchamp siblings – Jeanne and Leslie (known as 'Chummie') – were not as affected by Mansfield's moodiness and troublesome ways as the rest of the family. Leslie was away at boarding school for much of the year, though when he was at home, Mansfield clearly delighted in his company and he in hers: 'Chummie became a true friend, and the tie between brother and sister, who felt and thought alike, was strong in those years.'[33] And little Jeanne understood nothing of what was going on in the head of her older sister. Another consolation for the absence of London was that Harold, using his connections in Parliament, had managed to get Vera and Mansfield reading rights at the well-stocked parliamentary library. Records show that Mansfield in particular was a regular borrower, reading an eclectic mix of classic and modern fiction, as well as books on social reform.

In addition, as well as practising her music, Mansfield was now writing stories, the most polished of which were sent to an Australian periodical, the *Native Companion*, suggested by Tom Mills, a friend of her father's. Its editor from August to December 1907 was Edwin James Brady (1869–1952), who was immediately taken with Mansfield's work and published four stories: 'Vignettes' (October issue), 'Silhouettes' (November issue), 'In a Café' and 'In the Botanical Gardens' (both December issue). The first three were signed 'K. Mansfield' and the last one 'Julian Mark' (to disguise the fact that two of the stories in that issue were by the same author).

Brady's autobiography recounts his early misgivings that such a young woman could have written the stories, so he wrote to her asking for further biographical details. On 23 September 1907, Mansfield's response was brazen, to say the least, but it certainly marked her out as different and attracted Brady to the author and her stories:

> Dear Sir –
>
> Thank you for your letter – I liked the peremptory tone –
>
> With regard to the 'Vignettes' I am sorry that [they] resemble their illustrious relatives to so marked an extent – and assure you – they feel very much my own –This style of work absorbs me, at present – but – well – it <u>cannot</u> be said that anything you have of mine is 'cribbed' – – – Frankly – I hate plagiarism.
>
> I send you some more work – practically there is nothing local – except the 'Botanical Garden' Vignette – The reason is that for the last few years London has held me – very tightly indeed – and I've not yet escaped.
>
> You ask for some details as to myself. I am poor – obscure – just eighteen years of age – with a rapacious appetite for everything and principles as light as my purse – –

> If this pleases you – this MSS please know that there is a great deal more where this comes from –
>
> I am very grateful to you and very interested in your Magazine.
>
> Sincerely
>
> K. M. BEAUCHAMP.[34]

Once she had shown her father Brady's letter, Harold, without consulting his daughter, wrote to Brady himself, noting that

> you need never have any hesitation in accepting anything from her upon the assumption that it may not be original matter. She, herself, is, I think, a very original character, and writing – whether it be good or bad – comes to her quite naturally. [. . .] It may be that she inherits the literary talent of some members of our family, amongst them being my cousin, the authoress of Elizabeth and her German Garden, and other well-known books.[35]

It is to Harold's credit that he wrote to Brady, thereby encouraging the writing career of his daughter. Interesting, too, that Elizabeth, his cousin, was name-dropped into his response; the letter also indicates his change of heart, perhaps, for if his cousin could become a celebrated writer and marry a German aristocrat, why not his daughter? For Mansfield there was now a glimmer of hope that, with publishing success, her dream of returning to London would become a reality.

Mansfield's positioning of her characters by a window in 'Vignettes' and 'Silhouettes', two of the *Native Companion* stories, is quite marked, perhaps subconsciously revealing her own liminal position in life, since although her physical body was in Wellington, her emotional life (what she felt was her *real* life) was bound steadfastly to London. In 'Vignettes', she is back in her old room in Harley Street, before the narrative subconsciously shifts back to New Zealand 'with the hopeless note of a foghorn far out at sea'. The first three quotations below are from 'Vignettes', and the last two from 'Silhouettes':

> Away beyond the line of the dark houses there is a sound like the call of the sea after a storm – passionate, solemn, strong. I am leaning far out of my window in the warm, still night air. Down below, in the Mews, the little lamp is singing a silent song.

> I lean out of the window. The dark houses stare at me and above them a great sweep of sky. Where it meets the houses there is a strange lightness – a suggestion, a promise.
>
> I lean from my window in the tower. Through the stillness comes the hushed sound of the fountain. I fancy I can hear the rose petals in the garden falling softly.
>
> It is evening, and very cold. From my window the laurestinus bush, in this half light, looks weighted with snow.
>
> And I, leaning out of my window, alone, peering into the gloom, am seized by a passionate desire for everything that is hidden and forbidden. I want the night to come, and kiss me with her hot mouth, and lead me through an amethyst twilight to the place of the white gardenia . . .[36]

Clearly present is the influence of Oscar Wilde, with those notions of amethyst twilights and white gardenias. Even the first line of 'In the Botanical Gardens' could have been spoken by Lord Henry Wotton in *The Picture of Dorian Gray*: 'They are such a subtle combination of the artificial and the natural – that is, partly, the secret of their charm.'[37] 'In a Café' offers us a glimpse of the kind of writing Mansfield would develop as a mature artist, with its dialogue form exposing the personalities of the two protagonists, one of them clearly Mansfield herself:

> 'Do you think I should make a good wife?'
>
> 'That depends.' He stirred his coffee thoughtfully. 'Yes; why not? Interesting, certainly, beyond doubt; and who could do better than marry a problem? Misunderstanding keepeth Love alive.'
>
> 'I believe that, too,' she said, 'and yet, somehow, it's abominable. Oh! how I want and want things which are out of the question.'
>
> 'But not a husband, surely?'
>
> 'I hardly see myself settling down to sentimental domesticity and discussing the price of mutton.'
>
> 'Ah! now you are being foolish. You know that marriage need not mean that. Mine won't. And I certainly shall marry.'

> 'Oh! oh! oh! – then there are years of bachelorhood ahead of you, extravagant and reckless one.' A sudden tremendous happiness seemed to have sprung to birth in her heart. 'Oh! this adorable life,' she said. 'Oh! the infinite possibilities. Listen; can't you hear London knocking, knocking?'[38]

Sadly for Mansfield, London may have been knocking, but her father still had the key to the locked door firmly in his pocket.

November in New Zealand marks the beginning of summer. Millie Parker announced to Mansfield that she was to take a month-long caravan trip with six others through the mostly still-wild and spectacularly beautiful volcanic region in the middle of the North Island, sparsely inhabited by Māoris, with a few settler farms. Harold, perhaps thinking that a spell of separation between him and his daughter might cool down the inflamed tempers at no. 47, reluctantly agreed that Mansfield could accompany her, though he did not wholly approve of the mix of people she was to travel with, and it was certainly not his suggestion that she should go. Mansfield would famously keep a written record of the journey in what is now referred to as 'The Urewera Notebook'. The other members of the party were George Ebbett, a lawyer and sheep farmer; his wife, Eliza; another farmer, Hill, who was to be in charge of the horses; another single woman, Annie Leithead; and another couple – Herbert Webber, a Hastings pharmacist and his wife, Elsie. Elsie, who was only three years older than Mansfield (who, in turn, was the youngest member of the party), became close to Mansfield on the trip.

Mansfield and Millie left Wellington by train on 23 November 1907 for Hastings, a town just under 320 kilometres (200 mi.) from Wellington, on the northeast coast, where they stayed overnight with the Ebbetts and were joined by the rest of the party the following morning. From Hastings, the group made their way by horse-drawn coach to Napier (accompanied by a dray, which carried all their provisions and camping equipment), and then through the Esk Valley to the small sawmill town of Te Pohue. Mansfield, who had only ever known a life of servants and every convenience, initially found her first experience of camping difficult. On 26 November the party covered nearly 34 kilometres (21 mi.) of difficult and steep mountain terrain, which occasionally necessitated them dismounting and walking to relieve the horses. That evening the party visited its first hot spring, at Tarawera. The next day, after more arduous mountainous terrain, the road started to descend until they reached the Waipunga Falls and thence on to the Kaingaroa Plains, made up of volcanic pumice sand, eventually arriving at the tiny settlement of Rangitaiki. The next few days were spent travelling into the Urewera hills – densely forested, isolated mountain country – with its small Māori settlements. The party then retraced their steps back onto the Kaingaroa Plains, this time heading westwards towards the Waiotapu Valley, with its geothermal springs, lakes and craters. On 4 December they continued on towards the tourist town of Rotorua, where they spent four nights, with a stop en route at the spectacular geysers, silica terraces and pools of Whakarewarewa.

Over the next few days the travellers went from Rotorua to Atiamuri, in order to visit the celebrated Rainbow Falls, and from there to the Aratiatia Rapids and on to the town of Wairakei and its famous Geyser Valley. From Wairakei, the party continued on to Taupo, stopping at the Huka Falls en route, finally arriving at The Terraces Spa Hotel, 3 kilometres (2 mi.) beyond Taupo, where they spent the night of 10 December. From 11 to 15 December, the group retraced the beginning of the trip as they headed southwards towards Hastings, camping one night in the isolated Runanga Valley, with its solitary roadman's cottage and paddocks, the inspiration for one of Mansfield's stories, 'The Woman at the Store', published in 1912, but almost certainly drafted at this time.

On the train journey back to Wellington, Mansfield once more reverted to her old persona, with its Wildean posing, and started writing in her notebook as if the journey of the past month had barely happened: 'M. and I sitting opposite each other – I look perfectly charming. And I read a little book called The Book of Tea – it is wholly adorable.'[39] *The Book of Tea*, by Kakuzo Okakura, published in London in 1906, is a study of the art of the Japanese tea ceremony and, more broadly, of the customs and rituals of traditional Japanese life. An instant best-seller when first published, it is still in print today and would remain one of Mansfield's favourite books. And so it was a sunburnt, tired but, outwardly at least, still the same Mansfield who finally returned home a week before Christmas. Harold, who had been away on business, came back to find his wayward daughter as fractious and determined as ever to go back to London. Mansfield wrote to Martha Putnam, her father's secretary, who had been typing up some of her stories for publication: 'Castles have been tumbling about my ears since Father came home – Do not mention – I pray you – my London prospects to him – he feels very sensitive – but – willy nilly: – I GO – I'm determined.'[40]

In spite of all his domestic annoyances, as 1908 dawned Harold's reputation in Wellington continued on its upwards trajectory. On 11 April the *New Zealand Herald* reported that, the previous day, he had been re-elected as chairman of the Bank of New Zealand for a further year.[41] While she waited for her father's permission to leave New Zealand to return to London, on 8 May Mansfield enrolled at Wellington Technical School, taking classes in 'commercial subjects' – typing and bookkeeping. Perhaps this was done at her father's request – Harold, with his sensible business head on, thinking that these were skills that might stand her in good stead if she were to move to the other side of the world to try her hand as a writer. In fact, towards the end of her life, her little Corona portable typewriter would be a constant travel companion.

Eventually, embarrassed by Mansfield's behaviour and worn down by her constant badgering, by 19 June the decision was made that she could return to London; as Harold so calmly noted in his *Reminiscences* in 1937, completely overlooking the lengthy turmoil that had led up to his pronouncement: 'There could be no question of standing in her light.'[42] On 4 July, the *Free Lance* announced, 'Miss Kathleen Beauchamp leaves for England this week by the Papanui, to continue her literary studies.'[43] With freedom, which Mansfield had craved for so long, also came responsibility, but somehow, in the heady cocktail of London and liberty, this was overlooked. Even if the 'amethyst outlook', Mansfield's diary codename for her same-sex relationships, was now apparently a thing of the past, for the next three years at least she would make it her business to experience 'life', whatever the consequences. As a result, for many years afterwards, in the town of her birth, society ladies would speak her name in hushed tones. When Mantz interviewed Harold (now 'Sir' Harold) in 1931, 'fear lay at the back [of his] small blue eyes as he tried manfully to recall the childhood of his third daughter. "Her *Journal* hurt many people in New Zealand", he said; then he added, "But I don't think she meant it that way."'[44] It would take some time in New Zealand before embarrassment and condemnation would turn to admiration and veneration. Indeed, for many years, a story circulated in Wellington that Harold

> had the boats met as they swung at anchor in Wellington Harbor so the early books of his daughter, Kathleen, could be thrown overboard. Others denied the story as 'exaggerated'; in any case, her early published works could not be found in Wellington. Sir Harold had no copy of *Bliss* to leave to New Zealand.[45]

Mansfield left New Zealand a published writer, no longer 'Kathleen Beauchamp' but 'K. Mansfield', still uncertain perhaps of which direction her writing would go, but already with the knowledge that the Victorian style of commonplace analysis and description (and, later on, the late Victorian, theatrically opulent prose of Wilde and the Decadents) would not be her literary path. The Modernist revelation of character through narrative voice – through suggestion and symbolism – would become her method, in which she would offer glimpses into the lives of individuals and families, captured at a certain moment, frozen in time like a painting or photograph. And though she was not aware of it, as the SS *Papanui* steamed away from the shores of New Zealand towards Europe and the glittering lights of London, with Mansfield's eyes resolutely fixed on the horizon ahead and not on the coast left behind, it was New Zealand – mostly Wellington and the streets of Thorndon – that would eventually provide the inspiration for some of her finest stories.

2

London and Europe, 1908–9

It had been decided by her parents that on her arrival in London, Mansfield was to go back to her old boarding house at Queen's College for a few days, and then on to the appropriately named Beauchamp Lodge in Paddington, an unmarried women's hostel catering for music students. Uncle Henry Herron Beauchamp, who had died on 6 October 1907, aged 82, could no longer be of assistance, but his wife, Mansfield's Great-Aunt Louey, was charged with keeping an eye on her, as were her sons and in particular Henry again, who took on the nominal role of 'guardian' on behalf of her family. It was he who had recommended Beauchamp Lodge, since a number of his female students at the Royal College of Music boarded there and he could vouch for its suitability. Mansfield's allowance from her father was initially set at £100 per annum (roughly the average annual wage at the time), which was regularly increased during the rest of her life, until it reached £300. For the daughter of Harold Beauchamp, however, who had never had to skimp on anything, this allowance would leave her constantly short of money.

Mansfield's boat docked in Plymouth on 24 August 1908, and faithful Ida was there to welcome her. After staying for a few days in Ida's family's apartment off Baker Street, followed by her old boarding house, she moved in, as planned, to Beauchamp Lodge. Eager to see Tom Trowell and the rest of his family, who were all now living at 52 Carlton Hill, St John's Wood, she soon realized that although the family welcomed her into their home, her affections for Tom were most definitely not reciprocated. In fact, he was now seeing Gwen Rouse, Mansfield's close friend from Queen's College. Perhaps to save face, or because of her own insecurities, she very quickly turned her affections to Tom's twin brother Garnet instead.

Garnet was more than receptive to such attention, and soon Mansfield found herself head over heels in love, and spending far more time with Garnet and the rest of the Trowell family (and presumably the duplicitous Gwen Rouse) than at Beauchamp Lodge. Her amorous feelings were now, finally, being reciprocated, and passionate love letters were exchanged during Garnet's frequent absences as a travelling musician with the Moody Manners Opera Company. (There were two main singers in the company – Fanny Moody and Charles Manners – who toured the British Isles with their orchestra, other principals, players and chorus.) For her twentieth birthday on 14 October, Garnet sent her a little ring, the pair thenceforth believing themselves to be secretly engaged. They could not have been 'together' for more than about four weeks. Of course, it was all too much, too soon, but in these early months of her new-found freedom, Mansfield barely stopped to draw breath.

As noted earlier, Mansfield very quickly discovered that the initial allowance from her father of £100 per annum was inadequate for a young woman who had never really had to think about money – or find ways to economize. Harold, having left school at fourteen, had certainly undertaken domestic duties in his own childhood but had been determined that his own children would never know such privations; he was proud to bring them up with servants to do chores. As a result, one of the party on Mansfield's trip to the Ureweras in 1907 would recall that when Mansfield was presented with a potato to cook, she had no idea how to peel it: 'the same way as you peel an apple,' she was told.[1] She now, therefore, turned to her skills as a raconteur and actress in order to increase her allowance, and was soon being paid to entertain guests at society soirées. In the meantime, she was invited to spend five days in Paris, where she attended a wedding and visited Versailles for the first time, from 20 to 25 October, as the guest of Margaret Wishart, a friend from Beauchamp Lodge. On her return to London, fearing that she might have somehow become pregnant as a result of a dalliance in Montevideo on her voyage back to England from New Zealand, she visited a certain 'Mrs Charley Boyd,' who set her mind at rest. It was to be the first of numerous such visits. For the next three years, as C. K. Stead asserts, 'Lacking the pills and antibiotics which protected the new free women of the 1970s and 1980s, she suffered damaging consequences

Garnet Trowell, 1907.

– unintended pregnancies, venereal disease (which in turn lowered her resistance to TB).'[2]

In the meantime, Mansfield was still sending passionate letters and poems to Garnet, and spending time with him whenever he came home. Outwardly, of course, she led the suitable, appropriate existence expected by her family with her new Beauchamp Lodge friend, Margaret Wishart. In November 1908, together with Margaret, she attended the launch of the battleship HMS *Collingwood* in Devonport, hosted by Mrs Asquith, the prime minister's wife. Margaret was a young professional violinist, aged 29, who appeared to have much in common with Mansfield – they both came from well-off families, with powerful domineering fathers (Margaret's father was a rear admiral in the Royal Navy), and both were to fall in love with young men their parents would never approve of, facts which they had to hide – in Margaret's case, a piano teacher called George Woodhouse, and in Mansfield's a violinist in a travelling opera company. (Margaret eventually married her beau in August 1909, whereupon her family immediately cut her off.)

In 1948 Antony Alpers contacted Margaret and asked her to note down her recollections of this period – important because Mansfield systematically destroyed much of the evidence of the troubled years between 1908 and 1911, as we shall see. These recollections are therefore significant for biographers; Alpers used some – but not all – of them in his first biography of Mansfield, published in 1954. Margaret's full handwritten account was not discovered by her descendants until 2023.[3] Margaret wrote in her 'Notes',

> [Beauchamp Lodge] was excellently run by two busy musicians, Miss Rosamond Watson and Miss Ann Mukle, who were kindly, broadminded and tolerant and there were practically no rules or restrictions. I think there were about 20 or 30 of us, and we were of all kinds and ages, primarily it was intended for music students at the Royal Academy of Music, who largely predominated [...]. I found myself sitting next to K. M. at supper on my first night, and it seemed at once that we were destined to become close friends.[4]

Mansfield's uncanny ability to strike up close bonds almost immediately was certainly felt by Margaret; as she recorded, 'I have never shared such intimacy as in that period, with any friend before or since.'[5] A number of other people in Mansfield's life would come to know that sensation, especially in these early years. Ida, of course, was still very much in Mansfield's life, relied on in every moment of crisis, and there were to be many others, especially in the next three years. Margaret became jealous of the close relationship Ida had with Mansfield, which she manifested in her 'Notes':

> [Ida Baker] visited her frequently and was a great bore, but Kassie's kind heart (her own greatest enemy) made her tolerate this friend for the sake of her loyalty, even though it was almost suffocating at times. [. . . Ida] worshipped Kassie in an abnormal fashion and was frantically jealous of her having any other associates, so I kept out of her way whenever possible, and always disappeared soon after her arrival. At the same time I could not help hearing a good deal about her, and what an incubus she was even then.[6]

'Kassie's kind heart' was nothing more than dissembling on Mansfield's part. Even if driven to despair by her at certain moments in her life, Ida was – and would remain – the keeper of all of Mansfield's greatest secrets (well, the ones Ida was told about), but it didn't do to let people know that.

According to Margaret, Garnet Trowell was 'very tall and slender, dreamy, cultured and loving books almost as well as his violin', adding that 'K. M. was devoted to him.'[7] Mansfield was clearly in love, and felt herself invincible. Margaret also reported how at this time Mansfield was writing 'masses of short stories', which she read aloud to her friend: 'I remember how she would revel in sordid detail – there was one about a little dressmaker who had been seduced, dying of consumption in hot summer weather, in a slum tenement, and outside the window lay a pile of rotting bananas upset from a barrow.'[8] Perhaps not unhappily, that rather maudlin, sentimental story does not survive.

Towards the end of November, Mansfield, tiring of the strictures imposed on the boarders, and, contradicting Margaret's account, left Beauchamp Lodge in order to become the Trowells' lodger, thus providing the family with much-needed additional income, and herself with ever closer proximity to Garnet, which, when he was home, inevitably led to a sexual relationship. No one can be clear on dates because of Mansfield's systematic destruction of most of her personal letters and diaries from this period, but at some point in January 1909 the Trowell parents were shocked and angry to discover that Garnet and Mansfield had been sleeping together. What upset and embarrassed them even more was the fact that Harold Beauchamp had been instrumental in setting up the fund in Wellington that had allowed their twin sons to continue their musical studies in Europe in the first place. The news that one of them had now brought disgrace to the Beauchamp family was more than they could bear.

Mansfield's unfinished novel from 1913, *Maata*, which offers many parallels with events and people in her life from this time (discussed in detail in Chapter Four), provides evidence of how the Trowell parents discovered the sexual relationship. The principal character, Maata, the name taken from her Māori friend and lover in Wellington, is Mansfield herself, and the Close family represent the Trowells. In the story, Mansfield writes how Garnet's young sister Dolly (Maisie in the story) discovers and reveals to her parents Mansfield's sexual affair with her brother (which is, in fact, what happened). The character of Philip is drawn from Garnet, and Hal from his brother, Tom. In the chapter plan Mansfield drew up for the novel we find

> Chapter XXI. Maisie discovers them, but says nothing – she thinks they have been secretly married. She is full of the secret, and she can afford now to be nice to Maata and kiss her and hug her and help her to make Pip's bed.
> [. . .]
> Chapter XXIII. Maisie tells of their love episode. The silence explodes. They are violent, hysterical, half mad. She is denied the house immediately and she goes away to Rhoda who finds her a horrible little poor room.[9]

As the unfinished novel records, the Close/Trowell parents were outraged, and Maata/Mansfield was told to leave the house immediately.

At some point in January 1909, therefore, Mansfield returned to Beauchamp Lodge – clearly frightened and isolated, but comforted by faithful Ida. Believing, however, that Garnet would not abandon her, Mansfield continued to earn money through her recital work, in the vain hope that somehow everything would work out. But Garnet, young and inexperienced, had no idea what to do. There was also his job to consider. He therefore returned to the Moody Manners Opera

Company, while Mansfield hoped – longed – for reconciliation and marriage. Indeed, the lovers did meet when Garnet took a week off from touring in February 1909. References in Mansfield's papers to a liaison in Hull suggest they attended one of Tom's concerts there on 15 February, when he appeared alongside the singer John MacCormack. It was now that Mansfield discovered she was pregnant. She could no longer remain in limbo, waiting for Garnet to make a move. She had to act – and quickly.

In early February 1909, at one of her speaking engagements, Mansfield had met the man she would now go on to marry just a month later: George Bowden.[10] In previous biographies of Mansfield, his – admittedly brief – walk-on part in her life is seen as more of a footnote to an otherwise salacious story of unwanted pregnancy and double-crossing. Bowden's own full account of his relationship with Mansfield, written in the 1940s, some thirty years after the events it describes, and following a request by American researcher Lucy O'Brien, offers more or less the only evidence for what occurred between them, since Mansfield herself left almost no trace of her 'camping ground', as she termed it, for the years 1909–11.[11] However, in June 2024 John Wood discovered a sworn affidavit from 1917 in the National Archives in London dealing with Bowden's divorce from Mansfield, which had been strangely embargoed for one hundred years, and which Bowden had completely and deliberately ignored in his account of his brief relationship with Mansfield. Wood was the first person to recognize its importance in relation to Mansfield's life. Bowden's account in the affidavit of their

George Bowden, *c.* 1940s.

brief marriage and her personality is salacious, to say the least. But we digress. In early February 1909 he found himself rather attracted to this clever and flirtatious young woman from an impeccable and wealthy colonial background.

Born in 1877, Bowden was admitted as a choral scholar to King's College, Cambridge in 1899, at the age of 22, receiving his BA degree in 1902. After leaving Cambridge he became a lecturer on voice production and a teacher of singing, first in England and later in the USA. During the time Mansfield knew him, Bowden, with his fine tenor voice, was a performer at Henry Wood's Promenade Concerts. Bowden's second wife (after Mansfield) was Annie Frances Moore (known as Dina), and they were married on 22 March 1919 in Berkeley, California. She was 25 and Bowden 41 at the time of their marriage. He had gone to the USA in 1915 and taught music at the University of California in Berkeley from 1915 to 1918. He then moved to New York in 1918 and met Dina, who was studying music there. They spent nearly all their married life in Mallorca, Spain, and moved to the Isle of Man during the Second World War, as there was a general fear that Mussolini would take over Mallorca. They would go on to have one son and three grandchildren.

In fourteen typed pages, called 'A Biographical Note on Katherine Mansfield' and sent to American researcher Lucy O'Brien, Bowden supplied, for the first time, an account of his entire relationship with Mansfield – well, his bowdlerized version – in the accompanying letter for which he claimed they enjoyed 'a happy if short intellectual comradeship'.[12] He recounted his initial meeting with Mansfield at the home of Dr C. W. Saleeby, a music enthusiast whose wife was a daughter of the poet Alice Meynell. On introducing himself to Mansfield, Bowden found 'her wit was instantaneous and we had some rapid exchanges. Like others, I was to learn that [. . .] the demure air cloaked a very observant and critical eye.'[13] They discovered that they lived within walking distance of each other, for Mansfield was now back at Beauchamp Lodge in Paddington (having been thrown out of the Trowells' house in St John's Wood), and Bowden was in a nearby bachelor flat, which he shared with Lamont Shand (a great friend of the Saleebys), together with a manservant called Charles, 'our Admirable Crichton', who had once worked for the Marchioness of Aylesbury.[14] Bowden also explained his own career at the time and his reputation in musical circles in London, later stressing his connection to the important conductor Henry Wood, and noting that 'I gave the first public performance in London of Debussy's

"L'Enfant Prodigue" with his orchestra at the Promenade Concerts, Queen's Hall.'[15]

The two men invited Mansfield to their flat, but before she took up their invitation, she and Bowden met again at a tea party given by a young Continental soprano newly arrived in London. Bowden was surprised to see Mansfield dress

> more or less in Maori fashion. [. . .] There was something almost eerie about it, as though of a psychic transformation rather than a mere impersonation. At such times even her facial lineaments might seem altered, and in trying to understand her complex personality this is a factor to be reckoned with.[16]

Thereafter, Mansfield soon became a regular visitor to Bowden's flat, particularly for lunch: 'We chatted or made music as the spirit prompted and for love only.' She ate very little, having 'the appetite of a bird, and would peck daintily at her food, not so much with palatial savour as with an air of detachment'. She would eventually 'have the free run of the flat'.[17] According to Ida, Mansfield soon became the recipient of long letters from Bowden. Initially sympathetic, Ida recalled how

> Bowden was a kindly person, and, I believe, very much in love with Katherine. His letters were full of humble devotion and understanding, really beautifully expressed. I think he knew she did not love him, but he seemed to understand her and her needs, and offered security and a place where she would be sheltered and be able to work without anxiety.[18]

However, throughout her life, Mansfield hid much from Ida – and so we shall never know whether the astonishing contents of the divorce affidavit from 1917 (divulged in Chapter Five) were also hidden from her. Not a shred of substantive evidence remains – from Bowden himself, or Mansfield or Murry (who would have been served the same affidavit as co-respondent), or from Ida – of their response to the affidavit. And it appears that every single copy of the affidavit was destroyed, except for the one legally deposited at the National Archives.

But back to the time of happy comradeship. After Bowden had his tonsils removed in February 1909, it was Mansfield who collected him in a taxi and took him back to the flat. It was now that the pair became engaged (again, the speed with which Mansfield attached herself to Bowden is quite remarkable),

> the occasion being marked by a festive celebration at the next Saleeby dinner party. K. dutifully did her share of the honours, introducing me to those of her relatives living in London, among them her guardian uncle and the novelist, 'Elizabeth' [. . .] her cousin. But she was impatient with this side of her existence [. . .]. Nor did they on their part appear to be familiar with her way of life or her friends, few of whom were even known to me.[19]

Bowden recounted that Mansfield's guardian in London (Henry Beauchamp) had written to inform her parents of the engagement, but that she found the idea of having to wait for their consent – or worse, their arrival in London – 'repugnant', since 'it carried the unbearable suggestion of suffering again the domination from which she had only just escaped.'[20] Bowden noted that he was very sympathetic with the aims of women at that time and their struggle for enfranchisement, revealing himself to be both modern and enlightened in his political views. The real reason, of course, why Mansfield didn't want to wait was because of her discovery that she was pregnant with Garnet's child. The idea that her parents might want to delay the marriage for any reason was a horrific prospect. Even Ida reported that Mansfield initially had no interest in marrying Bowden, but that once she realized she was pregnant with Garnet Trowell's baby she knew she had to act. Mansfield therefore used all the not-inconsiderable charm at her disposal to attract the unsuspecting Bowden, who was clearly enchanted with the remarkable and alluring young Antipodean. In fact, he himself commented on the magnetic nature of her personality: 'she normally exercised a definitely positive attitude socially and must have found it easy to gain dominion if not domination in the intimate circle of her admirers. I fancy she knew on the instant where this power of hers was likely to be possible.'[21] Together the pair attended concerts, went to Rumpelmayer's for afternoon tea, or to Bowden's club, where they sat and wrote letters. Above all, Bowden recalled her determination to maintain her freedom and agency after their marriage:

> It was freedom in life itself that K. M. stood for so passionately. And no doubt it was this in the individual and bachelor character of life at the flat which attracted her. Immediately on our engagement I received a long letter warning me not to expect too much of her. We would meet at the casual roadside camp fire of an evening rather than share the life of the open road together. This was another of her frequent figures of speech, but only the sense of urgency or strain in the letter surprised me. [. . .] But I was to recall later the note of foreboding in this letter.[22]

Talking of Mansfield's 'dark humours', Bowden noted that on such occasions she became 'unapproachable', and 'she appeared rather to dramatize herself and to enjoy the ill-health of the soul.' One such mood produced the poem 'Loneliness', which she showed to Bowden, who, on returning the manuscript, had suggested changing the title to 'Solitude', which, as he now admitted, was outrageous, for it completely changed the tone of the poem: 'what followed was as near indignation as anything I ever saw in her.'[23] Such sensitivity to criticism, which John Middleton Murry would come to know only too well, manifested itself on another occasion regarding a piece of prose she had given Bowden to read. He made a suggestion about a comma:

> K. was standing at the other end of the room with her back to me facing a mirror. As I looked up I saw her head and neck rise as she slowly turned and said over her shoulder very distinctly indeed, 'You can't tell me anything about commas' And there seemed no doubt about it; I couldn't.[24]

Mansfield and Bowden were married at Paddington Register Office on 2 March 1909, with Ida Baker as the sole witness. The bride wore black. In his initial long account, Bowden appeared particularly reticent when it came to discussing what passed between them on that fateful marriage night, stating only that 'there came an abrupt end, for the time being at any rate, to the care-free comradeship of the flat with the realization of an incompatibility which made married life between us impossible.'[25] (Of course, he was completely ignorant of the fact that Mansfield was pregnant.) In subsequent letters to O'Brien, he provided further information:

> Ida Baker, whom I had not met up to this time, was K. M.'s witness. [. . .] We were to spend the day about town and K. wore the best street clothes she had, of which there was not much choice. If the dress itself was black, I remember her as becomingly and suitably clothed, for ordinarily she took little or no pains about her appearance. Certainly the impression on me was not a funereal one.
>
> [. . .] The marriage was not consummated. For reasons of her own which she never confided to me, she could not go through with it, and never came to live at the flat.
>
> [. . .] As already stated, she had her own reasons; possibly she had too much inner integrity to be able to go on with what she realised did not possess her heart. The marriage proved [. . .] an illogical conclusion.[26]

This description needs to be remembered when the 1917 affidavit is discussed later in this book. Bowden also provided more details about the wedding day:

> You must bear in mind what I have described as the 'bachelor' character of our relationship from the beginning, in which we never questioned each other's coming and going. There was a festive lunch after the ceremony, and I recall two items which K. M. would choose when out with me. It was a partiality influenced, no doubt, by nomenclature, for they were Creamed Jerusalem Artichokes, and an Italian wine known as Lagrima Christi. When we parted it was with the understanding that she would join me at the flat. That she did not do so, and without any explanation, was a painful mystery to me. Her marriage made her no longer eligible for Beauchamp Lodge, and it was a week or ten days before I was given an address. I found her in a miserable room. But all she would say in response to my concern was, 'I can't come'.
>
> Years afterwards when the LIFE was published, I drew the conclusion that she felt the nature of our relations would not stand the stress of a complete confidence on her part – had she been disposed to give it – while on the other hand she refused to face the duplicity which withholding it must have entailed.[27]

In 1949, learning that New Zealand author Antony Alpers was writing a biography of Mansfield, Bowden wrote to him on 16 November:

> Miss Baker's message in the dressing case, of which I now learn from your letter, may account for K. M.'s sudden and complete frigidity after we had reached the hotel suite where we were to spend the night. She had of her entirely free will entered into the marriage, we had had dinner and 'done a show' on our usual good terms, so that this anti-climactic denouement came as a complete surprise – not to say shock – to me.
>
> We left the hotel together the next morning, but instead of bringing her things from Beauchamp Lodge to the flat as arranged, she failed to appear, and it was something like a week before I could obtain an address.

The message Ida had placed in the dressing case she had lent Mansfield for the wedding read, 'Bear up.'

As noted above, Mansfield made deliberate and sustained efforts to destroy personal papers from the years 1909–11. However, we do have an enticing glimpse of her life at this time through an intriguing file of letters accumulated by Bowden during the two brief periods she lived with him – and therefore not personally destroyed by her – deposited in the Alexander Turnbull Library in New Zealand in 1986. The documents include three letters from Floryan Sobieniowski (more of him later); two letters sent by Mansfield to unknown recipients, almost certainly Ida; and a letter to Mansfield from a friend, Vera French, all of them written during this frustrating void of tangible biographical evidence, and which will be discussed in the next chapter. In addition, there is another item with biographical relevance that scholar Chris Mourant discovered in 2012: a hitherto-unknown complete story – 'A Little Episode' – written by Mansfield in the late spring of 1909, whose autobiographical plot also sheds new light on this obscure period.[28] In the story, written within a few weeks of this first marriage, she conveys all her bitterness and disillusionment with life. Alpers was not aware that a complete typescript existed in London when he mentioned the story in his 1980 biography, since he was working from a typescript held in Texas, which contains just very brief fragments.[29] He was able to conclude that 'In some way those fragments all seem related to the marriage and the events that preceded it.'[30] He was right; the complete story does indeed relate to Mansfield's marriage to Bowden. It offers perhaps the most detailed picture of events during that period in 1908–9, hinting at her bitterness over Garnet's abandonment of her and their unborn child, as perceived in the callous portrayal of the character of Jacques and his duplicitous behaviour towards Yvonne. The sentence 'By Lord Mandeville's pillow she saw a large bottle of Eucalyptus and two clean handkerchiefs' also hints at her distaste for the fastidious Bowden, who had a similar bedtime habit.[31] Thanks to 'A Little Episode', we now have more of a sense of her inner turmoil during this period.

In the story, Yvonne, Lady Mandeville, previously a penniless but beautiful orphan, has married well, but cannot get her former lover, Jacques Saint Pierre, out of her mind. Following one of his concerts, she makes her way backstage, and the two former lovers are reunited. He walks her back home, where, in a little gatehouse to which only she has access, she has set up a private shrine to her former life with Jacques. They make love:

> Never before had Yvonne needed so much love in her life. Primitive woman she felt – with primitive impulses – primitive needs – all conventions – all scruples were thrown to the four winds.
>
> Jacques flung off his coat. Then he came forward – – She could not look at him – but stood – suddenly silent.
>
> 'Here,' he said, 'let me help you off with this,' and caught hold of her cloak.
>
> 'Thank you,' she murmured – suddenly and absurdly glad that her dress was beautiful. Then he caught hold of her – kissed her – roughly – repeatedly.
>
> 'Let me go,' she said, 'let me go,' yet lay passive in his arms.
>
> 'Yvonne – Yvonne – look at me.'
>
> She put her arms round his neck, and held up her face.
>
> 'O, you are killing me,' she moaned.[32]

No wonder the story was never published, either by Mansfield or Murry; its Mills & Boon quality, with Yvonne's 'primitive needs' and Jacques's rough kissing, is certainly gauche in its presentation. After their secret assignation, Yvonne returns to the main house, 'dishevelled – flushed', her cut lip evidence of Jacques's rough and passionate handling of her, and where Lord Mandeville awaits her. As she prepares for bed, the realization that her husband expects conjugal relations fills her with disgust:

> 'O, I have lived – I have lived,' she cried – 'And I shall see Jacques tomorrow of course – something beautiful and stupendous is going to happen – O I am alive again – at last!'
>
> She threw off her clothes, hastily, brushed out her long hair, and then suddenly looked at the wide, empty bed. A feeling of intolerable disgust came over her. By Lord Mandeville's pillow she saw a large bottle of Eucalyptus and two clean handkerchiefs. From below in the hall she heard the sound of bolts being drawn – then the electric light switched off – –
>
> She sprang into bed – and suddenly, instinctively with a little childish gesture – she put one arm over her face – as though to hide something hideous and dreadful – as her husband's heavy ponderous footsteps sounded on the stairs . . .[33]

Here is evidence of Bowden, the singer, fastidious in his night-time habits in order to maintain his voice, which now repelled and disgusted Mansfield. Is this what she felt on her wedding night, while she longed for Garnet's embrace? Tragically for Yvonne, her story does not end happily, for Jacques Saint Pierre turns out to be a duplicitous rake:

> To-night – think of it – I saw Yvonne – she is quite a little Society lady – and I assure you – no longer one of us – But she bores me – she has the inevitable feminine passion for trying to relight fires that have long since been ashes – Take care, little one, that you do not – like wise. I hear her husband is very wealthy – and – what they call here – a 'howling bore'.
>
> Adieu – chérie – I shall be with you in two days – if I manage to avoid the charming Yvonne – There is the penalty, you see, for being so fascinating.[34]

The ending of the story mirrors the epigraph at the very beginning, taken from Wilde's *The Picture of Dorian Gray*: 'The one charm of the past is that it is past. But women never know when the curtain has fallen.' Here was Mansfield at one of the most traumatic moments of her life, pregnant – but not by her husband – deserted by the baby's father, and with no idea what would happen next.

In another twist, Mansfield's marriage to Bowden ran the risk of not being technically valid, given that she declared her age as '22 years' when she was only twenty. At the time, it was possible to marry under the age of 21 with parental consent, and even without it, being underage did not necessarily invalidate the marriage. If, however, she had told her parents and they had dissented, that would have created a legal bar to the marriage. In this case, it was Mansfield's guardian, Henry Beauchamp, who would most certainly have objected to the wedding and told her she must await formal consent from her parents. Marriage was a serious affair, and he would never have condoned such a thing without Harold Beauchamp's blessing. But as we know, being pregnant, Mansfield had no time to waste, and as a result did not wait for her parents' permission.

And so, the morning after the marriage, which – remember – according to Bowden himself, remained unconsummated, and having reconnected with Ida, Mansfield moved into a little room above a hairdressers' shop, where she remained in abject misery for a week. Desperately missing Garnet and fearful for her situation, she wrote to him, according to Ida, 'begging him to come and see her or to answer her letters'.[35] She now told Garnet of her pregnancy – but omitted to mention her marriage. Poor Garnet, going against his parents' wishes, did the gentlemanly thing and relented; by about 10 March, Mansfield was on a train to Glasgow, where the Moody Manners Opera Company was performing, now posing as Garnet's 'wife'. For a short time, Mansfield, who had a fine singing voice, became a member of the chorus. Many years later, she would regale writer friends, including Virginia Woolf, with tales of her life on the road with the company. By the end of March, the opera company had moved to Liverpool, with Garnet and Mansfield performing together, living together, she, like an ostrich with her head in the sand, ignoring the runaway train that was the mess she had made of her life hurtling at breakneck speed towards catastrophe.

The catastrophe, when it came, was in the form of a press cutting sent to Garnet by his parents, which announced Mansfield's marriage to one George Bowden. Her duplicity must have hurt Garnet to the core. Baby or no baby, he could not live openly with another man's wife. And so, in utter misery, with Garnet helpless in the face of so much adversity to their ever being together, Mansfield returned to London – and Ida – at the end of March, where, following a few days' refuge at the Baker family flat in Montagu Mansions, she found a tiny apartment of her own in Maida Vale. For Ida, this apartment left an impression of 'unpainted wood, bamboo furniture – the sort that tumbles over – and cotton curtains'.[36] As Jeffrey Meyers notes,

> Katherine's complete emotional and physical commitment to her first lover at the most vulnerable moment of her life, when her parents were 12,000 miles away and she could not confide in any adult, suggests that Garnet's betrayal and [his father] Thomas's condemnation had a profound effect. She was horribly shocked and permanently wounded by the rejection of her love, and this experience helps to explain why she became hard, tough, defensive and embittered.[37]

For reasons unknown, on 29 April Mansfield travelled alone to Brussels and remained there for several days; no clues exist as to the reason for this trip, but the possibility of obtaining an abortion cannot be ruled out. Perhaps the result was unsuccessful, or her nerve failed at the last minute; whatever the reason, she returned to Maida Vale still in despair, and still pregnant. She and Garnet never met again, but their correspondence continued for a while – on her side at least; a draft letter by Mansfield written in Brussels has morning sickness very much in evidence:

> In this room. Almost before this is written I shall read it from another room and such is Life. Packed again I leave for London. Shall I ever be a happy woman again. Je ne pense pas, je ne veux pas. Oh to be in New York. Hear me, I can't rest – that's the agonizing part.
>
> 'Tis a sweet day, Brother, but I see it not. My <u>body</u> is so self conscious – Je pense of all the frightful things possible – all this 'filthiness' – Sick at heart till I am physically sick – with no home – no place in which I can hang up my hat – & say here I belong – for there is no such place in the wide world for me.[38]

Had the word 'filthiness' been used by the Trowell parents, shocked at the sexual relations of the young couple? It was now a word imprinted on her very soul.

Of course, with the news of her hasty marriage having been communicated to them by her guardian, Henry Beauchamp, Mansfield's parents were in a despair of a different kind. They had the family reputation to maintain; Vera, their eldest daughter, was soon to be married to James Mackintosh Bell, a young Canadian geologist, and rumours of a wayward black sheep in the family, no matter how far away, were the last thing they needed. Accordingly, Annie Beauchamp sailed alone for England on 8 April on SS *Paparoa*. The journey, however, was hardly a trial: she loved sea voyages and was always a great favourite with the captain and other first-class guests on whatever ship she was on.

On 27 May Annie's boat train was met in London by a crowd of eager Beauchamp relatives, together with Mansfield, much less eager and half-hidden right at the back, in a completely unsuitable 'shiny black hat'.[39] Annie immediately moved her daughter into the smart hotel in Manchester Street where the family always stayed, giving the black hat to the chambermaid and buying her daughter a much more suitable fluffy tulle number. No one, of course, other than Garnet and Ida, knew that Mansfield was pregnant. Her parents, who had been aware of her 'fondness' for other girls, and especially her close friendship with Ida, were convinced that this was the reason for the abandonment of her marriage, as, it transpires, did Bowden himself. Bowden was duly summoned to meet Annie at the Bank of New Zealand offices, where he confirmed his own thoughts as to why Mansfield had left him – because she was 'sexually unbalanced' and attached in an unsavoury way to Ida. In his own 'Note', he stated that he felt 'bewildered' by events, and that details of Mansfield's subsequent trip to Bavaria (though not the reason why) came at a personal time of crisis for him, with, he claimed, the death of his father, which took up all his time. Of his meeting with Annie Beauchamp, he stated that there was 'constraint on both sides', and that the conversation had chiefly turned on the 'state of K's health. I gave my opinion that her manner of living had not conduced to a reasonable care of herself.'[40] It was quite clear to all concerned what he meant by that.

Ida's father, Colonel Baker, was then summoned, and everyone agreed it would be for the best if the two young women were separated. (Note that there is no evidence to suggest that any member of the Trowell family met with Annie Beauchamp; because of Mansfield's lies and deceptions, there was indeed nothing to summon them for.) Ida was despatched to the Canary Islands with her sister for a 'holiday', and Annie, who had done her homework on how such 'afflictions' were to be treated, accompanied Mansfield to Wörishofen in Bavaria to undertake the town's famous *Wasserkur* (water cure), created in the 1880s by

Catholic priest Sebastian Kneipp. In those days, such a treatment was deemed effective in 'curing' homosexuality. Nowadays, the town still attracts many thousands of visitors seeking the natural therapies, water treatments and vegetarian diet propounded by its founder to promote general health and well-being. Having arrived at the smart Hotel Kreuzer on 4 June, within a couple of days Annie left Mansfield there and travelled back to London in time for her return trip to New Zealand on 10 June, this time on SS *Tongariro*. She was back in Wellington by 13 August, whereupon she cut her wayward daughter out of her will, an act only discovered by Mansfield following her mother's death on 8 August 1918. The fact that Bowden so easily took Mansfield back into his home seven months later, as we shall see, makes it inconceivable that he had known about her pregnancy. It also explains why Annie Beauchamp stayed just a couple of days in Bavaria to settle her daughter into her 'cure', before returning immediately to Wellington. At no more than four months pregnant and, in her pre-tubercular days, still a portly figure, Mansfield could quite easily have hidden her pregnancy. If she had told her mother she was pregnant, Annie Beauchamp would surely have confronted Bowden with this news and the Trowell family would also have inevitably become involved once the truth was out. Bowden knew nothing, and neither did Annie.

Neither, of course, did Mansfield's friend Margaret Wishart, who was dismayed at Mansfield having abruptly ended their friendship:

> Margaret initially experienced a honeymoon period of intimate sharing followed by a shocking 'snap' disappearance, at the time of Mansfield's impulsive wedding to George Bowden on 2 March 1909, followed by her departure for Bavaria with her mother. In Margaret's words, 'she cut off like a clam in the last two days before disappearing, to my utter hurt and bewilderment'.[41]

Completely alone and now without any compulsion to hide her pregnancy, within a week of her mother's departure Mansfield had moved to the more anonymous and low-key Villa Pension Müller, a family-run guesthouse that inspired her first collection of short stories, *In a German Pension*, eventually published at the end of 1911. With her wedding ring firmly on, and using the name Bowden, she now passed herself off as an entirely upstanding married woman, residing in Wörishofen for her health. Within a few weeks, however, Mansfield hurt herself badly after trying to lift a heavy trunk onto the top of a cupboard and gave birth to a stillborn child: a dramatic climax to an emotionally traumatic few months.

A quick footnote on Garnet before we return to Mansfield in Wörishofen. Tom, his twin, who took the name Arnold Trowell in his professional life, went on to fulfil his promise of a successful musical career; Garnet, on the other hand, passed into obscurity. He eventually travelled as a musician to South Africa, where in 1923 (coincidentally, only after Mansfield's death) he married a Canadian woman, Marian Smith, and subsequently moved to Canada in 1929. He never discussed his earlier relationship with Mansfield with any member of his family, but, significantly, kept all her letters to him until his own death from cancer in 1947. They comprise possibly the most poignant extant collection of letters written by Mansfield, reflecting one of the defining emotional relationships of her entire life, with its catastrophic and unforgettable outcome. The fact that so many of Mansfield's letters to Garnet survive also points to the emotional attachment he himself had to this correspondence, which accompanied him on his travels around the world, before he ultimately settled in Canada. The raw, emotive, deeply felt – and at times sexual – passion that Mansfield describes in these letters is sometimes hard to read. It is too personal, and, because the reader knows how the love story ends, too painful. As early as 19 October 1908, just a few short weeks into their relationship, her sexual feelings manifested themselves, as in this letter, the second half of which (unpublished until my discovery of it in 2020) is quoted below:

> Oh, my darling, I do need you – I am waiting for you – Beloved, in your arms I find myself – Was ever Love so strong before – No, and I know why. There can only be one you. My darling – the night seems full of light. I kiss you passionately – Oh, I feel that when we are together, I shall truly die of joy and love – Garnet – I feel that my thoughts are on fire – you know the sensation? What would we be doing in our home now. You would be working and I should come into the dim, half-lighted room. We would throw open the window and lean out, smoking, and looked at the lighted streets – at the trees – their brown leaves bronzed with gold – verstehst du?[5] And then we would pull down the blind – and – Husband – the joy of thinking of it – takes my breath away. Oh, you have been gone so long

– darling – It's an eternity – and yet – it's nothing – at all – but I want you. Think of it – we two together – have all before us – I want to put my arms round you, & kiss your mouth. Let me come – close to you – Beloved – so close – I love you.

And now to work – yet tonight your kisses burn my lips – my mouth is hot – my hands tremble – I shake with passion. I wonder when we will be married – I wish I knew –

Garnet tonight – it is too strong for me – kiss me – kiss me – take me for I belong to you for ever

Kass.[42]

Mansfield, too, like Garnet, never forgot this relationship or her dead baby; as late as 1920, less than three years before her own death, she was writing in her diary, 'Oh misery! I cannot sleep. I lie retracing my steps – going over all the old life before. . . . The baby of Garnet's love.'[43]

So what of the following six months of 1909 spent in Bavaria? There is little firm biographical material to draw on, so thoroughly executed was Mansfield's mission to obliterate all traces of this period from her life. The rather breezy and affectionate postcards she continued to send her mother at this time do not hint at guilty secrets:

Wörishofen
The Church & a little white tower of the convent you can see, Janey dear. The large building opposite is the Kurhaus.

Wörishofen
And here the statue of Pfarrer Kneipp, & the fountain of Wörishofen water. That's the Kinderasyl behind and the Kneippianum.[44]

Janey was the family nickname for Mansfield's mother.[45] Both postcards show views of Wörishofen and the Wasserkur, once more affirming the fact that Mansfield had been sent to Germany for a water cure, not to give birth. As a result, it seems highly unlikely that her family ever knew of the events that actually took place in Bavaria until Ruth Elvish Mantz's research was published in the 1933 Mantz/Murry biography. If the family *had* subsequently found out, they certainly colluded in disseminating false information. A copy of an article written in 1933 by Tom Mills, an early Mansfield devotee in New Zealand, was read by Harold Beauchamp, who wrote, in returning the proof of the article,

> This I consider excellent, and I do not propose to suggest any alterations, as that would be tantamount to 'painting the lily and adorning the rose.' There is no one in New Zealand better qualified to speak of Kathleen's early efforts to get a footing on the rung of the literary ladder.[46]

In his article, Mills had written, 'Her instant success in London gave her the material for her first book, "In a German Pension", comprising a series of sketches she wrote for a London weekly journal, which sent her to Europe to write up the most famous and fashionable health resorts.'[47] Well, not quite. Mills had obviously not yet read Mantz and Murry's biography, also published in 1933, in which a portion of the truth was now finally revealed: '[Katherine] was told to return to her husband; and she refused. She had good reason for refusing; she was with child, and not by her husband.'[48] What this must have cost Harold Beauchamp emotionally, to have the truth about his deceased wayward daughter publicly revealed, can only be imagined; and then to read in Mantz, 'Katherine's child was fated to remain always a dream-child. It was born prematurely, and born dead.'[49]

And so we reset the stage. It is now the early summer of 1909. A twenty-year-old young married woman, separated from her husband, has just lost a baby in Wörishofen, Bavaria, ignored by her family, alone and in a foreign country. Emotionally overwrought, depression now took hold. A nurse friend of Ida's working in the slums of East London knew of a small boy called Walter, eight years old, who was recovering from pleurisy and who desperately needed a holiday. Ida records,

> I suggested that he convalesce with Katherine and she jumped at the idea. All Katherine's mother love flowed out to this boy. Arrangements were easier in those days; we got him a ticket, tied a label on him, and sent him across to her. She cared for him, loved him and kept him for two or three months, until he was able to return, healthy and well. She made him call her Sally.[50]

No one knows for certain when or from whom Mansfield contracted the tuberculosis that would eventually kill her, but surely little Walter must be a contender.

In depositing her daughter in Bavaria to 'take a cure', Annie Beauchamp had also left her with the monetary means to stay there. By moving from the expensive Hotel Kreuzer to the Pension Müller, and finally to lodgings with the Brechenmacher family, Mansfield was able to eke out this allowance until the end of the year (when Ida would eventually give her the money for her fare home). Wörishofen at this time was home to a group of émigrés, several of whom were Polish. Mansfield, already fascinated by Russia and Eastern Europe, naturally gravitated towards these Eastern Europeans. In 2018 a new poem by Mansfield, 'To You', written in Bavaria and offering tantalizing clues to Mansfield's life in Wörishofen at this time, was unearthed by Claire Davison and me. The poem is handwritten, signed and dated '09':

There are two portraits, sketched in this your Book;
The first has something of a Tigress air
But fascinating! And the second, look,
Profile, with just a flower in your hair

And, looking at these portraits, I can see
Your Modern Soul, the greatness of your Part.
Indeed, indeed, they both reveal to me
You are an Artist, with the Artist's heart.

I have not seen you play, but yet I know
How well you play, with what a grace – an air!
Till I am tempted to describe you so –
A Tigress with a Flower in your Hair.[51]

One lead as to a possible identity of the addressee is to be found in lines 5–6: 'And, looking at these portraits, I can see/ Your Modern Soul, the greatness of your Part'. She reinforces the theme of theatricality and performance, both directly and indirectly, pointing us in the direction of perhaps the most accomplished of her *German Pension* stories, itself titled 'The Modern Soul'. It is a story that blends pastiche, social satire and an archly poised authorial 'I' with an incisive, wicked eye for ridicule and a dramatic rendering of performers performing. Indeed, its sense of timing and voice is so artfully balanced that it could almost be a script for actors, as Mansfield targets her satire on the medley of hotel guests, rather than the local Bavarian citizens that feature in many of the other stories. It is similar to another story in the collection, 'The Luftbad', which also ridicules the pretensions and practices of the cure guests in the Bavarian spa town, with their barely concealed smouldering sexuality and greed.

The principal male character in 'The Modern Soul' is the trombone-playing Herr Professor who plays in the pine woods so as to be accompanied by the sighing delicacy of the trees, and who clutches a bag of worm-infested cherries between his knees. However, he is not the story's 'Modern Soul'. This privilege goes to Sonia Godowska from Vienna, a stage-struck, hyper-sensitive actress whom the trombone professor claims once to have 'described in her autograph album *as a tigress with a flower in the hair*' (my italics).[52] Miss Godowska teeters ardently on the brink of modernity – she recites Ibsen, entreats her audiences to go with her 'as lightly draped as possible' to the pine woods 'and bed with her among the pine needles', but almost swoons with horror when anything intimate about the body is mentioned.[53] As she tells her mother, 'I would rather my skirt dropped off my body' than hear any hint of down-to-earth vulgarity.[54]

Sonia Godowska herself has been read by some critics as a wickedly ironical self-portrait by Mansfield. Nothing could be more understandable: Mansfield frequently plays with literary masks and deflected identification, just as she doubtless joins Sonia in finding 'in all the works of all the greatest writers, especially in their unedited letters, some touch, some sign of myself'.[55] Now, however, with an autograph book and an evocation of a tigress in hand, things become more complicated. Could Sonia Godowska have been inspired by someone else residing at the Pension Müller, for she was clearly known to Mansfield? Might her name even suggest the presence in Bad Wörishofen of another 'modern soul', the passionate Polish harpsichordist Wanda Landowska (1879–1959), renowned for her heightened sense of dramatic performance and often hailed as the 'high priestess of the harpsichord'?[56] This makes sense when we recall the first two lines of the last stanza: 'I have not seen you play, but yet I know/ How well you play, with what a grace – an air!'

Wanda Landowska, a member of Natalie Clifford Barney's famed Parisian lesbian salon, was almost single-handedly responsible for the revival of the harpsichord as a performance instrument in the twentieth century. As Patricia Juliana Smith notes, 'In her enthusiastic research to uncover the forgotten music and performance styles of the seventeenth and eighteenth centuries, she paved the way for today's interest in authentic performances of early music on original instruments.'[57] Married to Polish folklorist Henry Lew in 1900, he encouraged her research and performance of early music, and assisted her in writing her book, *Musique ancienne* (1909).[58] Nevertheless, as Smith notes, 'While the relationship was a mostly supportive one, Landowska wished to be relieved of the sexual aspects of marriage.' At the beginning of the marriage, therefore, 'she arranged a ménage à trois, by hiring a maid who would also function as Lew's mistress. The situation was apparently satisfactory for all involved, and, even after Lew died in 1919, the maid remained in the musician's service until the latter's death.'[59] Thereafter, Landowska settled in Paris, 'often providing musical accompaniment for the various artistic functions of [Barney's] renowned lesbian salon'.[60] In the 1930s Landowska met Denise Restout, 'who became, in turn, her student, her life companion, and the preserver of her artistic legacy'.[61] It is entirely possible, then, that she could have been a 'cure' guest in Wörishofen at the same time as Mansfield and would undoubtedly have caused a stir in the small spa town. (She later taught harpsichord at the Berlin School of Music from 1912 to 1919.) And so, even though we know so little of her life during the second half of 1909, this little poem certainly seems to show Mansfield making the most of her time in Wörishofen, within a circle of bohemian friends and acquaintances, the most significant of whom was Floryan Sobieniowski.

Little is known of Sobieniowski's early life. Mantz and Murry's early biography provided details of a 'Polish literary critic', who was never named:

> Since it was cheap and unfashionable, beautiful and homely, Woerishofen attracted impecunious continental *littérateurs*. Among them was a Polish literary critic, charming, distinguished and completely untrustworthy. He might have served as the original of one of Dostoevsky's Poles. He had a magnificent singing voice, and a wonderful repertory of Polish and Russian songs. He had, also, a passion for Stanislas Wyspianski, which he strove to communicate to her; and with his help and a German text she began to translate one of Wyspianski's plays.[62]

Floryan Sobieniowski, *c.* 1930s.

Sobieniowski was born in 1881 in a southern part of Poland and studied at the prestigious Jagiellonian University in Kraków, founded in 1364 and one of the oldest universities in the world. He became a devotee of the Polish artist and polymath Stanisław Wyspiański and did much to promote him after his death in 1907. Inevitably, Mansfield soon developed an infatuation for Sobieniowski (not hard to imagine, given how vulnerable she was at this time), and they became lovers. She now found herself immersed in all things Polish, including the language and especially the work of Wyspiański. One of her rare letters still in existence from this period was written to her youngest sister Jeanne on 10 November:

> Your birthday gift, little Sister is here beside me on the table – it is a fat Polish dictionary with a green leather binding, and an air, already, of great weariness with life – in fact it goes about with me every day [. . .].
>
> Last night, sitting working here, the great jug of scarlet blackberry vine threw a twisted shadow on the wall – rather, my

> lamplight, more than a little fascinated, stencilled for me the trailing garlands with a wizard finger. And so I thought of you. Did you get the thought. Did you find it hanging on to the edge of your skirt ('Good gracious, is that a cotton .... Where can I have picked it up'.....) 'My dear, allow me to present you with a Bavarian mind wave!'[63]

What would young Jeanne, seventeen, safely and respectably at home in Wellington, have made of the exoticism of Polish dictionaries, weariness with life, twisted shadows, trailing garlands and wizard fingers, sent via a Bavarian mind wave? There is certainly an air of exuberance and confidence in the letter, but also a note of defiance in the bohemian and rather daring nature of the prose.

According to Alpers, Ida recalled in old age that Mansfield had '"made plans with the Pole" to go with him to his homeland, and then to go perhaps to Russia', but Ida only knew what Mansfield had told her, and an actual visit with Sobieniowski to Poland may well have been concealed from her, coming so soon as it did after all the disastrous events earlier in the year.[64] We know that Mansfield and Sobieniowski were lovers; we also know that she was fascinated by Russia and Eastern Europe and that she was itinerant by nature with a penchant for travelling, which would, later in her life, border on the compulsive. Therefore it is entirely possible that she and Sobieniowski did, in fact, travel to Poland together in November 1909; that they visited Kraków; that she saw the evidence of Wyspiański's artistic achievements visible everywhere in his home town, resulting in two poems, 'To Stanislaw Wyspiański' and 'To God the Father'; and that a third poem, dedicated to Floryan himself, 'Floryan Nachdenklich' ('Floryan Pensive'), was also written during this period.

Following a visit to Kraków a few years ago, I discovered by chance that Mansfield's poem 'To God the Father' was directly inspired by a monumental stained-glass window entitled 'God the Father – Let it Be' (*Bóg Ojciec – Stań się*), designed by Wyspiański for the church of St Francis, portraying a monumental figure of God in the act of creation. Mansfield's description of God in her poem directly refers to the image of the God figure as represented by Wyspiański. The window had been installed in the Franciscan church in 1904, three years before Wyspiański's death in 1907; Mansfield could only have heard of it through Sobieniowski, who may have shown her a photographic reproduction, if such an image existed, or, as mentioned earlier, and far more likely, she visited Kraków with Sobieniowski in the autumn of 1909, making full use of that Polish dictionary sent to her by her youngest sister. Mansfield was alone, carefree, and – yet again – in love. With the onset of winter, there was just one problem: she was now pregnant with Sobieniowski's child.

3

The *New Age*, 1910–11

We know so little about Mansfield's life during the following two years. These were her drug-taking, sexually provocative dark years – nearly all signs of which she obliterated – before her relationship with John Middleton Murry began, and when her interior decorating tastes ran to a couple of candles stuck inside a skull and a stone Buddha, as this chapter reveals.

Did Floryan Sobieniowski know Mansfield was pregnant? We do know that towards the end of 1909, the relationship took a more serious turn. Sobieniowski now wanted Mansfield to move in with him as his future wife, initially in Warsaw, with the intention of them both setting up home in Paris by the end of the year; Mansfield being pregnant certainly explains his now-urgent desire to put the relationship on a sounder footing. But suddenly – and perhaps the second pregnancy in less than a year precipitated such a revelation – Mansfield finally realized what the implications of becoming too involved with Sobieniowski meant. It was as if a veil had suddenly lifted from her eyes. She took fright on a train to Warsaw, made up some excuse and returned to Wörishofen via Munich, leaving Sobieniowski to travel on to Warsaw alone, she making empty promises about a romantic future together in Paris and divorce from Bowden. Her mind was in turmoil, and seeking an objective view, she now wrote for advice to an old Beauchamp Lodge friend Vera French, who sent her by return a ten-page letter, warning Mansfield against the steps she was planning to take. Mansfield's own letter to Vera, which does not survive, must have explained (without mentioning that she was pregnant) that she and Sobieniowski had hatched a plan whereby they would make an outward display of living together in Paris by the end of the year, so that Bowden would be forced to divorce her and leave her free to marry her Polish lover. But Vera's response to this plan was the warning that women are 'so constituted that if they love they can't bear to refuse the beloved his heart's desire' – that is, to sleep with them – and that this would be the ruin of her friend, if Sobieniowski then refused to marry her once her divorce was through. This response clearly indicates that she did not know that Mansfield had already given her Polish lover 'his heart's desire'. She continued: 'there may be an afterwards, which for you may be a Hell which will make you so desperate that you will not care what you do or what becomes of you.'[1] This letter would surely have reinforced in Mansfield's mind that divorce from Bowden and marriage to a penniless Pole would place her in an untenable social position and leave her permanently ostracized from her family.

In addition to Vera French's letter above, three letters from Sobieniowski exist from this time – inadvertently left at Bowden's flat in 62 Gloucester Place during the short time Mansfield lived there with Bowden in early 1910, more of which shortly. On 12 December Sobieniowski wrote to her in Wörishofen from Warsaw:

> Kathleen *Moja*! You don't want to speak a word to me today, the postman has been here three times and brought nothing, but I hope he'll come back in the evening. [. . .] You cannot guess how much I long for you, how full my thoughts are at every moment – where are you? what are you doing now . . . ?[2]

Sobieniowski wrote again the next day, a little happier as he had just received a letter from her:

> Kathleen! With what joy I open your letter from Friday. Oh thanks be to you dearest –[. . .] Then I was really with you in Paris with these words – and how can I thank you for these words – where you say that you love me and why it is not pronounced but you know – you know Kathleen – it is alive, it is mighty in me this feeling – I want to make it eternal for me, so that at any moment you can see that my whole being is with this love to you and that nothing extraneous is there.[3]

There then follows a detailed account of a party he had been to the night before, together with some abrasive comments on Walt Whitman's

Polish translator, before he closes: 'Good night, Kathleen, goodnight, and how will it be with the dream? The white forest I see now in your room – tells me, calls that I should come to it. Oh Kathleen maybe in 18 days – – – – – good night, give me your hands. Your Floryan'.[4] These are not the letters of a casual acquaintance or even a good friend. They are letters from a lover.

Vera French's warning letter of 12 December had come a little too late, however, since Mansfield now realized that she was pregnant – again. In the same Bowden file that contains the letters from Sobieniowski, there are two hastily scribbled letters from Ida, written to Mansfield in Wörishofen, replying to urgent cries for help. Ida had been tasked with finding accommodation and money, pending Mansfield's return to England, and possibly the name of someone who could arrange an abortion. Because of the events from earlier in the year, Ida's father, the irascible Colonel Baker, would not countenance any contact between the two and so Ida was having to think strategically:

> You know Miss Hanbury lives in tiny flats or suits of rooms – and she has told me she can take extra rooms when ever she wants anyone to stay there – well I thought that I would try to get a room there that you could have – because it would be simpler for me to come to you – & you see I thought if you were here on 31st [December] I could get her to ask me to 'see the Old Year out' there so that these people would be satisfied & I could be with you. [. . .] O dear – so much to say – do arrange to arrive in the morning the time the child did – because if it is evening – I don't see how I can come to you – and I could not possibly exist in the same town without doing so.
>
> I went straight to Vere [. . .?] and sent the dramatic message. & £6.0.0 – – – – this is absolutely all I can write at this minute – if I let myself think what it means – I shall – I don't know what – I can only wait to hear what you do and when – O Katie – – –[5]

That enigmatic request – 'do arrange to arrive in the morning the time the child did' – was perhaps, as John Wood suggests, a reference to little Walter, whom Mansfield had sent back to England from Bavaria a few months previously.[6] In another letter sent immediately after the first, Ida wrote more details about Miss Hanbury and how 'she loves her "patients" as she calls them – Rock no more! O Katie is it possible – is it not a dream –.'[7] Was Miss Hanbury a sort of back-street abortionist? Or perhaps someone who looked after unmarried mothers? Ida's anxiety and fears are clearly evident, and also her disbelief: 'if I let myself think what it means'. Something shocking had happened to her beloved Katie and – as so often happened – she had been asked to step in and help sort out the mess.

We have no firm details of what happened next. But we do know that instead of going to Paris with Sobieniowski, the impossibility of what she had promised him, together with the recently discovered disastrous state she was in, propelled Mansfield back to London instead, around the end of December 1909 or beginning of January 1910, with that £6 wired over by Ida. No records exist as to whether she went to Miss Hanbury's or not. But given her next move it seems not, since she stayed for a short time at the Strand Palace Hotel before, rather astonishingly, persuading George Bowden that she should move in with him – again. She told Ida that 'partly for the sake of the family' she was going to live with Mr Bowden and 'try to make it work'. This was confirmed by Mantz in the years following her biography, when she noted that the reason Mansfield went back to George Bowden was given to her by Ida: 'After K. M. returned from Bavaria, her father decreed that "since she was married" to George Bowden, she must return to him under threat of cancellation of her allowance of £100.'[8] Furthermore, Ida informed Mantz that Bowden 'had been lonely and had gone about', that is, had had multiple sexual partners since Mansfield had left him.[9] As a result, she suffered 'piercing pains' and was never well afterwards. It was of course possible that any subsequent venereal disease had been contracted because of her relationship with Floryan Sobieniowski, but if we are to believe the affidavit from 1917 (much more of which in Chapter Five), sexual relations with Bowden did now take place.

The simple fact was that Mansfield was pregnant on her return to England in January 1910, carrying Sobieniowski's child, the frightening circumstances of which, plus her family's threats, precipitated her return to her legal husband. In his 'Note', Bowden shies away from any mention of sexual relations with Mansfield, though his later affidavit affirms these took place. In sleeping with her legal husband, she may have thought she would provide legitimacy – of sorts – for this second unborn child. Of course, more lies were now told to Sobieniowski – that she was ill, but that she would return – in order to buy time while she decided how to deal with the latest predicament she now found herself in.

The Bowden papers contain a final letter written from Paris on Sunday, 9 January 1910, by a bewildered and frustrated Sobieniowski, offering incontrovertible proof that the relationship between him and Mansfield was serious and heartfelt – at least on his side:

> *Kathleen Dearest,* [. . .] I am dreadfully tired, but happy to be in Paris at last. If you could be mine already – this week will be as long as eternity for me. I shall be very patient though – just this worry – what's with you? Are you well already, or still ill? Oh write to me, *Dear*, straight away – write to me Kathleen that I can be tranquil. [. . .]
>
> How I long for you – Oh *my wife*, and for inner solitude – for truly we will live in complete solitude, there is so much to do – by spring I want to have my plays completed – to further my translations of Whitman – to write critical articles on a number of books [. . .] I have such a huge appetite for this work – I feel sufficiently prepared and strong – only I need you, Kathleen, in every moment more and more when it is possible, and I tell you quite openly and so simply that I cannot live without you – I cannot think and look without you – I cannot – because I love you and this love is now my life – – –[10]

This is powerful, emotive writing – Sobieniowski addresses her as 'my wife' – and even allowing for his subsequent ungentlemanly behaviour in the years that followed, as we shall discover, his ardour cannot fail to arouse a degree of pity and sympathy in the reader. But, her mind made up, Mansfield abandoned Sobieniowski to his fate in Paris, and moved on with her still-messy and complicated life. It was a brief but intense love affair that she ran away from, though for several years afterwards, perhaps guilt at her own shoddy behaviour, together with unease at what Sobieniowski might do next, meant that she found herself compromised and therefore in no position to deny him favours.

The letters quoted above from Sobieniowski and Vera French, together with several others, had been inadvertently left behind by Mansfield at Bowden's flat in Gloucester Place, following her second attempt at a 'relationship' with him, and had thus come into his possession. He kept them for the remainder of his life. In his 'Note', Bowden recounted how exactly Mansfield engineered this second attempt, early in 1910. One evening, while staying at a country house in Lincolnshire, he received two telegrams in quick succession, stating that Mansfield was back in London 'and urging me to see her'. Mansfield put on the charm and asked for a second chance at making the marriage work. Bowden continued:

> At the second attempt a year later, when her immediate trouble of which I was ignorant was over, she may have thought a return to our former footing possible. But though we could renew our mutual interests in music and literature, and again enjoy such things as Jerusalem artichokes and Lagrima Christi wine, the break had been too complete. There was a sense of lack of the confidence essential to real comradeship.[11]

Nevertheless, Mansfield accompanied Bowden to his studio in Bond Street and sang on a few occasions, as well as reciting some of her sketches at a concert at Hackney College, which was a huge success, and where the principal, Dr P. T. Forsyth, 'was particularly enthusiastic both with her writing and the literary quality of her subjects'. As Wood notes, 'Forsyth was a theologian, whose specialist interests seem to have been sin and guilty conscience.'[12]

But something had to be done about the baby. Mansfield, feigning appendicitis, left Bowden for a nursing home paid for by Ida, where an operation was performed for an ectopic pregnancy, as Kathleen Jones reveals.[13] She subsequently recuperated near the sea in Rottingdean, in a little flat above a grocer's shop, where Bowden went to see her, and 'where we had tea followed by a friendly talk in the cottage garden. Though she was far from well it was plain she had lost nothing [. . .] of her psychic fascination.'[14] Having felt she had done her duty by her parents and attempted a reconciliation with Bowden, as well as being relieved of her second pregnancy, she now considered herself free to pursue her own life once more. It is certainly an ironic twist of fate that the unsuspecting Bowden ended up as a temporary haven following her second pregnancy, as well as her first.

Before she left Bowden's flat, Mansfield had given him the *German Pension* sketches she had written in Bavaria a few months earlier, and at breakfast one morning, he suggested sending them to the *New Age*, a weekly political, arts and literature paper. Never one to let the grass grow under her feet, by dinnertime Mansfield had taken them to the editor, A. R. Orage, in person. Bowden recalled how 'She was full of the interview with Orage and the favourable impression her writing had made on him.'[15] Many years later, in conversation with Orage, Mantz discovered information that never made it into her 1933 biography of Mansfield, which had been co-authored with – and censored by – Murry. It appeared that Bowden and his second wife, Dina, had introduced themselves to Orage when he was lecturing in New York in 1925: 'Orage was incredulous [about the second Mrs Bowden] – the same build, the way of holding the head, the cut of the hair, the kind of clothes – they were Katherine's.'[16] As Mantz notes, Bowden then reminded Orage of the first time Mansfield had visited him at the offices of the *New Age* in February 1910:

> 'I was with her that day, pacing up and down before the stairway of 38 Cursitor Street'. Though Orage had completely forgotten his first meeting with Katherine, or how it came about, the details in Bowden's mind were vivid with insistent distinctness.
>
> 'She dashed up with her manuscript, and she was back so quickly that I thought she hadn't managed to see you; but she cried, all in one breath, "I gave him THE-CHILD-WHO-WAS-TIRED. He said 'I'll read it'. I said, 'When'? 'He said, 'Now'. Then he glanced through it and said, 'I'll print it.' I said 'When?' He said, 'Next week – if you'll make these corrections.'"
>
> Then she added in a childish voice: "I could kneel right here on this pavement!"'[17]

Wood, however, tells of another account of the meeting between Orage and Bowden, with a different outcome, as recorded by Gurdjieff adherent and friend of Orage Louise Welch:

> Many years later, when Orage had been in New York, for several years, a curious visitor, G. C. Bowden by name, called at his office, saying that he wanted to meet Orage, who had seriously affected his life. He turned out to be Katherine Mansfield's first husband, who told Orage that on a blustery day in February 1910, he had waited outside the office of the *New Age* while Katherine went to inquire whether her first short story was acceptable. When

> Orage affirmed this, she went out at once to her husband and told him that their marriage was over.[18]

We will never know which was the true version of events, but in any case, soon after meeting with Orage, Mansfield left Bowden for the second and final time.

On a much more positive note, and thanks to Bowden's suggestion, by early 1910 Mansfield's stories and poems started to be published in the *New Age* and elsewhere, and her career as a writer in London was launched. She soon became part of the circle surrounding the magazine's editor, Orage, and his mistress, Beatrice Hastings (1879–1943). Orage had grown up in Yorkshire with his widowed mother. Intelligent and hardworking, he initially trained as a teacher, joined the newly established Independent Labour Party and started writing political articles. He also developed a life-long interest in esoteric spiritual beliefs, philosophy and religion, which would later impact Mansfield's own life. Following a move to London in 1905, he became editor of the *New Age* in 1907, a position he held until the autumn of 1922. He would publish some of the most preeminent authors of the day, including Shaw,

A. R. Orage, New York, 1930.

Beatrice Hastings, *c.* 1910s.

Chesterton, Wells and Bennett, as well as less well-known authors who would eventually become celebrated, such as Ezra Pound, Richard Aldington and, of course, Mansfield herself. As Chris Mourant writes, 'T. S. Eliot described Orage's death as "a public loss": he will be remembered "as the best literary critic of that time in London", Eliot wrote, and "as the benevolent editor who encouraged merit and (what is still rarer) tolerated genius".'[19] Welch notes how Bernard Shaw characterized him as a 'desperado of genius', and how in 1912 he would become 'the first in England to publish Freud in a non-professional journal – a good year before the first English translation of *The Interpretation of Dreams*'.[20]

Orage's partner from 1907 to 1914, and unofficial co-editor of the *New Age* (in her own eyes, at least), was Beatrice Hastings, born Emily Alice Beatrice Haigh in Hackney, though brought up in South Africa. (Orage was technically married at this time but separated from his wife.) A complicated and feisty character, Hastings was, as Philip Mairet observed, 'the one woman who held her place for years amongst the regular writers of the paper and she did it by sheer force of character and volume of production'.[21] Indeed her overall contributions to the paper, sometimes hugely provocative, and written under a wide variety of pseudonyms, ran to almost four hundred pieces. Once she left Orage in 1914, she moved to Paris, where she became for a while the lover of Modigliani. Her consistently unstable temperament, previously held somewhat in check, eventually gave way to paranoia and madness. Her memoirs, published in 1936, were vituperative and spiteful; in them she claimed that Orage and others had undertaken 'a social cabale' and 'a literary boycott' against her and that *she* was the one to whom Mansfield had shown her first sketch.[22] Towards the end of her life, Hastings offered her huge archive of personal papers to the British Museum, but when they were rejected, she burnt them, before committing suicide in 1943.

This, then, was the couple with which Mansfield now allied herself. Exciting and avant-garde, they both steered the burgeoning young writer towards her successful writing career. For John Carswell, 'Orage's charm, knowledge, and personal magnetism; Beatrice's apparent strength and literary commitment; the fact that they were in a position to print her work; and above all, perhaps, their literary and sexual partnership with one another, made them almost unbeatable in Katherine's eyes.'[23] In addition, Wood believes that

> Orage would certainly have given her books to review (unidentified at present), some sub-editing, and generally involved her as part of the 'team'. This is supported by a notebook entry from 1921, where she wrote that she 'worked for some time for the New Age', suggesting a greater role than just a contributor.[24]

Following a period of convalescence in Rottingdean from April to July after her ectopic pregnancy operation, by which time six of her stories and a poem had appeared in the *New Age*, Mansfield moved back to London and for a few weeks was a lodger in Orage and Hastings's flat at Abingdon Mansions in Kensington. This would have troubled the jealous and paranoid Hastings, though she seemingly put up with it. Stephen Gray, the biographer of Hastings, notes how

> In 1910, once Katherine Mansfield was on the scene in London [. . .] there were joint runaway weekends for the two women to Ditchling-on-Sea (which Carl Bechhöfer identified as being close to Seaford and so forth). When he was sixteen, in late 1911, he lived with Beatrice and Orage at Pease Cottage, near Crawley in Sussex, where KM was a long-term guest as well.[25]

More of Bechhöfer shortly. On 29 July Ida wrote to Garnet Trowell on behalf of Mansfield, returning her 'engagement' ring, well over a year after the romance had ended. In the letter she wrote:

> – K. came to see me today & asked me to send you this – and also to give you her address. She is living just now with some literary friends also on the staff of the New Age – & perhaps later will be able to take a small flat for herself – She will never join G. Bowden again – she only did so at the beginning of the year because she thought it her duty for the sake of her mother & sister & brother – Now she is Katherine Mansfield – [. . .] That is her writing name – & she is taking it almost entirely now – I am so sorry – once more – we have not met – [. . .] – I feel there is so much to hear & say –[26]

As Ida poignantly notes at the end of her letter, there was clearly much 'to hear & say' – on both sides. What Mansfield's reasons might have been for wanting to reconnect with Garnet at this time remain unclear: possibly to assuage her own guilt, or perhaps to see if the relationship could be rekindled. Ida never discussed it in her memoirs, and no further contact with Garnet has been traced.

In late August 1910 Mansfield rented (with the help of Orage and Hastings) a two-room flat in Chelsea, at 132 Cheyne Walk, belonging to the painter Henry Bishop, who was taking an extended trip to North Africa. She recklessly bought a grand piano from the lady in the flat above and started practising singing. Now on intimate terms with Orage and Hastings, she would visit them regularly at their weekend cottage in Seaford, Sussex. Hastings, known to Mansfield as 'Biggie B', influenced many aspects of her life at this time. Indeed, Mansfield's sense of humour – an important feature of all her writing – is particularly evident in the parodies and pastiches the pair co-authored for the *New Age*. Both women had a mischievous and frequently mordant sense of humour, and while Hastings would end up taking her parodying to vindictive extremes later in life, Mansfield always retained a more measured, literary approach.

One of the main features of Mansfield's personal life during these two years, prior to her meeting Murry, was the sheer number of her sexual partners and liaisons. It was in early September that she met a young schoolmaster called William Orton (1889–1952) and embarked on a complicated love affair that Orton many years later 'fictionalized' in a chapter of his 1937 novel *The Last Romantic*.[27] However, letters and diary entries in his own notebooks that Mansfield had actually written herself were interpolated into the text, thereby adding authenticity to the autobiografictional account. Mansfield's black opal ring, which Ida believed 'had been given to her by the Maoris, and had some strange significance and occult power', was now given to Orton.[28]

Orton was a year younger than Mansfield, having been born in 1889, in Bromley, Kent, to a merchant grocer. He was only at Christ's College, Cambridge, for a year before the First World War broke out; wounded at the Battle of the Somme, he moved to the War Office, where he was posted until 1919. He eventually left England for the USA with his wife in 1922, to assume a faculty position at Smith College, Northampton, Massachusetts, where he remained until his retirement. When he first met Mansfield in the autumn of 1910 (at a weekend tennis party at the home of a German scientist and his Austrian wife), he held a position as a music and art teacher at the Skinners' School in Tunbridge Wells.

Orton affirmed to Alpers in 1948 that 'nothing in [*The Last Romantic*] is faked, although the temptation to alter was often very strong. It was meant to be as authentic a document as I could leave.'[29] He merely changed the names, so that he became 'Michael', his girlfriend, Edna Nixon (*née* Smith), became 'Lais', and Mansfield 'Catherine'. Edna Nixon (1892–1975) is herself a fascinating character. She was nineteen-year-old plain Edna Smith when she met Mansfield in 1910 through her then boyfriend, Orton. Mansfield entered their orbit like a bright shooting star and hung around in scintillating, sparkling fashion for several months, writing in Orton's journal until April 1912, before disappearing from view, never to return. Edna married James Nixon in 1916, and the couple moved to Geneva in 1920. According to her daughter, in the late 1950s Edna gave a short talk to the BBC about her relationship with Mansfield, in which she recorded how she became

> fascinated by her [Mansfield's] totally unconventional way of life [. . .]. She described her to me as beautiful & wearing her dark hair à la Trilby with a fringe & falling over her shoulders, which at the time was rather daring it seems. She would go thus to the Promenade concerts & make the acquaintance of strange men – or rather, men who were strangers. I believe that after about 6 months she tired of my mother & abruptly ended the friendship as they met one day in the street, by telling her they would never meet again. My mother was upset at the time & apparently destroyed all her letters, however one did survive.

> [. . .] Eventually my mother was to remember her fondly & I quote from a letter she wrote to a friend in 1928: 'At nineteen my love affair came to an end, for various reasons, one being Katherine Mansfield who rather took a fancy to my lover & myself. She played with us both for a little & then went on her way. She was a beautiful, wonderful creature, and I never bore her any grudge.'[30]

Wood believes that at this time Mansfield was possibly influenced in her lifestyle by George du Maurier's sensational book *Trilby*, first published in 1894 and renowned for being one of the most popular novels of its time, selling hundreds of thousands of copies in both England and America.[31] Set in the 1850s in an idyllic bohemian Paris, one of the most memorable characters is the rogue Svengali, a masterful musician and hypnotist. The novel was staged many times while Mansfield was living in London, and in 1914 was turned into a silent film starring Viva Birkett and Herbert Beerbohm Tree. We know Mansfield was acting in silent films at that time. Could she even have been one of the extras? It's a tempting prospect. In any case, her hairstyle was now apparently modelled on a character from the novel.

As for Orton and Edna, here were two more pawns to add to Mansfield's growing collection. In *The Last Romantic*, Catherine describes Lais (Edna) thus (and remember, these are all Mansfield's actual words, written down verbatim in the novel by Orton): 'Little Lais came. I met her and brought her home. I think she was happy: She made me feel eighteen. What very pretty hair! I expect I shall see her quite often and take her to concerts and I am sure I shall take her to the National Gallery.'[32] Later, in a beautifully expressive and detailed journal entry, 'Catherine' seems overcome by Lais's beauty:

> Lais has just been. She is so beautiful that I see no other beauty, and content myself with the sweet Lais. Her slim body in the grey frock – her hands cradling her vivid hair – she lay on the yellow pillows. When her voice speaks in laughter and her eyes shine, and a pink colour floods her cheeks, and her mouth is red as berries, I understand all the millions of reasons why God set the sun in the sky – that it might shine one day through closed curtains and light the beauty of Lais. We are the three eternities – Michael and Lais and I. For Michael is darkness and

> light and Lais is flame and snow and I am sea and sky. O, what a pity she is not a princess – with little white boots tipped with ermine and a silver shirt and a blue petticoat embroidered with pink apple blossom and a long flowing gown of pale green velvet worked with golden dragons and lined with vivid orange. A live snake for her girdle with eyes made of diamond-shaped emeralds – her hair flowing and caught at the ends with tassels of pink corals. She would ride in an ebony sleigh lined with the feathers of wild parrots – flamingos would fly over her head for a canopy. One day she shall be my inspiration for fairy tales.[33]

Indeed, in the story 'Something Childish But Very Natural' (1914), the innocent, childlike characters of Edna and Henry are loosely based on Orton and Edna. In his book, Orton described the way Mansfield had decorated the Cheyne Walk flat in her own exotic style: 'She had made the place look quite beautiful – a couple of candles stuck in a skull, another between the high windows, a lamp on the floor shining through yellow chrysanthemums, and herself accurately in the centre, in a patterned pink kimono and white flowered frock.'[34]

There were two major exhibitions in London in 1910, both of which would profoundly influence Mansfield – and her interior decorating tastes. The first was the enormous Japan–British exhibition held at White City in Shepherd's Bush from 14 May to 29 October 1910. It was the most concerted and systematic attempt by Japan to explain its traditional society and arts, modern industry and empire to its most important international ally, Great Britain, and was the culmination of the Anglo-Japanese Alliance of 1902. There were 'Japanese shrines and a village, miniature gardens, jugglers and wrestlers, prints and porcelain, the tea ceremony, the haiku'.[35] By the time the event closed in October, over 8 million visitors had attended. The Japanese gateway from this exhibition is still preserved in Kew Gardens today. In fact, 'Japonisme' – an interest in Japanese arts, crafts, literature and culture – had already impacted on British, French and American culture from the mid-nineteenth century onwards, particularly visible in the influence of Japanese print artists on the Post-Impressionist movement.

Mansfield visited the Japan exhibition and was entranced. She had already read Yone Noguchi's experimentally modern novel *The American Diary of a Japanese Girl*, first published in 1902. Noguchi was the first Japanese author to publish English-language novels and books of poetry. Born in 1875 near Nagoya, Japan, he travelled to the United States in 1893 and soon became part of the literary scene in San Francisco and later in London and New York City. Now it was his poetry that captivated Mansfield; she describes him as having a 'true authentic voice'. (Noguchi would go on to appear in five issues of *Rhythm*, during 1912–13, and issue 3 of the *Blue Review*. He only appeared once Mansfield had become a part of the editorial team, after June 1912 – her influence in this regard was therefore critical.) As a result, during 1910 Mansfield became obsessed with all things Japanese; she took to wearing a kimono at home, reread the poems of Noguchi, and invested in Japanese clothes and soft furnishings as described by Orton in *The Last Romantic*. Early in 1911 she would move to the Gray's Inn Road and decorate her flat in an entirely Japanese manner, with plain bamboo matting, floor cushions and a stone Buddha, in front of which she placed a bowl of water with bronze lizards in it.

Mansfield now presented Orton with a copy of the poems of Noguchi. Ida even recounts how also at this time, one night after Mansfield had gone to bed, she called out to Ida that she was 'thinking of going to Japan'.[36] She also acquired two Japanese dolls, O Hara San and Ribni, anthropomorphized into living little beings, as here in a letter to Murry of 25 December 1915: 'We are still quite babies enough to play with dolls and Id much rather pretend about Hara than about a real person – I would so see her, with her little hands in her kimono sleeves, very pale & wanting her hair brushed.'[37] J. Lawrence Mitchell notes that 'the name O Hara San must be a mis-recollection of O Hana San ('Miss Flower'), the title of a poem in Yone Noguchi's *From the Eastern Sea* (1903).'[38] Mansfield's 'Japonisme' continued throughout her life. Sylvia Lynd, who came to know her well in later life, claimed she looked 'not unlike one of those little dolls [. . . from] Japan's less commercial days, and Virginia Woolf, reminiscing after Mansfield's death about a visit she had paid to her in 1919, wrote, 'She had her look of a Japanese doll, with the fringe combed quite straight across her forehead.'[39] Mitchell talks of her 'love affair with things Japanese' and notes that 'her distinctive hairstyle, her Japanese dolls, her fondness for kimonos, and for Yone Noguchi's poetry – even perhaps her aesthetic of the miniature [. . .] – are all manifestations of this love affair.'[40]

Another Japanese influence that now came to the fore in her life was *The Book of Tea* (1906) by Kakuzo Okakura (which she had first read in 1907 back in Wellington following her three years' schooling at

Mansfield wearing a kimono, *c.* 1911.

Queen's College in London), the impact of which can be clearly seen in her personal writing. At the Japan–British exhibition, there was a tea house erected for visitors to witness authentic tea ceremonies and where, according to the official programme, 'fair maidens of Nippon serve tea and dainties to delighted visitors.'[41] Okakura's book was a popular purchase at the exhibition. Okakura himself was a highly respected scholar, who wrote in English and who helped both to promote and protect Japanese cultural heritage at this time. Outside Japan, he had an impact on a number of important figures, directly or indirectly, including the philosopher Martin Heidegger, Ezra Pound and especially the poet Rabindranath Tagore. Here, under the guise of explaining the intricacies of the tea ceremony, Okakura presents philosophies from East Asia in a clear and concise manner. He was

> unquestionably a man of genius, one of the great historical scholars of the modern world. He knew the Orient as few men ever have, for he combined the sharp focus of the West with a native knowledge of Japan, Korea, China, and other lands. His knowledge of all branches of Oriental art was, for its day, unequalled.[42]

The resonances in Mansfield's work from *The Book of Tea* are myriad. Taken at the most basic level, the word 'tea' itself occurs constantly in her creative writing, from the poem 'Camomile Tea' to the short story 'A Cup of Tea' (1922). Mansfield developed an almost-ritualistic approach to tea drinking that remained with her all her life.

The second exhibition that Mansfield attended in 1910 was Roger Fry's 'Manet and the Post-Impressionists', which ran from 8 November 1910 to 15 January 1911 at the Grafton Galleries in London. It was London's first real experience of 'modern art', and Mansfield never forgot it. On 8 December 1910 a review of it by Arnold Bennett was published in the *New Age*:

> The exhibition of the so-called 'Neo-Impressionists' over which the culture of London is now laughing, has an interest which is perhaps not confined to the art of painting. For me, personally, it has a slight, vague repercussion upon literature. [. . .] I have permitted myself to suspect that supposing some writer were to come along and do in words what these men have done in paint, I might conceivably be disgusted with nearly the whole of modern fiction, and I might have to begin again. This awkward experience will in all probability not happen, to me, but it might happen to a writer younger than me. At any rate it is a fine thought.[43]

The exhibition (followed by another in 1912) had an unprecedented impact on English artists and writers alike, including Mansfield, by introducing new modes of French aesthetic perception. However, it engendered the following hysterical response in the popular press: '[This is] a widespread plot to destroy the whole fabric of European painting.'[44] Mansfield was clearly modern and receptive enough to think otherwise. Ten years later, on 5 December 1921, she famously wrote the following:

> Wasn't that Van Gogh shown [...] ten years ago? Yellow flowers – brimming with sun in a pot? I wonder if it is the same. That picture seemed to reveal something that I hadn't realised before I saw it. It lived with me afterwards. It still does – that & another of a sea captain in a flat cap. They taught me something about writing, which was queer – a kind of freedom – or rather, a shaking free. When one has been working for a long stretch one begins to narrow ones vision a bit, to fine things down too much. And its only when something else breaks through, a picture, or something seen out of doors that one realises it.[45]

Mansfield's appreciation of Post-Impressionist art and Impressionistic technique would subsequently be transposed onto her own literary endeavours.

All in all, then, 1910 was a busy and fruitful year for Mansfield after its disastrous start. As well as seeing her Bavarian stories in print in the *New Age*, she now felt confident enough to send some of her poems off to a publisher. She had been writing poems since early childhood, and poetic verse would remain a creative outlet for her throughout her life. Eighty of the 217 poems in the 2016 volume of Mansfield's *Collected Poems* were written before she left New Zealand in 1908, attesting to the importance of poetry composition in her creative life from a young age. Now, during the early autumn of 1910, Mansfield sent her first book proposal to a London publisher, Elkin Mathews. It was not, as might be imagined, a book of short stories, but rather a poem-cycle called *The Earth Child*, comprising 28 numbered poems, and another eight poems, all written during 1909 and early 1910. Sadly, the publisher held on to the manuscript but did not offer to publish it. Most of the poems were never published elsewhere and remained unnoticed in the Newberry Library in Chicago until I discovered them in 2014. The poems reveal the development of her lyrical voice and poetic persona as she moved away from the influence of Wilde and *fin-de-siècle* Symbolism favoured by Walter Rippmann, towards the more complex neo-Romanticism and early Modernism of continental Europe. In addition, they provide a fascinating bridge from her earliest poems, sketches and vignettes through prose-poetry to narrative, offering new insights into her evolution and apprenticeship as a writer. The collection reveals that just when her stories were beginning to be accepted for publication in London journals, she was also taking herself *very* seriously as a poet.

Two letters from Mansfield accompany the *Earth Child* manuscript. Dated 8 November 1910 and 15 January 1911, they chronicle her failed efforts to persuade publisher Elkin Mathews to print the poems. The second letter is written in a tongue-in-cheek style, pleading with the publisher to put her out of her misery on whether her material will be accepted or not:

> Dear Mr Mathews
> May I hear from you soon the fate of my poor 'Earth Child' Poems – I really am worrying about her immediate future – yea or nay.
>
> Love her or hate her, Mr. Mathews, but do not leave her to languish!
>
> Sincerely yours
> Katharina Mansfield[46]

If Mansfield did receive a note of rejection, it has not survived.

Mansfield was still, of course, writing stories. In December 1910 'A Fairy Story' was published in a little magazine called the *Open Window* (perhaps having been rejected by Orage as not suitable for the *New Age*), signed 'Katherina Mansfield', a Modernist fairy tale of a woodcutter's daughter who moves to the great metropolis, thus betraying the love of her life. It is a partial homage to Hans Christian Andersen, a huge favourite of Mansfield's since her childhood, and indeed he is mentioned by name, as are a dozen or so of his fairy tales. Mimicking the fairy tale, imitating the gestures of children's literature, the story, beneath this whimsical surface, is far beyond both.

In January 1911 Mansfield wrote a piece called 'Sumurun: An Impression of Leopoldine Konstantin', signed 'Katharina Mansfield', which dates it to early 1911, and which I discovered in a mass of loose manuscript papers in Wellington in 2013. Mansfield had been to see the almost-silent play-pantomime *Sumurûn*, based on a story from the

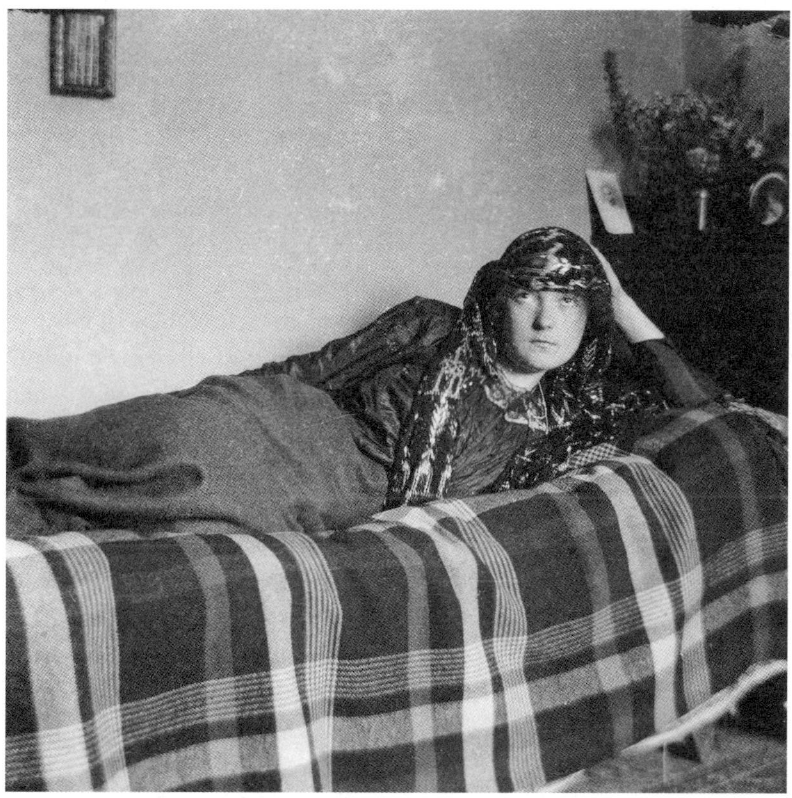

Mansfield, 1911.

Arabian Nights and directed by Max Reinhardt, which played to packed houses at the London Coliseum for six weeks from January 1911, with the Austrian actress Leopoldine Konstantin in the title role. Mansfield's piece is a creative impression – as the title says – of the play that she saw. There are dark images and even darker themes present, which is probably why Murry never used it in any of his posthumous publications of Mansfield's work. Open eroticism was the reason for the play's success, as well as its scandalous reputation, which would clearly have fascinated Mansfield. There are even a few extant photos from this time in which Mansfield is clearly trying to look like Leopoldine. In 'Sumurun', Mansfield writes,

> This little slave dancer of 'fatal fascination' moves through the strange drama of Sumurun utterly indifferent to everything about her which she does not want to possess – greedy for wealth and hungry for love – thrilling with that curious half cruel joy

> in herself and her own beauty – using these weapons of joy and beauty with the passionate courage of youth. The mournful figure of the hunchback is not tragic to her – he is disgusting and his love is disgusting. When he is seriously in her way she tries to throttle him – gropes at his twisted neck with her brown fingers – shakes him to and fro – tosses back her hair, heartlessly laughing.[47]

This is so much more than a review. As she herself titles it, it's a 'creative impression', with Mansfield vicariously positioning herself as Sumurun. She would surely have enjoyed knowing that on 21 January 1912, when the production had moved to New York, Konstantin was interviewed by the *New York Times*; the reporter notes Konstantin was looking forward to a trip 'to Chinatown where the young lady hopes to pick up some Japanese prints and to see the interior of an opium den'. The 'creative impression' was possibly yet another piece intended for the *New Age* but rejected by Orage.

Mansfield's love life, of course, remained as complicated as ever, since as well as dallying with Orton and Edna, she was now conducting an affair with a very handsome young man called Francis Heinemann. Their relationship forms the backdrop to the story 'A Dill Pickle', which would be published in the *New Age* in 1917. Of Heinemann, Ida recounts how Mansfield

> was much attracted by him, and he fell in love with her. They were young, and happy, intended to marry, and soon became lovers. However, the affair was short-lived: his family disapproved. They looked on Katherine as a potential danger, a married woman who was living alone. They must have forbidden him to see her for he did not come to her again.[48]

Of course, it's not hard to see where this would end: Mansfield's extraordinary fecundity at this time (and which contrasts so starkly with those later, barren years, when she dreamt so much of having a child with Murry) led, unbelievably, to her becoming pregnant again. But was the unborn baby Heinemann's? As well as a relationship with Heinemann (and Orton and Edna), Mansfield was also conducting an affair with J. M. Kennedy, the *New Age*'s charismatic foreign correspondent (who had taken over the role from Clarence H. Norman, for a time chairman of the New Age Press, formed in November 1908). Much later, Norman reported that 'one day Kennedy burst in upon him and threatened him with a revolver, because he alleged he had taken Katherine away from him.'[49] Had marriage even been mooted? Alpers notes how 'Orage's secretary Alice Marks, who was fond of Kennedy, always resented on his behalf the fact that Katherine had accepted his gift of an expensive fur coat before she jilted him.'[50] As far as Norman was concerned, he 'told Kennedy he had never seen K M in his life which was probably true.'[51] According to Alpers, Kennedy had told Edmund d'Auvergne that 'he feared he had "put a girl in the family way"'.[52] Wood notes that Beatrice Hastings suggested that Mansfield had made 'a mess' of Kennedy and seemed to imply this may have brought about his premature death.[53] In fact, Kennedy moved on and attempted a relationship with a young Rebecca West (who called him a 'poached egg') before dying as a result of the 1918 flu pandemic. What a tangled web Mansfield was weaving.

Meanwhile, in early January 1911, with the imminent return of Henry Bishop, Mansfield moved out of his Chelsea flat to one at 69 Clovelly Mansions on the Gray's Inn Road, found for her by Orage. The rent for the fourth floor, four-room flat was £52 a year, more than half her then annual income from her father. On the lease, she signed herself 'Katerina Mansfield', yet another Eastern European version of her name. The daily woman who cleaned the flat, Mrs Bates, would long be remembered by Mansfield, who memorialized her in the story 'Life of Ma Parker' (1921).

With Mansfield still pregnant and assuming the child was Heinemann's, Ida was now used as a go-between to try and persuade him to return to Mansfield. Ida went to try to talk to him at his office, but he didn't turn up, 'So he never knew of his child.'[54] Heinemann had no intention of reigniting the relationship, but Mansfield's heartbreak – if, indeed, she felt any such thing given the number of men then in her life, and now in full nesting mode in her new flat – was softened by the thought of the baby she was carrying. This baby was one she was determined to keep. When Ida was summoned to Rhodesia in April 1911 by her father, and worried about her precious friend, she deposited some money in a bank account for Mansfield's use, in case of emergencies. As she subsequently recounted, 'I was gone for about five months and when I returned in the autumn I found no baby and a closed bank account. We never discussed the matter; obviously it had all been horrible,' and then in a parting remark, 'I am sure that Beatrice Hastings had been in some way responsible.'[55] Ida never did like Beatrice. There would be one further pregnancy and abortion, but the baby Mansfield subsequently longed for during the rest of her life never materialized.

On the night of Sunday, 2 April 1911, the ten-yearly census was taken of the British population.[56] Mansfield's completed census form provides a glimpse into her mindset at that moment in her life. Under 'name and surname', she wrote, illegally, 'Katharina Mansfield', that regular pseudonym she was using at this time, confirming her fascination with all things Russian. (Her legal name at the time, as we know, was Kathleen Mansfield Bowden, following her marriage to Bowden on 2 March 1909.) She confirmed on the form that she was married, stating the marriage had lasted 'three' years, when it had only lasted two 'completed years', and even that was a gross misrepresentation. She stated her occupation as 'Author', her birthplace as 'Wellington, New Zealand' and declared herself to be a 'British subject by parentage'.

However, another census form paints a far bleaker picture. By the time of the 1911 census, the Trowell family had moved from Carlton Hill to 60 Springfield Road, two streets to the north. There were six people listed on their form, including Thomas Trowell (Senior) and his wife, Kate. Three children were listed as having been born during the marriage, two living and one dead; therein lies an inexplicable and deliberate omission. The Trowells had four children altogether: their eldest son Lynley, who had sadly died at the age of ten in New Zealand, the twins, Garnet and Tom, and a daughter, Dorothy (Dolly). It would seem that following the events of 1909–10 the family had disowned Garnet completely. Tom was still at home, aged 23, single, his occupation listed as 'violoncellist', born in New Zealand. Dolly was now seventeen, single, no profession listed and also still at home.

What of Garnet? On the night of the census, he was in Leeds, still travelling with the Moody Manners Opera Company, staying at 15 Quarry Mount Terrace, Woodhouse, which was owned by a widow, Mary Jane Flower, aged 52. He listed himself as 23, single, a musician, born in Wellington, New Zealand. Did he know of his family's decision to disown his existence on their own census form? Were his siblings aware of their parents' decision? We do not know. It seems likely that his son's conduct led Thomas to cut him out of the family, strangely mirroring Mansfield's own mother, who, after having deposited her wayward daughter at a convent in Bavaria at the beginning of June

1909, returned immediately to New Zealand on 10 June, and rewrote her will.

Mansfield had not yet met John Middleton Murry, her second husband; this meeting would take place in December 1911 at the home of W. L. George. Murry did not appear anywhere in the 1911 census, since he was in Paris during the spring of 1911, making the acquaintance of the painter J. D. Fergusson, hatching the idea for a new magazine to be called *Rhythm* (the first issue of which would be published in June 1911), and generally 'hanging out' in the seedier parts of Paris with people such as Aleister Crowley and Francis Carco, both of whom would go on to make appearances in Mansfield's own life.

The census documents discussed above go some way to underlining how difficult this period was in Mansfield's life. No biographer has mentioned how the Trowell family were so bitter over the relationship between their son and the 'fast and loose' Kathleen Beauchamp that they disowned him, to the extent of denying his existence. Mansfield herself was now leading her life under a variety of pseudonyms, trying to come to terms with recent events, cut out of her mother's will forever and pregnant – again. Her meeting with Murry was just a few short months away. Patient, tolerant Ida was putting up with a boarding-house existence in the Home Counties with her sister, still at the mercy of her irascible father in Africa. George Bowden was married, separated and back with his mother in Harrow. The Murry family were at home in Hampton Wick, no doubt worried sick about their wayward son Jack, who did not appear to be interested in continuing his studies at Oxford, and who would shortly meet a married woman with a very difficult past, move in with her and destroy all his father's hopes and aspirations.

In May 1911 Mansfield's mother and siblings – initially minus Harold, who could not spare the time from his many business concerns in New Zealand – arrived in London for the coronation of King George V on 22 June 1911, renting a grand furnished house at 34 Norfolk Square 'for the season'.[57] On the same trip, Mansfield's older sisters, Vera and Chaddie, were presented at court, but Mansfield, already now officially the 'black sheep' of the family, was not invited. In July she suffered a severe attack of pleurisy, perhaps the first overt sign of her incipient tuberculosis. As soon as she was able, she took off for Bruges and then Geneva in order to recuperate, remaining for several weeks, where Ida, having recently returned from her visit to her father in Rhodesia, joined her. It was while he was in England with the rest of the Beauchamp family that Mansfield became close to her brother Leslie (Chummie); she even introduced him to Orage and gave him the key to her flat in Clovelly Mansions so that he could come and go as he pleased. As Ida later recounted, at this time, Mansfield and Leslie 'were wholly at one with each other and spent much time together in the flat. Katherine wrote to me in Rhodesia saying how complete their love and understanding were. I believe that her feeling for him was one of the greatest joys of her life.'[58] Indeed, before the Beauchamps left London on 8 March 1912 to return to New Zealand, Chummie was the only member of the family to have actually met Murry.

Meanwhile, Mansfield was still carrying on with her rather sordid private life. Beatrice Hastings noted that from about the spring of 1911 'Orage stayed about four months with friends in town while I house-hunted.'[59] Of course, this gave him and Mansfield ample opportunity to conduct an affair, which they now actively embarked upon, the pair having always been attracted to one another. As Louise Welch affirms, 'for a time before her marriage to Murry, their friendship became a love affair.'[60] On 6 September 1911 Mansfield wrote a very sexually explicit diary entry (published verbatim in Orton's *The Last Romantic*) referring to an encounter with 'the Man', who was not Orton himself:

> When the bells were striking five the Man came to see me. He gathered me up in his arms and carried me to the Black Bed. Very brown and strong was he . . . . It grew dark. I crouched against him like a wild cat. Quite impersonally I admired my silver stockings bound beneath the knee with spiked ribbons, my yellow suede shoes fringed with white fur. How vicious I looked! We made love to each other like two wild beasts.[61]

In her diary at the time she also wrote of the same episode with the unnamed 'Man':

> *September* 6, 1911, *Wednesday* Michael came yesterday afternoon and asked me for Black Opal. I quickly took Black Opal off my finger. He was dressed in pale grey with that delightful vivid tie. I promised to see him later at Queen's Hall – yes, yes, I wished to go. When I lit a candle – the world faded away. I acted. He tore my clothes from my shoulders. I laughed – bent forward

> – graceful and lithe – blew out the candle and stood naked to the waist in the moon-lit room. 'My beautiful, my wonder!' He knelt before me, his arms round my body. I crushed him against me – shook back my hair and laughed at the moon. I felt mad with passion – I wanted to kill. . . . By and by he left me.[62]

There are three possibilities for the Man's identity – a different person to Michael (Orton himself). Alpers believed it was her old German teacher, Walter Rippmann, with whom Mansfield had recently been in contact and on whom she had always had a crush. Ida herself affirmed that Mansfield did *not* have a relationship with Rippmann while she was at Bishop's flat: 'Katherine would not start with him the new relationship that he seemed to want.'[63] Of course, it is possible that Mansfield felt it necessary to deny such a rumour to Ida, which is interesting in itself. Wood notes,

> The *New Age* (largely Orage and Beatrice Hastings) did not like Rippmann and Rippmann did not like the *New Age*. They dubbed the Simplified Spelling Society with which he was associated the 'Simplified Speling Sosieti' (*New Age*, 15 Jan 1914) and Orage described him as 'the phonetical drill-instructor who would have the English language learn his goose-step' (*New Age*, 28 Jan 1915). Rippmann himself described the *New Age* as 'clotted nonsense' (a quote from Dryden). Orage insisted on very high standards of writing in the *New Age* and would not have liked messy spelling. On the other hand, he was a great believer that good written English derived from the oral tradition and should be able to be read aloud easily. This may well be why Mansfield used to read her work aloud once she had written something.[64]

It seems unlikely, therefore, that Mansfield would have conducted an affair with someone so derided in the *New Age* offices. Indeed, her biographer Claire Tomalin believed that a far more likely candidate was the Austrian journalist Geza Silberer (1876–1938), better known in the literary world by his pseudonym Sil-Vara, who was living in London at the time, 'collecting material for articles on English life and characters. He was also interested in the theatre, and looking for plays to translate; his version of Synge's *Playboy of the Western World* was published in

Germany in 1912.'[65] In fact, Wood believes that the story 'The Mating of Gwendolyn', published in the *New Age* on 2 November 1911, signed Mouche (and recently attributed to Mansfield), was co-authored by her with Sil-Vara. In the early 1930s Murry would send Ida a letter, enquiring, 'When was the love affair with Sil Vara? She once gave me all his letters to her to read and then burned them.'[66] The letters apparently were burnt in the late summer of 1912, while Mansfield and Murry were at their cottage in Runcton, West Sussex. In 1929 Sil-Vara published a play called *Caprice*, which, as Wood notes, may well reference Mansfield herself.[67]

Sil-Vara might have been another one of Mansfield's connections from her long stay in Bavaria, or, as Wood believes, she may well have met him at the home of society hostess Gwen Otter (1896–1958), whose Chelsea home at that time was a renowned meeting place for writers, musicians and theosophists.[68] Gwen was also a long-standing friend of Aleister Crowley. For a short time, she and Mansfield became friends. As James Laver notes, 'They [. . .] wrote a little play, or sketch, together called *Mimi and the Major*, which they acted, with Gwen as the Major and Katherine Mansfield as Mimi.'[69] Years later, in January 1921, Mansfield would recall Gwen in a letter to Anne Estelle Rice: 'I tremendously enjoyed hearing of the Gwen Otter dinner. I could see it & hear it. Gwen in gold trousers & that long long après midi d'un Faune. Poor dear! it will never be over for me. I have a warm corner in my heart for that woman always.'[70]

A third possibility for the 'Man' as far as Ruth Mantz was concerned, and the most likely according to Wood, was Orage himself, which would explain Mansfield's need to hide his identity, since he was at the time not only married, but involved with Beatrice Hastings. As Wood reminds us, Ruth Mantz reported how Orage had told her that

> B was jealous of KM; if they started to talk, she came in; kept them watched. O says he had to cater to B because she was so important to the paper. *The Maids' Comedy* shows her at her best; she did have charm then; wrote much better than KM. She was important to the N A because she wrote so much. Yet she demanded to be the center. She even went so far as to suggest KM live with them (so she could keep an eye on her).
>
> O says in spite of the triteness of saying 'marriages are made in heaven', it is true. People live together, but there are few, few

> real marriages. BH demanded marriage from him; but they could never have married in that sense. He and KM never could have been either (he says), even though there was something between them.[71]

And there was definitely 'something' between them – an instant attraction that over the years transmuted into jealousy and rejection on both sides, then rapprochement once more, and which by the end of Mansfield's life would transform again into something intensely precious and enduring, as this biography reveals.

Soon after they met, Orage had presented Mansfield with a copy of *Five Dialogues of Plato Bearing on Poetic Inspiration*, translated by Percy Bysshe Shelley, first published in 1910; inside, in her own handwriting, is the inscription 'Katherina Mansfield 1910'. In the section called 'The Symposium' Mansfield underscored passages defining the varied aspects of love, both material and spiritual. Wood is convinced – and so am I – that Orage was in love with Mansfield during 1910–11 and that the relationship became physical. Given Mansfield's promiscuity at this time, it's not a difficult scenario to imagine. No wonder Hastings was constantly on her guard with Mansfield. Orage also gave Mansfield another book at this time: *Light on the Path and Karma* by Mabel Collins, a theosophical treatise that had appeared in a new edition in 1911. With its subtitle, 'A treatise written for the personal use of those who are ignorant of the eastern wisdom, and who desire to enter within its influence', the text provides rules that serve as rungs of a ladder in the progress of a spiritual life, which would certainly have appealed to Mansfield. She, in turn, gifted the copy to Ida that same year, writing a poem called 'The Secret',[72] 'inscribing it', as the latter notes, 'inside the cover of a small book of occult wisdom, which was always one of my treasures'.[73] Wood questions whether Mansfield had intended to return the book to Orage, with the poem written for him, 'but instead gave it to Ida at the last minute as a sop for disappointing her over an aborted plan to spend a weekend together'.[74] 'The Secret', of course, was the love affair between Mansfield and Orage.[75] Those who think Mansfield suddenly came upon spiritualism in 1921–2 when reading *Cosmic Anatomy* need to understand that from her earliest days in London she was surrounded by those drawn to esoterica in all its manifestations, such as Orage and Crowley. Indeed, as Wood affirms,

> Mansfield would in fact have read much of *Cosmic Anatomy* during 1911, before she was sent it at the end of her life. The book was an amplified version of M. B. Oxon's articles called 'Theology', which ran in the *New Age* from 2 February 1911 for nine instalments to 30 March 1911, while Mansfield was still very much involved with the paper. A subsequent anonymous reviewer in the *New Age* concluded: 'This is a book that will have far more influence than it will achieve of fame. Those who read it will know it is profound'.[76]

And all the while, Orton and Edna were still being dallied with. Margaret Wishart's 'Notes re K. M.' describe her meeting Orton in about 1915, of whom she wrote,

> [Orton] knew K[atherine] very well and told [...] of a strange era just before for some years when K[atherine] was being very eccentric wearing flowing robes & sandals and taking strange drugs. Also I am sorry to say, living with quite a number of different people – but she just could not bear to hurt or disappoint people, she was quite too soft-hearted. She was never 'wanton' but as Will described her 'amoral' not 'immoral'.[77]

It's hard to reconcile Margaret's image of this 'tart with a heart' (apparently too 'soft-hearted' to say 'no') with what we actually know of Mansfield's character.

However, Beatrice Hastings was certainly a formative – and dangerous – influence at this time, as Ida rightly noted (although it's ironic that towards the end of 1911, Hastings would distance herself from Mansfield because of what she perceived as her flagrant promiscuity). Hastings had become a regular at the séance evenings led by the now-notorious occultist Aleister Crowley (1875–1947), another contributor to the *New Age* and friend to Orage and Gwen Otter, and took Mansfield along with her. In her vituperative memoir, Hastings recorded,

> I first met Orage at a theosophical lecture he gave in 1906, when on a visit to London from Leeds. Afterwards, in the smoking-room, I rallied him on his perverse loquacity (of the which I later detected every trick). A year or so after, when Aphrodite

had amused herself at our expense, I found in his rooms a collection of works on sorcery. Up to this time, Orage's intimate friend was not Mr. Holbrook Jackson, who thought he was, but Mr. Aleister Crowley.

[. . .]

A few months before I came on the paper, Orage published a long review of one of Mr. Crowley's works, describing him in the terms belonging to Masters and concluding: 'Will he excite that life-long animosity that is accorded only to the most dangerous thinkers?'[78]

But Mansfield already had her own connection to Crowley – the Australian violinist Leila Waddell (1880–1932). In October 1923, Waddell would write an account of her brief relationship with Mansfield in the *Shadowland Magazine*: 'Two Anzacs Meet in London: Some Personal Impressions of Katherine Mansfield'.[79] Eight years older than Mansfield, she had arrived from Australia to start a new life in London in 1908 – the same year as Mansfield. It was at a concert by Vladimir de Pachmann at the Queen's Hall in London in early 1909 that she met Mansfield for the first time:

Her eyes were dark brown and very penetrating, with occult depths. They seemed to look thru one rather than at one, and when her gaze was directed towards me, I felt that, altho we were sitting in the Queen's Hall awaiting the appearance of a famous European artist, she could see me from under the Southern Cross and read my innermost secrets, tho with kindly interest. [. . .] I, as an artist, was enraptured by her beauty. My interest was distinctly divided between the great De Pachmann, who was playing Chopin so exquisitely, and this girl's baffling personality, which attracted and fascinated me like some strange exotic bird.[80]

As Cynthia Crosse notes, 'The two women were immediate friends. They had a love of music in common, of course, with Mansfield playing cello and her sisters also musical.' However, Mansfield was at her most enigmatic at this time (as well as being pregnant with Garnet's child and courting the hapless Bowden). She was 'difficult – even a little uncanny, with her level, unblinking, unsmiling glance and monotonous, inflectionless voice'.[81] It is unknown whether the pair kept up a correspondence once Mansfield left for Bavaria, but Bayreuth, where the annual Wagner festival was held every July, was only a couple of hours away by train from Wörishofen, so it is not impossible that the two young women might have met up that summer.

During 1910, Waddell met Crowley for the first time, becoming one of his most important acolytes. As well as being a concert-level violinist, Waddell was also an accomplished writer and magician. During October and November 1910, Crowley used Waddell and other members of his magical order, the Argenteum Astrum, in his series of dramatic planetary-based magical rites, the 'Rites of Eleusis', at London's Caxton Hall. It is perfectly possible that Mansfield herself attended such performances once she had returned from Wörishofen in January 1910. Other places they might have met included the notorious and short-lived nightclub the Cave of the Golden Calf, which opened in Heddon Street, just behind the Café Royal in central London in early 1912, and closed just two years later:

> It was decorated by Spencer Gore in Russian Ballet-inspired murals, with contributions by Jacob Epstein and Wyndham Lewis; Eric Gill designed the club's motif, a phallic Golden Calf, symbol of biblical dissipation and idolatry. Here the cult of Wilde could continue to worship. The club's self-advertised aim was to be 'a place given up to gaiety', its art-subversive interiors 'brazenly expressive of the libertarian pleasure principle'.[82]

Wood records how 'On 3 July 1913 the *New Age* published a report of a performance of 'Mozart in a Cabaret'. Although described in the review as the 'Cabaret Theatre Club Ltd.' and 'this Heddon Street cabaret', it was actually a performance at 'the famous Cave of the Golden Calf''.[83] Rebecca West recalled seeing Mansfield at the Cave of the Golden Calf in 1913:

> I saw KM only once, when she was *compere* at a cabaret show in a night club in Regent St., run by one of Strindberg's wives. She did not do it very well, but looked very pretty in a Chinese costume. She was very attractive, with her beautiful dark hair.[84]

As Wood notes, another spectator gave Mansfield an equally poor review:

> Rebecca West's recollection of Katherine's performance accords with that of the contemporaneous *New Age* reviewer, 'John Playford': 'No one who knows anything about cabarets would have permitted bright Miss Katherine Mansfield, or Masefield, to play the part of the call-boy-master-of-ceremonies in the silly and affected way she did.'[85]

Later on, in 1915, at one of the low points in their relationship, Murry wrote to Mansfield remembering her frequenting cabarets with Beatrice Hastings in the early months of their relationship: 'that used to terrify me and almost killed me dead – I mean the Cabaret bit.'[86]

But back to Crowley. At his séances, which Mansfield attended – with Waddell, with Gwen Otter and with Hastings – Crowley apparently encouraged use of a 'South American drug' said to have come from Mexico and to have the property of intensifying visual imagination. In fact, as James Laver asserts, 'Crowley's disciples used to take analonium [derived from the mescal button cactus, plus belladonna], the effect of which was to enlarge the consciousness and give "a different dimension". Even those who weren't exactly disciples were sometimes given packets of the drug.'[87] Mansfield, never needing any encouragement to play a part, would attend such evenings dressed in a loose, richly coloured Oriental robe borrowed from Ida. With her new shorter hairstyle 'à la Trilby' (which Hastings always claimed was a copy of her own, and which indeed made them look uncannily alike), her red-lipsticked mouth and her enigmatic smile, she looked every inch the Eastern charmer. One evening, at a séance Gwen Otter held for Crowley, sitting cross-legged among the cushions, Mansfield tasted the drug:

> Both Gwen and Katherine took a dose of analonium [. . .]. Katherine lay on the sofa and lit a cigarette. She threw the match on the floor and it lay crookedly on the carpet. This caused her such acute distress that Gwen put it straight. 'That's much better,' said K M. 'Pity that stuff had no effect.' Then she began to talk, about a princess who lived at the edge of the sea and when she wanted to bathe she just called to the waves [. . .] Gwen got rid of the last guests and returned to find K M standing rather unsteadily in the middle of the room. 'Where are the others?'

> she said. 'Have they gone on deck? It's lucky it is such a smooth night. Pity that stuff had no effect'.[88]

What a time Mansfield was having, all the while playing the role of dutiful daughter and sister during the Beauchamp family's long residence in London during 1911–12.

One curious result of this brief entrée into the world of Crowley and his acolytes was the eventual publication in 1914 of two songs for tenor and piano, 'Your Grave Grey Eyes' and 'Cinnamon Curls', composed by Bernard F. Page, with words by Crowley himself. Strangely, both songs were dedicated to Mansfield's youngest sister, Jeanne Beauchamp. Did Crowley ever meet Jeanne during the Beauchamp family's visit to London in 1911? It seems unlikely. Page himself moved to New Zealand in 1913 to take up a position as the Wellington City Organist, 'and was soon in the thick of musical activity in the capital, conducting the Wellington Municipal Orchestra, the Royal Choral Union and the Wellington Amateur Operatic Society. He was a popular recitalist, particularly among the women, as he was considered a very handsome man.'[89] For both songs to be dedicated to Jeanne points to a relationship between both parties, however innocent. Page was married, whereas Jeanne, at the time the songs were composed, was the unmarried 22-year-old daughter of one of Wellington's wealthiest and most prominent citizens. The handwritten inscription on the music manuscript reads, 'To my dear friend Jeanne, with every good wish from BFP 18 November 1914'. But as to Crowley's involvement? It's a bizarre conundrum.

Let's return briefly to Carl Erich Bechhöfer (1894–1949), who also saw a great deal of Mansfield during 1911. Six years younger than Mansfield, he was just sixteen when he first met her at the *New Age* offices. At age fifteen, he had been sent to Germany by his father to study, and 'While still a student he began sending things to *The New Age*, beginning with letters to the Editor and soon adding parodies, verse, and reports on theatrical events in Germany.'[90] During his holidays in 1911 he met Orage and some of the other contributors to the *New Age*, and for a few months, as Gray asserts, Bechhöfer was more or less adopted by Orage and Hastings. Paul Selver recorded meeting him:

> Of the others [regular contributors to the journal] I discern, very much in the foreground, a fattish, red-faced youth who, when I entered the circle, was about eighteen. In those days he

> still signed himself Carl Bechhöfer (sometimes thinly disguised as Charles Brookfarmer). After the war of 1914–18, in which he served in the Lancers and later made an adventurous trip to Soviet Russia, he shed his umlaut and became Bechhofer-Roberts. Before his umlaut vanished he had a knack of writing lampoons which bubbled with undergraduatish fun. One of his happiest efforts in this manner was a set of skits on the leading London periodicals, and we all felt that when he, so to speak, had graduated as a writer, he ought to accomplish something considerable.[91]

Bechhöfer subsequently led the most extraordinary life for such a young man, travelling for ten years, including to Russia both before and after the Revolution, all of which he recorded in a number of books, before becoming an adherent of Gurdjieff, whom he met for the first time in Tiflis (now Tbilisi) in 1919. As Sullivan notes,

> His *In Denikin's Russia and the Caucasus, 1919–1920*, contains the first description of Gurdjieff published in English. He warmly recounts being guided by Gurdjieff on an unusual tour of Tiflis, especially the baths and restaurants. Roberts notes that this 'curious individual named Georgi Ivanovitch Gurdjieff [...] was still surrounded by this strange entourage of philosophers, doctors, poets and dancers. He was not exploiting them; on the contrary, several of them were living on his diminishing means.' Later in this journey, Roberts describes listening to his long-time journalistic acquaintance, P. D. Ouspensky's engaging renditions of light-hearted Moscow and Essentuki adventures while they shared a bottle of vodka that Ouspensky prepared from pure white spirit and orange peel. Subsequently, out of curiosity, he made several visits to Gurdjieff's Institute at the Prieuré but 'preferred to remain an intimate and disinterested spectator.'[92]

Here then was an early link to Gurdjieff, a man with whom Orage would come to be closely allied. As Sullivan affirms,

> It seems likely that Bechhöfer had something to do with this development, though, in Orage's case, it is probably over-determined, with his long-standing interest in Theosophy

> playing a role as well. At any rate, the 'fattish red-faced youth' left his mark on the journal and its editor, as, no doubt, they did on him.[93]

Gray recounts how on 20 May 1911,

> Carl Bechhöfer found a note on the door that, due to a slight cold, KM and Mrs H were off to the seaside for a few days and would be back on the Monday morning. There they jointly put up this piece addressed to their common lover Orage as editor of The New Age:
>
> > Sir, – Finding ourselves on Sunday in Ditchling-on-Sea, without any literature, we were driven to rely upon memories of our favourite authors. We forward our summaries for the benefit of your readers who may sometime find themselves in a similar situation.[94]

The piece was, of course, the fascinatingly mordant 'A.P.S.A.' (the acronym for 'A Pleasant Sunday Afternoon'), published in the *New Age* on 25 May 1911, parodying, among others, the works of G. K. Chesterton, Arnold Bennett and H. G. Wells. As Gray concludes, 'Theirs was a matchless, needling sisterhood.'[95]

Mansfield certainly left her own mark on Bechhöfer. Wood records how in 1949 Alpers interviewed him for his first biography of Mansfield and was told how Mansfield had 'treated Murry with contempt – when she was not with him. She probably slept with Orage, often, to show her contempt.'[96] Gray goes further, stating

> Alpers [. . .] omits much of the material he did uncover; because he finds it unsuitable, although he did at least preserve it for the use of future researchers. For example, he leaves out the story that [. . .] Katherine Mansfield tried to seduce the hapless fifteen-year-old little Carl Bechhofer, still in school.'[97]

Bechhöfer records an attempted seduction in his semi-autobiographical novel *Let's Begin Again*:

> She shifted her chair nearer, and I felt her knee against mine. Her dressing-gown gaped open and I could not help seeing

> her shapely little breasts. Then she seized my hand, pressed it to them, placed her other hand around my shoulder and, her face transfigured, kissed me wildly. I was flabbergasted. I tried uneasily to disengage myself, but she clung tightly to me.
>
> 'Hold me in your arms! Kiss me! Do what you like with me!'
>
> I did not want to do anything with her.[98]

Bechhöfer's cameo role in Mansfield's life remains a rather strange and bizarre one. Later on, Mansfield certainly expressed some affection for him, but subsequently thought he had become 'terribly conceited': 'Before he was spoiled he was very nice – I mean as a boy.'[99]

On 5 October 1911 Orage published, as a letter, a short piece by Mansfield titled 'Along the Gray's Inn Road'.[100] As Wood notes,

> It can be read as a full blooded attack on the *New Age* and its staff, who Mansfield may have been told might possibly move to the new socialist *Daily Herald*. This may be the moment that Orage eased her out of the *New Age* editorial team. Beatrice Hastings had returned from the country. He may have tried to soften the blow by suggesting that it was time for her to move on to 'seek an editorial feather in her cap', as he was also thinking of doing. Against this background Mansfield's piece can be read rather differently. 'A little procession' she described it, 'in front, a man [Orage] between the shafts of a hand-barrow that creaks under the weight of a piano-organ [...] bright red [the socialist *New Age*].' The man is followed by a 'big bundle' of a woman, [Hastings], holding a 'little bundle' [Bechhöfer] and 'two small boys,' [Kennedy and Randall]. 'They are like pilgrims' the piece concludes, 'straining forward to Nowhere [a poem by William Morris had appeared in the first *Daily Herald* news sheet], dragging, and holding to, and following after that bright red, triumphant thing [Socialism]'. Katherine was clearly upset by her rejection and Orage was not afraid to publish her outgoing protest as the final item of that number of the *New Age*. Orage gave Katherine the last word.[101]

Regarding the implications of the above piece, Murry later suggested that 'Katherine [was] presented with a kind of ultimatum, calling upon her to choose between the two journals, and she chose *Rhythm*.'[102] But as Wood observes, Murry waited until after the death of Orage before suggesting this. In fact, 'Along the Gray's Inn Road', published in October 1911, was her last piece in the *New Age* that year.

In December 1911 Mansfield's first collection of thirteen short stories, *In a German Pension*, ten of which had already appeared in the *New Age*, was published by Stephen Swift & Co., and widely reviewed – concrete evidence of her success in her chosen career. The collection is a perfect example of a place-based story cycle and demonstrates her natural proclivity for the genre. Set in a German spa town, an unnamed female narrator describes the daily routines of the guests in a typical German pension or boarding house as they undertake their various 'cures'. The narrator is 'othered' by the fact that she is English-speaking (though, being a New Zealander, is not actually English), and is therefore different from the other residents. The stories have many themes in common, aside from their location in a German spa town, one of the most obvious being the failure to communicate, both between the sexes, and between German- and English-speaking people. Another theme is the revelation of the true horrors of childbirth, as well as the condemnation of voracious male sexual appetites. The unnamed first-person colonial narrator of several of the stories is herself a mystery (for she speaks English but is *not* English – exactly Mansfield's own situation), and offers a subversive element to the cycle. Nowhere do we learn why she has come to the spa town; her reasons are never clarified in the way they are with some of the other pension residents.

Three of the stories, 'At Lehmann's', 'A Birthday' and 'The Child-Who-Was-Tired', are different from the others, since their most overt theme is childbirth. In 'At Lehmann's', an innocent young servant is left traumatized, both by the terrifying realities of her mistress's pregnancy and labour, and the sexual advances of a predatory male. The physical pain of childbirth is also revealed in 'A Birthday', where a selfish husband considers his own mental strain during the process of childbirth rather than his wife's physical pain. In the most depressing and distressing story of them all, 'The Child-Who-Was-Tired', a very young, overworked and underfed servant girl resorts to the suffocation of one of the babies in her charge when she finds out her mistress is pregnant again.

In a fourth story, 'Frau Brechenmacher Attends a Wedding', the constant assertion of conjugal rights leaves Frau Brechenmacher at the mercy of her husband's sexual appetites. Here Mansfield sends out a clear message about gender relationships, the general unhappiness, subjugation and physical suffering of the female in contrast to the selfishness, greed and sexual appetites of the male. In this cycle of stories, the setting is semi-autobiographical, as are a number of the themes. The horrific experience Mansfield underwent during 1909 – giving birth in Bavaria to a stillborn child – is interwoven with an insightful mockery of the hypochondriac 'cure' residents.

In the final story of the collection, 'A Blaze', all previous assumptions are turned on their head. Here the predator is not a man but a cold and calculating married woman who is conducting an affair with her husband's best friend, the implication being that, for once, the woman is the one in control. It's a clever twist by Mansfield to end the collection on, implying, perhaps, that neither extreme is to be welcomed. Moreover, even though these stories rely on hegemonic, imperial undertones, the unnamed, first-person colonial narrator offers a subversive element to the cycle.

Tellingly, the volume was marketed by the publishers as a 'six-shilling novel', rather than a collection of short stories, as well as a 'delightful literary novelty', thus asserting the cyclical nature of the stories themselves.[103] Indeed, the story cycle, in a tradition going back to Homer, Boccaccio and Chaucer, was particularly popular at this time, as Dominic Head attests, filling 'the need of readers for brevity in an increasingly fast-paced and distracting culture, while also supplying the kind of explanatory framework found in the novel'.[104] Reviewers were positive, calling the collection 'impish', 'lively', 'caustic', 'amusing' and 'original'.[105] Mansfield, then, with her first published book under her belt at the age of just 23, was receptive to new literary challenges.

At a dinner party in the same month, Mansfield met John Middleton Murry, a 22-year-old Oxford undergraduate, for the first time, having recently sent him 'The Woman at the Store' (the story from 1908 based on her experiences of her camping trip to the Ureweras in the remote part of New Zealand's North Island), for his recently founded little magazine, *Rhythm*. He was soon invited to Clovelly Mansions, and a new chapter in Mansfield's life began, though the chaos did not immediately disappear.

Looking back over this early period of Mansfield's life (of which most details remained unknown to him until Alpers's first biography in 1954), Murry wrote in his journal in 1953,

> It seems to me now that at first she was enchanted by my innocence, and wanted to preserve it, and (to be in harmony) to put away her own 'experience', which was considerable and much of it an unhappy memory. She wanted to annihilate her past. Of that I am *sure*. She never mentioned it to me – her past (I mean) so far as it consisted of relations with men – and I was made to feel that any reference to, or curiosity about, it would be unwelcome, and hurting. [. . .] I was deeply conscious that she wanted to start afresh, and that she was in some way afraid of my making any contact with her past.[106]

Rejecting her past, however, was not something Mansfield was easily able to achieve.

4

Rhythm and the *Blue Review*, 1912–14

In December 1911 (the same month that *In a German Pension* was published), Mansfield sent a story, 'The Woman at the Store', to a recently founded little magazine called *Rhythm*. Its co-editors, John Middleton Murry (still an undergraduate at Oxford), his Oxford friend Michael Sadleir and J. D. Fergusson (a Scottish artist whom Murry had met in Paris earlier in 1911), had produced the first issue in the summer of 1911. From the very outset, *Rhythm*'s editorial slant was towards 'the ideal of a new art'. As the editors famously stated in the first issue,

> 'Before art can be human it must learn to be brutal.' Our intention is to provide art, be it drawing, literature or criticism, which shall be vigorous, determined, which shall have its roots below the surface, and be the rhythmical echo of the life with which it is in touch.[1]

The initial, ambitious, aim of the magazine was to champion new French art, literature and philosophy for an English audience; this included the philosophy of Henri Bergson, fauvism and the French literary *fantaisistes*. Many of the artistic contributors, alive and dead – such as Picasso, Goncharova, Derain and Van Gogh – would go on to become establishment names. Moreover, roughly half of the regular contributors to *Rhythm* were, unusually, women: they would include Mansfield herself, Fergusson's then partner the American artist Anne Estelle Rice, Jessica Dismorr, and Dorothy 'Georges' Banks. As Peter Brooker notes, discussing 'this woven cultured alliance' in Paris between 1907 and 1914, 'one senses [. . .] the rare existence of a mixed and congenial, relatively democratically organized, male and female artistic community.'[2] Mansfield's story, 'The Woman at the Store', fitted the brief of the new magazine perfectly. Raw, stark, with a brutal subplot, it captured colonial life at its most primitive and was a marked departure from the *Pension* stories, which had all been set in 'civilized' Europe. It was Mansfield's entry into the European avant-garde: a 'modern' colonial writer, offering a new mode of writing direct from the farthest-flung outpost of the empire.

In the first issue, Murry himself attempted to clarify the editors' ideals with one of the very first printed references to the word 'modernism':

> The artist attains to the pure form, refining and intensifying his vision till all that is unessential dissolves away [. . .]. He must return to the moment of pure perception to see the essential forms, the essential harmonies of line and colour, the essential music of the world. Modernism [. . .] penetrates beneath the outward surface of the world, and disengages the rhythms that lie at the heart of things, rhythms strange to the eye, unaccustomed to the ear, primitive harmonies of the world that is and lives.[3]

Discernible in this early statement of belief from June 1911 is an uncanny resemblance to Mansfield's own later artistic philosophy. Her memory of seeing a Van Gogh painting, quoted in the preceding chapter, inspiring the notion of 'shaking free', revealed those 'moments of pure perception' expounded here by Murry. So, what of *Rhythm*'s main editor? John Middleton Murry, born in 1889 into a lower-middle-class family in Peckham, then a mean little suburb in southeast London, had been a precocious child, a quality that eventually won him a scholarship to the prestigious Christ's Hospital, near Horsham in West Sussex, a public school with a royal charter, founded in 1552. Its mission was – and still is – to offer children from disadvantaged backgrounds the chance of a private education. His essay 'Literature and Journalism' would win him the school's Charles Lamb medal at aged sixteen, before he went up to Brasenose College, Oxford; it seems that Murry was destined to be a literary editor almost from childhood.

The success of the first issue of *Rhythm* in the summer of 1911 meant that Murry soon abandoned his studies at Oxford in order to become

John Middleton Murry, 1912.

a full-time editor. He met Mansfield for the first time towards the end of December 1911, at the home of W. L. George (1882–1926), a novelist and essayist. George had been brought up in Paris by Jewish-British parents and was twenty before he learnt English. In 1905 he moved to London to become a journalist. His first novel, *A Bed of Roses* (1911), with its subject-matter of a woman's descent into prostitution, was an instant success, going through nine impressions in its first year of publication; George had now made his mark on the London literary scene and could afford to be magnanimous to those younger authors on the way up. At a dinner party at George's house, Murry was excited to meet Mansfield, the author of the 'brutal' story he had been sent. Afterwards, the two started corresponding; sadly, none of Mansfield's early letters to Murry during 1912 exist – the ones still extant begin in April 1913. We do, however, have a few of Murry's letters to her from 1912, in one of which he responded to her having asked him what he knew of Victor Neuburg (1883–1940), an English poet and writer whose latest collection, *The Triumph of Pan*, Murry had sent her to review. In his reply, sent on 27 January from Oxford, Murry wrote,

> I don't know very much about the man Neuberg – but what I do I'll try to tell you. He is or rather was one of Aleister Crowley's push in the advanced spiritualist – obscene yet divine – stunt; and so far as I know he was Crowley's lover. [...] Then for some reason they quarrelled – over some money matter, and

> at present Neuberg is, I am told, holding over Crowley's head some books that he had privately published, and which are for England the ne plus ultra of dirt. [. . .] I believe he looks a very bedraggled weed but I never saw him, since when I knew Crowley in Paris he had some other fellow, Kennedy.[4]

A Cambridge graduate, Victor Neuburg was an intimate associate of Crowley, who wrote on the subject of occultism, including theosophy, and this brought him into the orbit of Orage. At this early stage of their friendship, it would be very unlikely that Mansfield had told Murry of her own connection either to Crowley or his acolyte, Leila Waddell, and needless to say there is no subsequent mention of Crowley in Murry's autobiography or biography: by the time such volumes were written, any connection to the louche and disreputable 'magician' was not something to be foregrounded. Mansfield's review would appear in the July 1912 issue of *Rhythm*, signed 'K. M'.

But what about the *New Age*? Even though towards the end of 1911 Orage and Hastings had sensed it was time for Mansfield to go, nevertheless they were not happy that, after all their nurturing, she had seemingly moved on to another journal *quite* so quickly and easily. On 18 January 1912 Hastings wrote a vituperative piece in the *New Age* called 'Modernism' using the name 'Alice Morning', one of her many pseudonyms. As John Wood notes,

> It would be one of a series of similar pieces by Hastings that appeared over the next three years or so. Internally disjointed, they nonetheless contain snippets of biographical material which appear as though culled at random from her notebooks, including phrases such as 'This Greek God is just down from Oxford and is mad on poetry', an overt reference to Murry.[5]

According to Murry, 'Katherine had broken with *The New Age*; she had been presented with a kind of ultimatum, calling upon her to choose between the two journals, and she had chosen *Rhythm*,' which rather spoke to his own narrative after Mansfield's death, rather than to the facts.[6] Gray notes how '*Rhythm* was drearily serious about itself – except when Murry's acquaintance, natty Francis Carco, contributed his frivolous letters from Paris – and not fully suited to Katherine's exuberant comic skills.'[7] And, of course, Murry *was* wrong about the rupture:

covertly, Orage was still very much attracted to – if not still in love – with Mansfield, and she either continued to supply material for the *New Age*, or else he published material she had already supplied him; four pieces – 'A Marriage of Passion', 'Pastiche: At the Club', 'Pastiche: Puzzle: Find the Book' and 'Pastiche: Green Goggles', were all published between March and July 1912, and those exuberant comic skills were thus given an outlet.

After almost a year in England, the Beauchamp family finally returned to New Zealand in March 1912. At Mansfield's invitation, and with her stuffy parents now out of the way, Murry moved into a room at 69 Clovelly Mansions, initially as a formal arrangement but some weeks later they became lovers. Wood, however, notes how there might have been a more complex motive for her decision. Murry himself wrote how prior to him moving in, Mansfield had planned to relocate to the country, specifically 'Cherry Tree Cottage, Heronsgate', and indeed, according to Wood's research, there is a Cherry Cottage and a Cherry Tree Lane in Heronsgate, just outside Rickmansworth.[8] The name Heronsgate itself would have appealed to her, since 'Heron' was the middle name of her beloved younger brother Leslie. But it did seem a strange moment to want to leave London, having just started to establish herself as a writer. Wood believes this move may have had something to do with Orage,

> since Heronsgate was originally a Chartist settlement, which would certainly have appealed to Orage himself. Were Orage and Katherine in fact thinking of running off there together? But then Katherine met Murry and everything changed. Whatever the reason, in May 1912 Orage would launch his 'Mrs Foisacre' attack on Katherine in the *New Age* using the pseudonym R. H. Congreve, with Mansfield referred to as 'Marcia Foisacre'.[9]

There had definitely been some sort of rupture between her and Orage, and Mansfield now turned to Murry, both professionally and personally.

Thus it was that in issue 6, Spring 1912, Mansfield made her first appearance in *Rhythm* with 'The Woman at the Store', that brutal exposé of colonial life. In the story, three travellers ask to set up their tent for the night at a dusty backblocks store in the middle of nowhere, run only by a haggard woman, old before her time, and her dim-witted, traumatized, small daughter, the husband having, according to the woman, gone 'shearing'. One of the travellers remembers the woman from before her marriage, when she was much prettier and less careworn, and sleeps with her. The other two travellers engage with the young child, who, in a drawing, reveals exactly what happened to her father, in an image showing him being shot and then buried by her mother.

From the outset, the story is immediately recognizable as colonial in subject-matter because of its 'othered' descriptions:

> All that day the heat was terrible. The wind blew close to the ground [. . .] so that the white pumice dust swirled in our faces [. . .]. There was nothing to be seen but wave after wave of tussock grass – patched with purple orchids and manuka bushes covered with thick spider webs.[10]

This was certainly not London. As she wrote the story, Mansfield must have had on her desk in front of her the Urewera notebook in which she recorded every detail of her camping trip. As Ian A. Gordon notes, the language in the notebook and the story is frequently identical, with phrases and incidents transferred from one to the other: 'The "heat" and the "chuffing" horses, the "shrilling" larks, the collocation of tussock and orchid and manuka, the rider's "blue duck" trousers, the whare's "horsehair sofa", the "swampy creek", the absent man who is "away shearing" [. . .] all are in the notebook in virtually the same words.'[11] In an interview many years after Mansfield's death, Tom Seddon, the former New Zealand prime minister's son, remembered bumping into Mansfield in Rotorua, during the Urewera trip, where he was also staying at that time: 'Sitting on a bench under some willows in the drizzling rain, and looking very despondent, was Kass. She said, "I'm travelling in a caravan with some people father doesn't approve of and I feel miserable but I've written a marvellous story".'[12] That story was almost certainly 'The Woman at the Store'.

The ambiguously female-gendered narrator (for much of the story, at least), unnamed, like 'the woman', but unlike the two male travellers, Jo and Hin, complicates the subversive element of the text. The story also demonstrates many embryonic features of Mansfield's later Modernist style, as she synthesized and reworked late nineteenth-century techniques, together with this early colonial content, into her own 'special prose'. As a reminder of the colonial aspect of the story, the walls of the store are 'plastered with old pages of English periodicals. Queen Victoria's Jubilee appeared to be the most recent number.'[13] The Golden Jubilee had taken place in 1887 and the Diamond Jubilee in 1897; whichever Jubilee is being referred to, the scene depicted points to poverty, a place where magazines, long out of date, having travelled many thousands of miles throughout the Empire, are deemed a suitable replacement for expensive wallpaper. The contrast between the dazzling scenes of pomp and majesty on the pages themselves and the dirty, impoverished walls they now cover, in one of the most remote outposts of empire, is deliberate.

In this story (and 'Millie', published the following year in 1913), the effects of colonialism on women are key. Mansfield reveals how the woman has clearly been abused by her husband, her teeth knocked out and having had several miscarriages as a result of being battered. In turn, the woman abuses the living things around her, kicking and beating animals and her own small child. Jo remembers when the woman had had 'blue eyes and yellow hair' and 'knew one hundred and twenty-five different ways of kissing'.[14] Brutalized, the woman is still, nevertheless, prepared to sleep with him, taking comfort where she can. In this story, Mansfield depicts the frequently cruel repercussions of colonialism, with its legacy of violence for many women at the edge of empire.

Now part of the *Rhythm* editorial team, as well as being Murry's partner, would Mansfield have tried to flaunt her contacts to Murry and his Oxford colleagues by telling them that she personally knew a Polish writer, with sound knowledge of European literature, who could act as *Rhythm*'s Polish agent and help the little magazine to spread its influence into Eastern Europe? Or had Floryan Sobieniowski perhaps started making a nuisance of himself, asking her for help? Whatever the truth, by issue 6, July 1912, Sobieniowski was listed as the magazine's 'Polish correspondent'. During the month of May, Mansfield and Murry, now firmly in love, travelled to Paris on a sort of honeymoon, with Mansfield not just a tourist but a published author, having had her first collection of stories – *In a German Pension* – published in 1911. The pair thus found themselves with a certain literary cachet, and Murry took his new partner to the Latin Quarter and introduced her to his many literary acquaintances there. The 'Paris correspondent' of *Rhythm* at that time was Francis Carco, an impoverished young *fantaisiste* poet and journalist whom Murry had made friends with on a previous visit and whom he hailed as the new Rimbaud.

Carco (1886–1958), born in Nouméa on the French island of New Caledonia in the South Pacific, always liked to claim his 'South Sea' connection with Mansfield. Together with his Corsican parents, he moved back to France at the age of ten. During the First World War, he became Corporal Carco (holding the same rank as 'le petit caporal' in Mansfield's story 'An Indiscreet Journey' from 1915). Bohemianism in Paris, as a lifestyle choice for Carco and a horde of similar writers, artists, performers and hangers-on, seems largely to have been a matter of surviving on boiled eggs and devising increasingly ingenious ways to shock the bourgeoisie. But they also had serious ambitions to liberate and educate society at large, by rejecting the intellectual, emotional and sexual strictures inherited from the previous generation. Carco's connections at that time included Picasso, Modigliani, Apollinaire and, significantly for Mansfield, Colette. He became one of the founders and guiding lights of the *poètes fantaisistes*, as well as an art critic, novelist, essayist, memoirist, biographer, cabaret performer, songwriter and film script writer. He would become particularly famous for his novels depicting Montmartre and the Paris underworld; indeed, it was Carco specifically who helped to shape our popular image of Montmartre in the early twentieth century as a place of drug addicts and opium dens, homosexuality, pimps, prostitutes, brothels and criminals.

Hence, on their few days' 'honeymoon' in Paris in May 1912, Murry was eager to introduce Mansfield to his friend. Mansfield and Carco instantly hit it off, and Carco noted Mansfield's apologetic 'je ne parle pas français' to him when they were introduced (and which Mansfield subsequently drew on for her celebrated, cynical story loosely based on this meeting, titled 'Je ne parle pas français' (1918), with its seedy male protagonist based on Carco). The threesome now spent several evenings in each other's company, roaming the streets of Montmartre, as later depicted by Carco in his autobiography of 1938, *Montmartre à vingt ans*: 'It suited us to go out in the evenings as comrades, to haunt the bal-musettes on Montagne-Sainte-Geneviève or the little café-concerts on Place d'Italie, and sometimes to return at dawn.'[15] Carco even offered to give the pretty young Antipodean French lessons, which must surely have worried Murry. It was also on this same trip that Mansfield first met Murry's friend and co-founder of *Rhythm* the painter J. D. Fergusson; she was in much safer hands there, and Fergusson would go on to become one of her most trusted friends. Back in London, from issue 5 of *Rhythm*, June 1912, Mansfield was officially listed as an editorial assistant to Murry, and now more able to bring her own contacts and specific literary interests to the attention of *Rhythm*'s readers – especially with regard to Eastern Europe and Russia. In fact, she, Murry and their ever-widening social circle held strong convictions about the singular importance of Russian literature, and these were reflected in many of their creative endeavours.

It was now, some two years after their second attempt at living together, that George Bowden re-entered Mansfield's life, regarding a possible divorce. According to Ida, who – let's face it – mostly only ever knew what Mansfield spoon-fed her, 'at the end of April 1912, they had written to Katherine's husband, George Bowden, to ask him to divorce her. He arrived one day to see her and there was much talk; but in the end he did nothing. So Murry and Katherine decided to live as man and wife without legal consent.'[16] Here we see, in a gesture now all too familiar, how Mansfield, after such a short time living with Murry (barely a month), was already considering marriage. The only extant letter from Mansfield to Bowden (there are none from him to her still in existence), written on 23 May 1912, was friendly and professional:

> Dear G.
> I called at the Bank of New Zealand this afternoon and saw Mr Kay who gave me your letter and told me of his interview with you. Thank you for your letter. I should very much like to see you if it can be arranged and discuss your project with reference to an American divorce – I think it is in every way the wisest plan for us both. But arrange a time for us to meet, G. will you? I was sorry not to see you on Saturday afternoon –
> Believe me,
>
> Sincerely yours
> K.[17]

Clearly, they did now meet, for in response to a query from Alpers in 1949, Bowden related how he had called on Mansfield and Murry at Clovelly Mansions, in mid-1912:

> She did not seem to be concerned about any proceedings that would make remarriage possible for her [. . .]. For on leaving

> I asked her in [Murry's] presence – half jokingly – if they wanted to marry, and she looked quizzically at him and said something like, 'Do we, J. M.?' Incidentally [. . .] it had happened that K. M., with the easy manner of a good hostess asked me if I would not sing something for them. And on finding a volume of Schumann's songs – for low voice, however – I went to the piano and played and sang one or two.[18]

This all seems very jolly and grown up. But evidently Bowden did not leave it there. The sworn affidavit from 1917 records a second, apparently much less friendly visit in 1912:

> On the 14th August 1912 I, in company with my Solicitor, Mr. Bartlett, attended at 69 Clovelly Mansions Grays Inn Road London, where my said wife rented a flat. The door was answered by my wife and I immediately entered the flat accompanied by Mr. Bartlett. I told my wife that Mr. Bartlett was my Solicitor. My wife asked what he wanted and he said he wanted to see her alone. They went into the drawing room. I was left in the hall. I saw the Co-Respondent there. I had seen him before. He looked as if he had just got up. My wife was also as far as I can remember attired in a kind of dressing gown. Not long afterwards, I left the flat with my Solicitor. I held no further conversation with my wife and have never since seen her or had any relations of any kind with her.[19]

Clearly, Bowden was trying to convey the impression that Mansfield was now co-habiting with her latest conquest – Murry – which was true. He then went on to claim that his

> domestic troubles impaired my ability to make a living at my profession and in the hope of bettering my financial position in a community where I was a stranger I took the advice of friends and came to California arriving in San Francisco towards the end of 1912. I have since supported myself by teaching music and voice culture.[20]

Mansfield's desertion, he seemed to be suggesting, was to blame for his inability to make a living and the root cause of his abandoning his life in

England, making for California instead. He concluded by stating, 'My straightened [*sic*] means have compelled me to delay these proceedings. I have not sooner been able to save sufficient money to pay the necessary costs and have now only managed to lay aside the requisite sum with the strictest economy.'[21] The affidavit was sworn at the British Consulate in San Francisco in the presence of the Acting British Vice Consul.

So what was going on in August 1912? From Bowden himself stating in 1949 that all was well and the friendship between them was maintained during that first meeting, to a subsequent, much less friendly, almost-sordid encounter in mid-August, written in detail for the courts, there is a huge disparity in tone and bonhomie. There may be one reason, and it might have been instigated by Mansfield herself: unbelievably, she was now pregnant again and had changed her mind about the divorce. Bowden's subsequent visit with a solicitor would, therefore, have served both their interests. This might also explain what happened next.

In September, there having been embarrassing remarks made by other tenants at Clovelly Mansions concerning Mansfield and Murry's unmarried state, the couple decided to move to a little cottage in Runcton, near Chichester. It was to be their first proper home together, and to this end they invested in good-quality furniture from Maples, on hire purchase. But the real reason for the move, according to Mantz, was the fact, as noted above, that Mansfield was pregnant once more, this time with Murry's child, hence the need to make a more permanent home, away from prying Beauchamp relatives' eyes.[22] No one can know for sure how Mansfield eventually lost the child she was carrying, but Mantz was told that the poem 'Firelight', published in the *Athenaeum* on 25 April 1919 under the pseudonym Elizabeth Stanley, and, more importantly, the story 'This Flower' from 1920 make covert references to this tumultuous time.

In the story, a woman has a shady, back-street doctor secretly terminate a pregnancy, and then asks him to tell her partner that there was nothing wrong with her after all – just her heart playing up:

> 'Well,' said the doctor, taking up his hat, holding it against his chest and beating a tattoo on it, 'all I've got to say is that Mrs. – h'm – Madam wants a bit of a rest. She's a bit run down. Her heart's a bit strained. Nothing else wrong.' [. . .]
>
> She saw Roy's smile deepen; his eyes took fire. He gave a little 'Ah!' of relief and happiness. [. . .]

> She heard the front door close and then – rapid, rapid steps along the passage. This time he simply burst into her room, and she was in his arms, crushed up small while he kissed her with warm quick kisses, murmuring between them, 'My darling, my beauty, my delight. You're mine, you're safe.' And then three soft groans. 'Oh! Oh! Oh! the relief!' Still keeping his arms round her he leant his head against her shoulder as though exhausted. 'If you knew how frightened I've been,' he murmured. 'I thought we were in for it this time. I really did. And it would have been so – fatal – so fatal!'[23]

Is this what happened? It's certainly curious that Murry chose a rather obscure Shakespeare quotation from *Henry IV, Part 1* for Mansfield's gravestone: 'But I tell you, my lord fool, out of this nettle danger, we pluck this flower, safety.' Perhaps now we can understand why, for it is the epigraph Mansfield chose for this very story, and was, therefore, possibly Murry's covert way of commemorating, on her grave, their unborn child. The poem 'Firelight' comprises a short little daydream about a mother and a young son, hinting at Mansfield's sorrow over the lost child:

> Playing in the fire and twilight together,
> My little son and I,
> Suddenly – woefully – I stoop to catch him.
> 'Try, mother, try!'
>
> Old Nurse Silence lifts a silent finger:
> 'Hush! cease your play!'
> What happened? What in that tiny moment
> Flew away?[24]

With no baby, there was no longer any pressing need for a divorce, and everything on the Bowden front went quiet again, but Mansfield's messy past just would not go away. It was now that Sobieniowski decided to make a nuisance of himself, and Murry recorded his own reaction to the magazine's 'Polish correspondent' turning up in Runcton: 'Suddenly a Slavonic friend of Mansfield's came to England, and being penniless, came to us, with two big black trunks full of books and manuscripts, for he was a writer. [. . .]. We made him welcome, though he was a burden to our purse as well as our spirit.'[25]

A calamitous event now occurred when, at the end of September, the financial backer of *Rhythm*, Charles Granville (who had published *In a German Pension* under the name Stephen Swift), fled the country, having been accused of embezzlement and bigamy. He was subsequently brought back, tried and imprisoned, and his publishing company was liquidated. The only one of the editors with any regular income was Mansfield, who now gave over her entire monthly allowance to keeping the magazine afloat, and Martin Secker and Edward Marsh stepped in to help as financial backers. With a sound business head, Mansfield now 'worked hard at canvassing advertising which Murry [. . .] had earlier blithely declared as "unessentials"'.[26] (Nevertheless, the debts left by Swift eventually led to Murry declaring himself bankrupt in February 1914.)

The cottage in Runcton was, of course, now proving far too expensive. By November, with the baby no more, and therefore no need to be holed up away from prying eyes, they abandoned the cottage, sent back the Maples furniture bought on hire purchase and returned to London, this time to a one-room flat in Chancery Lane, Holborn, and then to a slightly larger flat at 57 Chancery Lane, which now doubled as *Rhythm*'s office. Sobieniowski was still rather a millstone around their necks, according to Murry:

> Ever since the break up of our home in Runcton we had been supporting him. He was indeed nominally our lodger at 15*s* a week; but since his method of paying this sum was to borrow from us at the rate of 25*s* a week; we were not notably profited. By the time that we ceased to keep a reckoning he owed us more than £40, and when we finally plucked up the courage to declare that we would support him no longer, we had not merely to move again in order to get rid of him, but to 'lend' him a further £15 to make him go.[27]

Mansfield and Murry certainly needed a holiday, and so they eagerly took up the offer to spend their first Christmas together in Paris, with friends Gilbert and Mary Cannan and Gordon and Beatrice Campbell, where Mansfield first met the artist Anne Estelle Rice, the then-partner of J. D. Fergusson. Beatrice Campbell subsequently remembered in her memoirs a vibrant, bold and confident Mansfield during this trip:

> I remember her gaiety, the way she would flounce into a restaurant and sweep her wide black hat from her bobbed head and hang it among the men's hats on the rack. I remember a group of men at a table running their tongues round their lips saying 'Oh la la' and her little muted laugh, delighted with herself [. . .] At night we went from café to café; there always seemed to be some terrific psychological drama going on, and we had to keep avoiding someone or other.[28]

This description, written by a close friend at the time, demonstrates the freedom of expression – in appearance, emotions and situations – that Mansfield manifested at this moment in her life. Her recklessness had brought her much suffering, but she was still a show-off at heart, and relished being the centre of attention.

In the final two issues of *Rhythm*, Mansfield and Murry were officially listed as joint editors. Issue 12, published in January 1913, featured mainly regular contributors, with, in addition, a painting by Cézanne. Mansfield herself contributed her seventh – and final – story for *Rhythm*: 'Ole Underwood'. Sobieniowski, however, was still making a nuisance of himself. Alexander Janta observed how

> Despite the distress Floryan caused her, Katherine Mansfield was willing to work with him. She helped him try to introduce the poet and playwright Stanislaw Wyspianski to the English stage. There was a plan to devote an entire issue of *Rhythm* to Wyspianski, but the magazine collapsed before it could be effected.[29]

Of course Mansfield agreed to help him. By this time, she had absolutely no choice – he knew far too much. As Jeffrey Meyers confirms,

> [Floryan's] power over them [. . .] was based on his past sexual relations with Mansfield. Since Floryan threatened Mansfield, and Murry (who never suspected she had been Floryan's mistress) was passive by nature, they were forced to tolerate him until they could pay what he demanded.[30]

Murry, even if frustratingly passive by nature (as later chapters reveal), must surely have found the relationship perplexing. Intriguingly, though, the above document by Janta records the fact that an entire issue of *Rhythm* devoted to the work of Stanislaw Wyspiański was planned. It would have been a considerable achievement and done much to raise early awareness of Wyspiański's genius outside his native land. It is also worth noting that Sobieniowski remained the 'Polish correspondent' until the very last issue of *Rhythm* in March 1913.

Meanwhile, between March and April 1913, Murry and Mansfield had taken on 'The Gables', a cottage in Cholesbury, Buckinghamshire, near to Gilbert and Mary Cannan, who owned a much grander converted windmill nearby; Mansfield now moved into the cottage, with Murry joining her at weekends. It was during this period that her poem 'Floryan Nachdenklich' ('Floryan Pensive') appeared in the Wellington *Dominion* on 3 March 1913.[31] After Mansfield's death, Murry always assumed that it must therefore have been written around 1913, but in fact the original manuscript is to be found on a page torn out of a diary for 1909 and was therefore proof that it had been written by Mansfield in Bavaria in 1909, at the height of her love affair with Sobieniowski. How or why she decided to publish it in Wellington as late as 1913 remains a mystery. And of course, Sobieniowski was still hanging around, a dangerous reminder of a period in her life Mansfield would have given anything to obliterate. On 13 May 1913 she wrote to Murry:

> Floryan is taking this for me. Will you phone Ida to come to Chancery Lane and see about his box, because some things of his are in the top of my box and he had better have them all. The story is really, rather what Id thought. He has had false promises and believed them: its no good discussing it. He promises to pay you back in little sums of £1 and £2.[32]

More deception: more lies told to Murry. In a letter written by Murry on 19 May 1913, we see how his patience must have reached breaking point when he declared, 'what a liar & Scoundrel Floryan is, and how he'll get us into trouble everywhere.'[33] Sobieniowski now disappeared out of their lives for several years. By August 1913 he had made contact with George Bernard Shaw; he would go on to translate forty of Shaw's plays and become as much of a nuisance to Shaw as he ever was to Mansfield and Murry.

Mansfield's contributions to *Rhythm* over the course of the magazine's short life had consisted of eleven poems, seven stories, six book reviews and two editorials co-written with Murry. This was in addition to her duties as an assistant editor and then joint editor, when her influence on the magazine's contents and contributions was marked; many items that did not bear her authorial name would, nevertheless, have been edited or revised by her. The little magazine's short-lived successor, the *Blue Review*, which ran for only three months from May to July 1913, was edited by Murry, with Mansfield as an associate editor (though with far less influence than before), her role seemingly limited to correspondence. It was now that the couple first came into contact with D. H. Lawrence and his wife, Frieda, then living in Italy, when they requested a story from him; Lawrence suggested 'The Soiled Rose', which appeared in the first issue. As well as Lawrence, the eventual list of contributors included Gilbert Cannan, Rupert Brooke and a few minor poets, with contributions by Murry and Mansfield, together with some drawings and cartoons. However, the little magazine lacked the international scope and visual excitement of its predecessor; there was a complete absence of foreign correspondents, so noticeable in *Rhythm*, and indeed of foreign contributors in general. The avant-garde feel had gone, and gone too that sense of being at the threshold of something new and original. On 26 June the *New Age*, which had been more or less positive about the *Blue Review*'s first issue, now, as Gray notes, put out a much less positive notice, written 'by a sulking Orage':[34]

> People who dissented from our praise of Miss Mansfield's sketch in the last number of 'The Blue Review' will be crowing over us this month. It seems to be true that women's talents are as fleeting as their beauty, and as little under their own control. There was in Miss Mansfield's first epilogue a momentary poise upon the gay good-humour which balanced her best early work; without this quality she becomes as in her two present sketches, either coarsely cynical or coarsely sentimental, inartistic.[35]

Finally, in June, the couple met Lawrence and Frieda in person, when the latter visited the *Blue Review* offices in Chancery Lane, having returned to England following their elopement. As Alpers observes, 'so began the famous alliance filled with danger that was to alter, and at times govern, Jack Murry's life for the next twenty years, and Katherine's for three.'[36] All four now started spending time together – the bond was instantaneous, and they clearly had much in common. Both Frieda and

Mansfield and John Middleton Murry at Chaucer Mansions, 1913.

Mansfield were technically married to other men when they first met their then-husbands, and the families of Murry and Lawrence were shocked at the women their precious sons had taken up with. By July, Mansfield and Murry had abandoned Cholesbury and moved back to London, residing at 8 Chaucer Mansions, West Kensington.

It was now that Mansfield made a second attempt at a novel, *Maata* (as noted in Chapter Two), drafted between August and November 1913, of which, once more, only fragments were eventually written.[37] Of course, by now Mansfield was an established author, and a very different person from the author of *Juliet*, her first attempt at a novel from 1906. Nevertheless, the plot and characters revisit Mansfield's relationship with the Trowell (here 'Close') family during the autumn and winter of 1908–9, almost as if she was still attempting to process that dramatic and painful period. She also intertwined characters from her more recent past.

Mansfield's written plan for the novel, comprising 35 chapters, was drafted by the beginning of August 1913, and by the end of the second week in August she had written the first chapter. However, the many complications of her life at this time, with constant house moves, plus dealing with the aftermath of *Rhythm*'s publisher absconding, leaving Murry liable for all the debts incurred, must have made fiction writing almost impossible. The second chapter of the novel was completed in mid-November before the whole thing was abandoned. Kaplan calls the novel Mansfield's second attempt at a *Bildungsroman*, claiming as a formative influence Lawrence's own autobiographical novel *Sons and Lovers*, which she and Murry had read during the summer of 1913.[38] Tomalin also believes Lawrence's novel was the impetus for Mansfield's beginning *Maata*:

> One or two touches suggest that Lawrence had put his fingerprint on her imagination: Maata's skin 'flames like yellow roses' when she undresses, and when Rhoda leans out of her bedroom window in the morning, "'Ah-ah' she breathed, in a surge of ecstasy. 'I am baptized. I am baptized into a new day,'" which certainly does not sound like anything else in Mansfield.[39]

And, of course, in naming herself Maata in the novel, Mansfield was recalling her youthful, intense relationship with her former schoolfriend, the exotic and glamorous Māori princess Maata Mahupuku.[40] Margaret Scott also notes that the novel has affinities with the strange story 'Brave Love', written in January 1915:

> In both stories the heroine is beautiful, cynical, self-absorbed, drawn to the innocent young lover, but destructive of him too. In both cases, the young man is not only betrayed but also punished. [. . .] it does seem likely that Evershed in both stories was suggested by George Bowden, and that Mildred in one and Rachael West in the other were suggested by Beatrice Hastings.[41]

As noted previously, the character of Rhoda Bendall in the novel is clearly based on Ida, and for Scott 'represents the only attempt K. M. made to describe Ida Baker's feelings for her. It is important for that alone.'[42] The first name reflects Ida's Rhodesian colonial origins, and Bendall was the surname of Mansfield's close friend Edith during the time she spent in Wellington in 1907–8 before returning to London. Here in *Maata*, Dolly Trowell is called Maisie; as Scott reveals, where

Mrs Close says, 'the one you had afterwards Maisie,' Mansfield had 'started to write "Dolly", crossed it out and substituted "Maisie", thus confirming that it was the Trowells she had in mind'.[43] This, of course, and other similar instances of real names crossed out, reaffirms the autobiografictional basis of the text, and was precisely what Mansfield did in *Juliet*, where real names such as Vere and Caesar (Mansfield's nickname for Tom Trowell) pepper the story.

Chapter One begins in Rhoda Bendall's bedroom, as Rhoda wakes up to the sound of rain. Today is the day that her dearest friend Maata, who has been away for two years in some far-off, unnamed place, is to return to London, and later she is to go to the station to meet her off the boat train. The language Rhoda uses as she paces her bedroom betrays her intense emotions towards her friend: 'My treasure, my beloved one, the day is beautiful with you. Your breath is in this wind and the same rain falls on us both. *On us both*. Oh God, bring her quickly. Bring her quickly. [. . .] She is your spirit, your essence. She is God in woman.'[44] Such extreme devotion sets the tone for their entire relationship. Mansfield paints an unflattering portrait of Rhoda herself, 'big and heavy', and with a 'violent bodily hunger and a wavering sense of shame', again features of Ida's true appearance and her need for comfort eating.[45]

In Chapter Two we are introduced to Philip and Maisie Close. In *Juliet*, the Mansfield character had been in love with David the cellist; now, in *Maata*, she is in love with Philip the violinist, echoing, as noted earlier, Mansfield's real-life transference of affection from Tom Trowell (cellist) to Garnet Trowell (violinist). Philip and Maisie, like Rhoda, have come to the station to meet Maata from the boat train. Completely forgetting Rhoda, it is to Philip and Maisie that Maata rushes, enveloping Maisie in her arms. Rhoda is eventually spotted, and Maata apologizes for having forgotten about her. Yet, ever practical, it is Rhoda who has seen to Maata's luggage and hired a waiting hansom cab, which Maata completely takes for granted. Here, it is Rhoda's emotions that Mansfield portrays, using free indirect discourse to expose Maata's selfish character: 'Those moments at the station hurt her still. Her throat ached and tears pressed into her eyeballs.'[46] The two opening chapters could almost be perceived as a hymn to Ida's unswerving devotion to Mansfield, who could not know, in 1913, that this devotion would last for the rest of her life. However, glimpses of the excess of it are painted here: 'Rhoda knelt on the floor and handled her darling's possessions as though these were all – every one – more precious than gold.'[47]

The rest of the manuscript, bar one small section at the end, takes place at the Close family's house. Philip (Pip) and Hal are twins, and both musical, as is their father (exactly like the Trowell family). But it is clear that the family has little money, and that socially they are beneath the glamorous Maata, as Mansfield's portrait of Mrs Close reveals:

> By the table sat Mrs Close, darning whole new feet into a pair of Hal's socks. Her skirt was turned back over her lap, her little slippered feet curled round the chair legs. Now and again she leant forward and opened her mouth for Maisie to pop in a 'beautifully soft one' [roasted chestnut], but she was, for the most part, pale and tired.[48]

Maata and Philip contrive to be alone together in his room, where 'The violin case lying open on the white bed was like a little coffin' (presaging, perhaps, the unhappy denouement of their relationship, for according to the chapter plan, when Maata eventually marries not for love but for social position, Philip kills himself).[49] The two lovers sit and talk, but all the time with a sense of foreboding, as though such talk will ultimately be futile, as here in Maata's speech to Philip:

> 'You know sometimes I feel I am pursued by a sort of Fate – you know – by an impending disaster that spreads its wings over my heart – or maybe only the shadow of its wings – but it's so black and terrible I can't describe it. Sometimes I think it is [. . .], foreboding, telling me that what I am facing in the future – is –' she shrugged her shoulders – 'just *darkness*.'[50]

This speech echoes the numerous occasions in her life when Mansfield wrote of darkness in her future, using the word 'wings' to describe her fluttering heart, which she always thought would kill her, and subsequently, following her diagnosis of tuberculosis, her lungs. The last fragment of the novel ends with a similar foreboding atmosphere, as Maata reflects on her own character, her secret self and the sham that is her outer world:

> Standing there in the dark she drifted away to that shadowy loneliness which sometimes seemed to her to be her only true life, the only changeless truth – the thing that she was never

> really certain was not reality after all. How extraordinary! She saw herself all these last weeks, playing a part – being Maata, being herself, caring for things that after all don't matter at all. Why, only that afternoon, a minute or two ago, she had believed in it all – and it was all nothing, nothing.[51]

In *Maata* Mansfield does not victimize her protagonist as she does in the more youthful *Juliet*. This time she has agency and it is the man who is destroyed, for the chapter plan tells us that Philip will ultimately commit suicide after learning of Maata's marriage to Evershed (in reality, Mansfield's marriage to Bowden): 'His heart bursts with grief. He listens to Hal and by and bye he takes out the revolver and puts the spout in his mouth and shoots himself.'[52] As Kaplan notes, however, 'In terms of creative power, the assertions of artistic freedom in the later novel seem to lead to a confusing and ambivalent impasse, and to a corresponding diminishment of energy.'[53] Mansfield's inability to continue with the novel points as much to her personal emotions regarding the story's autobiografictional elements as to her outward, difficult circumstances. She would never forget the deep passion between herself and Garnet, her first true relationship, and of course the anguish over the loss of their ill-fated child. *Maata* was the last time that her creative energies were directed towards a *recherche du temps perdu* of the Trowell family.

After her two previous attempts at novel-writing, Mansfield would try just once more – with 'The Aloe' – to extend the length of her short fiction narratives. She more than once referred to 'The Aloe' as her 'book' as she was writing it, although its final length is actually more that of a novella.[54] As a story cycle, her Burnell family stories, 'Prelude' (the later, revised, published version of 'The Aloe'), 'At the Bay' and 'The Doll's House', in effect, create a short novel. *Juliet*, written when she was still a teenager, is immature in both form and content, although glimpses can be seen of Mansfield's love of interiority – free indirect discourse – that is the hallmark of her mature style. Nevertheless, for Kaplan, it remains 'of special interest as a version of Mansfield's self-development in that it is both a fairly transparent account of her early adolescence and an unnervingly prescient projection into a life she had not lived.'[55] *Maata* represents that uncanny projection brought to life, this time via a recall of actual events lived, rather than describing an indeterminate fantasy future. Both fragmentary novels deserve their place in any critical discussion of Mansfield's oeuvre, not least because of the autobiografictional basis of each narrative, as well as for revealing evidence of the proto-Modernist writer Mansfield was in the process of becoming.

By December 1913, their finances in a precarious state, Mansfield and Murry decided on a permanent move to Paris, naive in their belief that they would be able to live more cheaply there, that Murry would be able to both review French books for the *Times Literary Supplement* and write a best-selling novel. The couple moved into a flat at 31 rue de Tournon, initially accompanied by Murry's good friend Frederick Goodyear. In fact, it was Mansfield who settled easily into Paris life and Murry who floundered, unable to find work, harassed by Carco and other impoverished French associates who believed he could find them work writing for English papers.

Despite this, Mansfield soon wrote to her sister Chaddie in an ebullient mood:

> The weather is icy but Paris looks beautiful [...] I am going to enjoy life in Paris I know. It is so human and there is something noble in the city – Then the river is so much more a part of it than the Thames. It is a real city, old and fine and life plays in it for every one to see. Jack and I are dropping into speaking French together and leaving English alone until we have really mastered the other.[56]

During this month, she wrote the story 'Something Childish But Very Natural', a much longer story than any she had written up to that point and her first attempt at writing in 'episodes'. Her new situation had helped to turn her creative processes in a different direction and made her experimental both in scope and vision.

Carco, of course, was now constantly on hand, and the relationship between him and Mansfield developed as a consequence. In his later memoirs, he recorded the following impression of her at this time: 'The young woman, among her trunks, in the large room in the rue de Tournon, smiled at me and made me swear that I'd move to London as soon as everything went well.'[57] These memoirs, however, were written in 1938, almost 25 years after the events described and with an eye for upholding the cult that had by then enveloped the personality of Mansfield in France.[58] In Murry's own first novel, *Still Life*, published in 1916 but started during this trip to France, the character Dupont, who is Carco's fictional equivalent, tells the character named 'Morry' that he 'must never love a woman more than three or four days', but that during those three or four days he must 'Never think of anything else, never leave her for a moment, and thus, knowing her to the last hiding-places of her mind, break with her once and for all, leaving no thread of the unknown or the unexplored to bind you to her.'[59] From what we know of Carco historically, this cynical advice would have fallen easily from his own lips and therefore tallies with how Mansfield was eventually to present him in her own fiction. It was also exactly what was to happen in Gray, France, in 1915, more of which in the next chapter.

However, within a few short weeks of their arrival, financial complications were about to scupper Mansfield and Murry's plans. It was now becoming obvious that Murry could not make a living in Paris and, in addition, bankruptcy proceedings arising out of the *Rhythm* fiasco were threatening in England; he returned briefly to London in an attempt to sort out his affairs, but to no avail. With their hopes for a new life in Paris dashed, after only three months away, on 24 January 1914, the couple were forced to return to England, having disposed of all their worldly goods – and some of Ida's precious family furniture – for a pittance to brothel owners helpfully provided by Carco. In a letter to a friend, Mansfield merely noted, 'I have given Carco a few souvenirs – the egg timer which charmed him and some odd little pieces like that.'[60] However, the most important outcome of this stay in Paris was the relationship that would continue to develop between Mansfield and Carco, which led to a further – and now famous – clandestine meeting between them a year later, and all of which culminated in the production of two stories: 'An Indiscreet Journey' and 'Je ne parle pas français'.

Returning to London on 24 February 1914, the couple took a furnished flat at 119 Beaufort Mansions, Chelsea. Ida, from whom Mansfield had become somewhat estranged at this time, returned to Rhodesia to see her father and would remain there for two years. In April the couple moved yet again, this time to less expensive but more miserable rooms at 102 Edith Grove, off the Fulham Road, where they both quickly succumbed to pleurisy; there then followed a move to an even cheaper flat at 111 Arthur Street, Chelsea, which, they discovered, was infested by bugs. It was a wretched time all round.

And yet, one of the defining relationships of Mansfield's life began in the summer of 1914, when she met the Russian émigré Samuel

Mansfield, *c.* 1914.

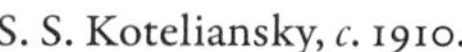

S. S. Koteliansky, *c.* 1910.

Solomonovich Koteliansky (1880–1955), known to literary London simply as 'Kot', who remained devoted to Mansfield, despite the occasional period of estrangement, until her death and indeed for the rest of his own life. Kot was a Russian Jew from Ukraine who had immigrated to England in 1911 following political harassment by the then-Tsarist government. Dorothy Brett would later describe him in 1915 as 'so broad-shouldered that he looks short, his black hair brushed straight up "en brosse", his dark eyes set perhaps a trifle too close to his nose, the nose a delicate well-made arch, gold eyeglasses pinched onto it'.[61] In 1914 he came into the sphere of Mansfield and Murry, having been introduced to them by Lawrence. Although literature was where Kot's real interest lay, he was, by then, working in an office known as the Russian Law Bureau, translating Russian legal documents. In fact, John Carswell notes how, with 'the growing passion for all things Russian, [Kot] was beginning to be recognized not only as a translator but as a finder of new Russian material'.[62] Darya Protopopova underlines his importance in this regard, claiming that

> Koteliansky was an infinite resource on the whole range of Russian literature; he translated not only the authors who were already well known in England, but also the contemporary Russian writers who left Russia after the revolution, but

> remained undiscovered by English readers, e.g. Ivan Bunin and Alexander Kuprin.[63]

This, of course, would explain how he came into the sphere of the Bloomsbury Group and its fringes, whose 'fascination with Russia', as Galya Diment notes, 'had two major components: the Ballets Russes and Russian literature'; Kot's Russianness would have been attractive to them all.[64] For Claire Davison,

> Koteliansky's involvement in these circles was not as a bystander but as an active participant, even instigator, and specialist. [. . .] He informed Lawrence's dream of a utopian community, 'Rananim', Virginia Woolf's reading of the Russians, Leonard Woolf's knowledge of the harsher political truths of the Bolshevist regime, Murry's study of Dostoevsky, and Mansfield's understanding of the revolution.[65]

Participant he may have been, but apart from his intimate friendships with Mansfield and Lawrence, Kot's relationship with Bloomsbury proper remained troubled (and the same could be said for Mansfield, Murry and the Lawrences). Indeed, in a letter to Mansfield composed much later on 9 December 1919, he wrote, 'there is no one who cares a bit or is to the smallest degree interested in what happens to me. [. . .] But left with myself, quite alone, for very long stretches of time, I feel as if I have already ceased to live.'[66] This state of affairs was underpinned by a comment made by Beatrice Campbell, who noted, 'He was dazzled by them [Bloomsbury], but with few exceptions they had no real friendship or affection for him.'[67] Nevertheless, Kot would go on to collaborate on a number of literary translations from Russian with several different writers, including both Leonard and Virginia Woolf, Lawrence, Murry and Mansfield herself. Indeed, the gossip in Bloomsbury squares about the antics of a rather forward young New Zealander called Katherine Mansfield would have been augmented by pumping Kot for information. Strangely, in June 1914, Murry, already gaining a reputation as an expert on Russian literature, had been offered a job at the British Embassy Library in St Petersburg; he turned it down, having been commissioned to write his critical book on Dostoevsky by the publisher Martin Secker. Later, during the winter of 1914, Kot and Murry would begin collaborating together on a series of projects for a

D. H. Lawrence and Frieda's wedding day,
with Mansfield and John Middleton Murry, 1914.

publisher called Maunsel, translating Russian works into English for £20 a piece and dividing the fee between them, with Kot doing the initial translation and Murry polishing and perfecting the English; their first such venture was *The Bet and Other Stories* by Chekhov.[68]

Meanwhile – and emphasizing how close the two couples had become – on 13 July Mansfield and Murry attended the wedding of Lawrence and Frieda at Kensington Register Office. Frieda gave Mansfield her old wedding ring, which she would wear for the rest of her life and which she took to her grave. In fact, Frieda had only meant for Mansfield to borrow the ring until she and Murry could marry. As Catherine Carswell records:

> Long afterwards Frieda, laughing, told me how that day Lawrence's infectious insistence on the importance of fidelity, and so of marriage, had given Katherine Mansfield the desire to wear a wedding ring herself. But such trifles cost something, and money with the Murrys, too, was scarce. So Frieda lent Katherine her discarded ring to wear till Murry could give her

> one of her own. Frieda had looked to have it back. But Katherine misunderstood and nothing more was ever said.[69]

After many rumblings, war was declared on 4 August 1914. Murry, carried away by initial patriotic fervour, enlisted in a cyclists' battalion but, having second thoughts, quickly obtained medical exemption. In September, after briefly holidaying in Cornwall, he and Mansfield moved to a cottage at Udimore, near Rye, Sussex, and by the end of October they had moved again to Rose Tree Cottage, The Lee, near Great Missenden, where they began to experience the violent quarrels between Lawrence and Frieda, who lived just 5 kilometres (3 mi.) away. Joanna Woods records one such quarrel:

> Shortly after Katherine and Murry moved to Rose Tree Cottage, the Lawrences had one of their rows in full view of Koteliansky who had been invited to stay. Koteliansky took Lawrence's part and Frieda stormed out into the pouring rain to walk the three miles which separated their cottage from the Murrys'. Several hours later, Lawrence and Koteliansky were surprised by the arrival of Katherine, drenched to the skin in wellington boots with her skirt tucked up to keep it out of the mud. She announced that Frieda would not be coming back and vanished into the night.[70]

The Lawrences might have been quarrelling, but so too were the 'Murrys'. Mansfield was now disillusioned with her life and more specifically with her relationship with Murry, which began to go sour as he disappeared into his work and his own circle of male friends, leaving her feeling isolated and demoralized. In this disaffected state, when a letter arrived from Carco addressed to Murry, Mansfield, receptive and emotionally in need, wrote in a notebook,

> A letter from Carco. I had not expected it and yet when it came it seemed quite inevitable – the writing – the way the letters were made, his confidence and his warm sensational life. I wish he were my friend – he's very near me. His personality comes right through his letters to Jack – & I want to laugh and run into the road.[71]

According to Carco's memoirs, her feelings were more than reciprocated. As noted earlier, Carco would eventually become renowned for his novels depicting the seedier side of Parisian life, one of which, *Les Innocents* (1916), would include a not very flattering portrait of Mansfield herself as the character Winnie. We know now how his much later published 'souvenirs' of Mansfield were very much developed to fit an image, an icon, in whose life he had fortuitously found himself playing a minor – if significant – role. As the couple now started corresponding, he later somewhat disingenuously recorded,

> I knew nothing of the friendship that a man can feel towards a woman, and such a complex feeling, to which, without my suspecting it, Katherine Mansfield had initiated me, suddenly developed in such a way that at first I understood nothing of what was happening to me. I didn't dare talk to anyone about it.[72]

It is hard not to laugh out loud at such blatant whitewashing of his own manipulation of Mansfield's burgeoning feelings for him. But her own notebook entries from this time now showed a marked disaffection for Murry as her interest in Carco grew, the tone ever more urgent:

> F. may be leaving Besancon soon for the front, he told me, & he said – every day I love you more – & he told me that all the while we had been in Paris he had loved me. Well, he thinks so now, and that he would like to live in a little hut on the edge of the world where no one would ever come, and that at times now he has merely an awful sensation of emptiness, he would like to lie in the road & let the world pass over him and when I fall asleep, I take you in my arms – and I feel a terrible sadness – and – ever so much more. The day after this letter he sent me another, very short – Dear Katherine, I want only you. You are and will be my whole life.[73]

The notebook continues in this vein for several entries, spread over a number of weeks.

Meanwhile, at Christmas 1914, an infamous house party led to the beginnings of an entry into Bloomsbury for Mansfield and Murry. Present at Gilbert and Mary Cannan's converted windmill in Buckinghamshire were Lawrence and Frieda, Mansfield and Murry, the painter

Mark Gertler and Kot. Everyone got drunk, to the extent that no one was in a fit state to even carve the suckling pig that had been ordered for the occasion. Two short plays were performed, centred around the relationship between a cynical husband and a wife who wants to comfort a sentimental foreigner. The acting became rather too realistic. Mansfield's 'comforting' of Gertler and her refusal to stop kissing him led to Frieda taking Gertler outside onto the road in front of the house and telling him that Mansfield was a bad woman and he should leave her alone. Gertler then burst into tears. Gilbert Cannan later described the evening to Lady Ottoline Morrell as akin to something out of a Dostoevsky novel, and the whole episode was recounted with glee by the gossipmongers of Bloomsbury and beyond. The 'Murrys' were becoming an interesting couple. The problem was that Mansfield, her relationship with Orage now seemingly in the past, wasn't sure she wanted to be with Murry anymore. It spelt a complicated end to a fractured, unsatisfactory year.

5

Death and Disillusionment, 1915–17

Still living in Rose Tree Cottage, the 'Murrys' (in Mansfield's eyes at least) were barely a couple anymore. Murry had turned to the men in his life, especially Lawrence and Gordon Campbell, for intellectual comradeship, and so Mansfield now turned to Carco for everything she felt was lacking in her relationship with Murry. As early as 6 January 1915, following a trip to London, she explored in a notebook her burgeoning feelings for Carco:

> He has haunted me all day. I have seen for him and with him all day long. As I went to Piccadilly in the evening on top of a bus I nearly got up & called out his name. I longed for him so, & yet I dare not push my thoughts as far as they will go. [. . .] Had my photo taken for him.[1]

She also sent him a lock of her hair. Even though she and Murry were still making love, Mansfield now fantasized about Carco during their lovemaking. It was clear their relationship was reaching a crisis point. Murry, for his part, had resigned himself to the fact that she was going to leave him. Kot briefly came to stay, and it was around this time that Lawrence's idea of 'Rananim' (the word taken from a Hebrew song Kot was fond of singing) came into being – a mystical, remote island to which a group of like-minded people would retreat from the world and live a communal life in absolute harmony. So ran Lawrence's dream, anyway.

Mansfield discussed her plans to meet Carco with Beatrice Campbell:

> Katherine told me of how she was planning to leave Murry and go to Carco at Gray, where he was stationed in barracks in the military zone of France. Though she and Murry were not yet married, as her first husband had not divorced her, I had looked on them as inseparable and was worried about her. It seemed like one of her 'stunts'.
>
> To convince me of the seriousness of her love affair with Carco, Katherine brought me one of his letters, but I felt she was trying to convince herself as well as me.[2]

This was indeed a strange and unsettling time; Carco wanted Mansfield to visit him in France, but she didn't have the means to get there. Her trump card came via her brother Leslie, who had just arrived from New Zealand to join up; following his training, he would hold the rank of a bombing officer in the South Lancashire Regiment. Why he joined this rather unusual regiment is unclear. J. Lawrence Mitchell writes that 'At the suggestion of Uncle Harry (Trinder), Leslie met with a member of Lord Kitchener's staff in the War Office, flourished his discharge papers from New Zealand and within 24 hours had secured a commission in the South Lancashire Regiment.' This may well be true, but there is another possibility, as revealed by John Wood.[3] In July 1902 Richard Seddon, the then prime minister of New Zealand and a great friend of the Beauchamp family, visited England, accompanied by his daughter Phoebe and her husband, Frank Dyer (Mansfield's uncle). During the trip, they went to St Helens in southern Lancashire, where Richard Seddon had been born. They attended a ceremony at the town hall along with all the civic dignitaries, where Seddon was given the Freedom of St Helens. Nearly all the other young men from New Zealand involved in the First World War joined the New Zealand Expeditionary Force, whereas the soldiers for the South Lancashire Regiment were almost exclusively recruited from St Helens and the surrounding area. The Seddon/Dyer connection may thus have resulted in his enlistment into this regiment, which otherwise seems a very strange choice.

But back to Mansfield. On about 10 February, during another trip to London to retrieve her monthly allowance from Mr Kay at the Bank of New Zealand, she bumped into none other than Leslie himself, unaware that he had just arrived in England. Here was just the chance she needed to escape Murry and travel to see Carco. She now duplicitously told Leslie that she had a contract for a series of 'war sketches' with a

Leslie Beauchamp in uniform, 1915.

newspaper, but that her allowance didn't run to a trip over to France. The lies got bigger, with innocent Leslie reporting in a letter to his parents back home in Wellington:

> She is more than ever in love with J. M. Murray which is a thing to be thankful for and with a new contract with one of the monthlies for a series of war sketches, they have prospects of a little money coming in, though these times are exceptionally trying for their itinerant sort of writings. They are going over to Paris at the end of this week to collect materials for the new job. I do not expect to see K. again for some time.[4]

Poor old Chummie. Of course he would lend dear Kass the money she needed. This was exactly the impetus Mansfield needed, and by 15 February she was on her way to Paris.

Unknown to Murry, on arrival in Paris Mansfield went straight to the Closerie des Lilas, a famous Parisian brasserie, and a favourite of hers, to lunch with the other Beatrice in her life – Beatrice Hastings, Orage having given her some packages to deliver (indicating that Mansfield had been seeing him as well on those recent trips to London). Wood notes, 'On 1 February, Mansfield recorded that she had read *The Lonely Nietzsche*, the second volume of Nietzsche's biography by his sister. Orage was to comment on this in his "Readers and Writers" column on 11 February, so she may have been given it to read by him.'[5] It's very unlikely that Murry knew that she had met up with Orage. As Wood notes, 'Hastings and Orage had separated and become estranged after she had left him in 1914, initially for Wyndham Lewis. She was now living in Paris with (and being immortalized in paintings by) Modigliani.'[6] Mansfield now told Hastings of her troubles with Murry, both financial and emotional (which must have pleased her erstwhile friend enormously), adding that her new French beau had not been able to meet her in Paris, and could she therefore borrow some money from Beatrice to get to Gray, where he was now stationed as a postman to a unit of military bakers (not the most glamorous of war roles). Hastings obliged, and thus it was that on 19 February Mansfield travelled to Gray, undertaking a difficult journey to the battlefront (generally forbidden to women), hoodwinking the French army officials by falling back on the old tale of a sick relative.

On arrival, the new lovers – each emotionally ravenous, though for different reasons – fell upon one another, Carco having taken a room in a village house. She describes their encounter quite dispassionately in a notebook:

> It was like an elopement [. . .] Laughing and trembling we pressed against each other a long, long kiss [. . .] the whole affair seemed somehow so ridiculous and at the same time so utterly natural [. . .] In the most natural manner we slowly undressed by the stove. F swung into the bed. 'Is it cold?' I said. 'No, not at all cold. Viens, ma bébé, don't be frightened. The waves are quite small.' His laughing face and his pretty hair, one hand with a bangle over the sheets, he looked like a girl [. . .] The sword, the big ugly sword, but not between us, lying in a chair.
>
> The act of love seemed somehow quite incidental, we talked so much. It was so warm and delicious, lying curled in each other's arms, by the light of the tiny lamp [. . .] only the clock and the fire to be heard. A whole life passed in the night: other people, other things, but we lay like two old people coughing faintly under the eiderdown, and laughing at each other.[7]

Francis Carco, 'vaguemestre' (non-commissioned officer in charge of the postal service) for sector 45, in his room at the Gray cantonment near Besançon, 1915.

The story 'An Indiscreet Journey', never published in Mansfield's lifetime, is a biographical account of that trip to the war zone in France to see Carco, rewritten as a short story, with parts of the text replicating her own notebook entries. Its importance lies in the fact that it is one of the earliest fictional accounts of the First World War written in English, and, what is more, written by a woman, one with first-hand experience of the scenes she is describing. From Gray, for example, she penned a diary entry describing the sight that greeted her and Carco as they made their way to dinner: 'The wounded were coming down the hill. They were all bandaged up. One man looked as though he had 2 red carnations over his ears, one man as though his hand was covered in black sealing wax.'[8]

Mansfield's trip was risky, not just physically but also for her reputation. As Angela K. Smith notes, 'there is a sense of anarchy inspired by the implied amorality of the narrator [of the story], which reinforces the notion that the war could be a dangerously liberating experience for women.'[9] Though lightly handled on the surface, as with so much of Mansfield's work, this 'simple' story is made the vehicle for a rich freight of ideas and impressions. With admirable economy, Mansfield summons up the peculiar atmosphere of ordinary village life in France caught up in the middle of a war that was still in its infancy at the time she was writing. Take, for example, this description of Mansfield's unnamed female protagonist's view of the passing landscape from the window of her railway carriage:

> What beautiful cemeteries we are passing! They flash gay in the sun. They seem to be full of cornflowers and poppies and daisies. How can there be so many flowers at this time of the year? But they are not flowers at all. They are bunches of ribbons tied onto the soldier's graves.[10]

That sense of surface brightness and gaiety, as the train flashes past freshly dug graves of the war dead, the temporary wooden markers decorated with ribbons by loved ones, seems almost hallucinatory, given the true horrors of the war all around. Indeed, Con Coroneos claims that 'the story has the disconcerting effect of seeming to aestheticize or trivialize the war,' but it would be an obtuse reader indeed who could not reach beneath the surface and view the story as a polemic against the war and its horrors, which the author had witnessed at first hand.[11]

More importantly, here we find, in fiction and possibly for the first time, a description of the after-effects of gas poisoning on a soldier and added to the story of her escapade. It was most probable that Mansfield witnessed the effect of this gassing (chlorine gas having only been introduced by the Germans for the first time on 22 April 1915 at Ypres) while she was residing in Paris in May of that year at Carco's flat – for it was to Paris that the dying and injured from the trenches were brought in their thousands – and thus she was able to incorporate what she saw directly into a story that perhaps might be more correctly termed 'literary journalism'.

As with so many of Mansfield's stories – and much Modernist fiction – very little happens in the way of action. Yet it remains a moving eulogy to the suffering of the soldiers of the Great War since Mansfield's skills as a writer, including her syntax and imagery, offer a pitch-perfect exposé of the horrors of war and especially, as here, for those soldiers who survive:

> The café slowly filled [. . .] In the din the door sounded again. It opened to let in a weed of a fellow, who stood with his back against it, one hand shading his eyes.
>
> 'Hullo! You've got the bandage off?'
>
> 'How does it feel, *mon vieux*?'
>
> 'Let's have a look at them.'
>
> But he made no reply. He shrugged and walked unsteadily to a table, sat down and leant against the wall. Slowly his hand

> fell. In his white face, his eyes showed, pink as a rabbit's. They brimmed and spilled, brimmed and spilled. He dragged a white cloth out of his pocket and wiped them. [. . .]
>
> His comrades watched him a bit, watched his eyes fill again, again brim over. The water ran down his face, off his chin on to the table. He rubbed the place with his coat-sleeve, and then, as though forgetful, went on rubbing, rubbing with his hand across the table, staring in front of him.
>
> And then he started shaking his head to the movement of his hand. He gave a loud strange groan and dragged out the cloth again. [. . .]
>
> 'Ooof!' groaned the man with the eyes, rocking and mopping. But nobody paid any attention to him except Madame. She made a little grimace at her two soldiers.
>
> '*Mais vous savez, c'est un peu dégoutant, ça*,' she said severely.[12]

This piece of writing is remarkable on many levels. The description of the gas-poisoned soldier is almost clinical in its detail – vivid and unforgettable and made to seem even more awful by the sobriety of Mansfield's laconic account. This is a man in considerable pain and discomfort – who may indeed be dying – initially acknowledged by the other soldiers in the bar, but soon forgotten as they return to their card game and their flirting, until he is reduced to little more than an object of disgust by the proprietress, whereupon the other soldiers wholeheartedly agree with her – she is a much prettier and coquettish sight than their sick comrade. Even the two main characters, engrossed in each other, ignore the plight of the stricken soldier – they are more interested in what is on the menu.

It is obvious that even at this early stage of the war, Mansfield was able to appreciate and describe its inhuman consequences, and yet to show how it is a human defence mechanism to be perceived as carrying on as normal. Her story, beneath the notional superficiality of the plot, opens a disturbing window onto the devastating consequences of war and exposes the long, dark shadow that it casts over people's lives. As Mitchell observes, 'Mansfield had caught a disquieting glimpse of what might await her brother at the front,' and Murry went further, explaining in an editorial note to the 1954 edition of Mansfield's *Journal*, 'No single one of Katherine's friends who went to the war returned alive from it. This will explain the profound and ineradicable impression made upon her by the war.'[13]

After just four nights with her new lover, Mansfield returned to London and Murry on 25 February, disillusioned, but with plenty of copy (and of course, Carco appeared to be following his own rules to the letter regarding the way to treat women, as set down by him for Murry). Murry recounts how four days after the episode, in Gray,

> suddenly, I received a telegram from Katherine to say that she was returning and would be at Victoria at 8 a.m. on the next day. I went up to London to meet her. She was strange, her hair was cut short, and she was aggressively defensive. I was not to imagine that she had returned to *me*.[14]

And yet, gradually, her anger and general frustration diminished enough for them to find rooms together in London, at 95 Elgin Crescent, which Murry set about decorating while she escaped once more to Paris, in order to write. Though Mansfield may have been disillusioned with Carco as a lover, she clung onto the relationship for a few more months – long enough to make use of his apartment in Paris on the Quai aux Fleurs, overlooking the Seine on the Île de la Cité. At this point in her life, she was both disillusioned by the selfishness of Carco and wounded by the indifference of Murry:

> I don't miss Jack at all now. I don't want to go home. I feel quite content to live here in a furnished room & watch. [...] Life with other people becomes a blur: it does with Jack, but its enormously valuable & marvellous when I'm alone – the detail of life – the life of life. Carco feels that too – but nobody else.[15]

In fact, as we can see, the trip to Gray having somehow not fulfilled her expectations, she had returned to Murry, only to leave him again a few days later to return to Paris and Carco's flat. Two weeks later she was back in England, and a month later she was back at Carco's flat again. And all the while, she was writing cheery, loving letters to Murry and breezy, vaguely flirtatious ones to Carco (having told Murry she was no longer in contact with him), perhaps, cynically, because she wanted the use of his flat, perhaps because she still held a candle for their relationship. But there were undercurrents of disapproval starting to appear: on 9 May she wrote to Murry,

> I went out on the landing just now to get some water. The concierge was sweeping the stairs & the woman below me came out to talk to her. 'The little lady upstairs came in very late last night,' said she – 'Who.' 'La maîtresse de Francis Carco,' bawled the voice. [. . .] I am still trembling with fury.[16]

To add to an already duplicitous picture, Carco too was writing back, perhaps hoping for another visit from his new lover, since I discovered the following unpublished letter from him, dated 26 March 1915, sent using a female pseudonym, claiming to be a relative with an invitation to stay, which would certainly have facilitated another journey to the front:

> My dear friend
> Thank you very much for your last letter. I'm very happy to see you in Paris. This will allow me to visit you after the war, as we promised, and to spend some excellent days with you. But while I'm waiting for my trip, I'd like to remind you that Mum has put a room at your disposal here for as long as you like. I know that Chez Gray isn't very interesting, especially in wartime. But the weather is fine, and perhaps you won't be upset to find it quieter here than in Paris, where the zeppelins are a fright. Come and see us. Mum would be delighted [. . .] In that case, get a valid pass for a certain time. I don't think the consulate will have any trouble getting it [. . .]. Marguerite Bompard[17]

There would appear to be all sorts of promises and expectations hidden in this letter and in the game of cat-and-mouse that was being played. It is certainly unclear as to who exactly was playing the predatory role in the relationship. Mansfield never did go back to her French soldier but made full use of the flat on offer. Tomalin, however, notes how Carco had possibly given her more than just 'copy' for her stories:

> According to Karen Usborne's study of 'Elizabeth', her companion A. S. Frere heard Murry telling her that Katherine had contracted syphilis after her visit to Carco at the front in 1915, when she is alleged to have had her hair cropped like a soldier's and visited the trenches in uniform. Apart from the fact that she did come back with her hair cropped very short, this seems

> an unreliable bit of reporting by someone known to be hostile to Katherine, as Frere was; but it may be a garbled version of Katherine's gonorrhoea, which very possibly flared up again as a result of the Carco episode. It does suggest that Murry spoke of his wife in less exalted terms during her lifetime than later.[18]

As Tomalin intimates above, Murry glossed over Mansfield's misdemeanours after her death in order to sanctify her personality, but he was not above criticizing her while she was alive. The gonorrhoea – the symptoms of which she always thought were due to rheumatism – would not be formally diagnosed until 1918.

The ramifications of the Mansfield/Carco relationship are to be felt in the annals of French as well as English literature, for in Carco's novel *Les Innocents*, as noted in the previous chapter, he portrays Mansfield unsympathetically as the wholly unlikeable Winnie Campbell. Many years later, backtracking on his original denigratory characterization, Carco said of this portrayal, 'And yet, I owe my best book to Katherine Mansfield, because she provided some of the elements. Although she is recognizable in many of the details of Winnie, she has taken from the character only what is pure and intact.'[19] There is, however, very little 'pure and intact' about the character of Winnie, who comes across as predatory and exploitative. A curious fact unearthed by Wood concerns an issue of the *New Age* from 2 March 1922, when Orage was still editor, and where a long review of *Les Innocents* appears, written by Pierre Robert. It offers a much more flattering interpretation of Winnie's character, and, given that Mansfield and Orage were now drawing close again, may have been commissioned following a discussion between them.[20]

In 'An Indiscreet Journey', the personality of Carco is drawn with a light pen, but in the 1918 story 'Je ne parle pas français', the unsavoury character of Duquette is much more easily recognizable as having been drawn from Mansfield's memories of him. Mansfield went so far as to mention his name in connection with the story, in a letter she wrote to Murry: 'The subject I mean lui qui parle is of course taken from – Carco & Gertler & God knows who. It has been more or less in my mind ever since I first felt strongly about the french.'[21] Carco is depicted as a writer, a gigolo and possibly bisexual. This may well have been a measured and deliberate response by Mansfield to Carco's portrayal of

Winnie (Mansfield) as bisexual in *Les Innocents*. She also satirizes Carco's literary endeavours at this time through the titles she invents for Duquette's novels: 'False Coins', 'Wrong Doors' and 'Left Umbrellas'. Carco comments on the story in his autobiography:

> I recognize myself and her future husband, John Middleton-Murry [. . .] For me, it's a bit like a tale I could have written and never will. The three portraits have a strange air about them, so striking that it seems almost hallucinatory. In this story, Souris is Katherine Mansfield.[22]

So many games; so much dissembling. In the meantime, while she was in Paris, Mansfield was seeing a good deal of Hastings, which would surely have got back to Orage in London. In a letter to Murry on 21 March, though she was complimentary about Hastings's apartment – 'really very jolly. [. . .] All her furniture is second hand and rather nice [. . .] – really very charming'– Mansfield was not complimentary about Hastings herself:

> Strange and really beautiful though she is still with the fairy air about her & her pretty little head still so fine – she is ruined. There is no doubt of it – I love her, but I take an intense, cold interest in noting the signs. [. . .]
>
> Myself, I am dead off drink – I mean the idea of being drunk revolts me horribly. Last time I was drunk was with Beatrice here and the memory stays and shames me even now – We were drunk with the wrong people [. . .] Of course everybody she ever knew has died a grisly death in this war – & the fact that Carco is going to Turkey seems to delight her beyond measure. Il ne reviendra jamais![23]

In fact, as Gray affirms,

> Carco was spared annihilation on the Eastern Front and trained as an aviator instead. Between practice runs he began to spin his novel, *Les Innocents*, featuring KM as the coldly life-sucking Winnie, stuck in a cramped apartment on the Seine and writing up the lives around her, reinforced by her reporter friend, that liberated woman (from Argentina) whom Carco had not yet

> met. His portrait of the terrifying Beatrice was based entirely on the hearsay Katherine had gathered for him.[24]

The renewal of her relationship with Hastings now culminated in a huge row, which finally brought the friendship to a permanent halt:

> At B.'s this afternoon there arrived 'du monde' including a very lovely young woman – married & curious – blonde – passionate – We danced together. I was so angry about the horrid state of things. [. . .] It ended in a great row. I enjoyed it in a way, but Beatrice was very impossible – she must have drunk nearly a bottle of brandy & when at 9 o'clock I left & refused either to stay any longer or to spend the night here she flared up in a fury & we parted for life again.[25]

In another letter to Murry, the old game-playing Mansfield returned: 'To tell you the truth, both of them [Orage and Hastings] are bitter because they have nearly known love and broken and we know love and are happy,' which of course was far from the truth at this complex time.[26] Murry, meanwhile, faking a breezy attitude, had written to Mansfield on 22 March, telling her that – in despair – he had written to Orage asking for paid work:

> I wrote to Orage a really very nice letter – I got a reply 'No thanks'. I won't pretend I'm not hurt about it. I am very deeply hurt. And it rankles nastily in my brain. I had never dreamt that it was possible that he should give me a slap in the eye like that. [. . .]
>
> Only now I feel sure that what you admire in Orage – or rather your admiration – belongs to you of three years ago.[27]

Mansfield replied on 26 March: 'I think Orage wants kicking – Just that – Of course what is so peculiarly detestable is his habit of lying so charmingly – his "I should be delighted, Katherina", rings in my ears.'[28] Did she mean all this? Unlikely. As we know, she had only recently seen Orage before setting off for Paris, taking some parcels for Hastings. Murry almost certainly had no idea, and Mansfield's dialogue piece 'Stay-Laces' would be published in the *New Age* later that year, on 4 November, when she was away in Bandol. As Wood explains,

> Murry clearly did not understand why Orage should be antagonistic to him. Mansfield, on the other hand, seemed just a little amused by Orage's reaction, and her response to Murry's protestations about his treatment by Orage, muted. She may have been secretly pleased that Murry, who would have had greater prominence than her in literary circles at this time, had been prevented from making 'daisy-chains' in what she still considered her 'meadow'. Within a few months, Orage was publishing her work once more.[29]

Anyway, her life still as complicated as ever, quarrelling with Hastings, dissembling with regard to her relationship with both Orage and Hastings and with zeppelin raids ringing in her ears, Mansfield nevertheless somehow found time to begin drafting 'The Aloe', writing to Murry on 25 March: 'I had a great day yesterday. The Muses descended in a ring like the angels on the Botticelli Nativity roof – or so it seemed to "humble" little Tig and I fell into the open arms of my first novel.'[30] This was not, in fact, her first attempt at a novel, but her third; as Wood observes, 'perhaps now, for the first time, she could see her way to a more coherent whole.'[31]

By the end of the month Mansfield was back in London with Murry at Elgin Crescent. Rupert Brooke, whom they had first come to know through Eddie Marsh, had sailed with the British Mediterranean Expeditionary Force in February 1915. He was reported dead from septicaemia on 23 April 1915, the result of an infected mosquito bite on a ship moored off the Greek island of Skyros, while on his way to the landings at Gallipoli. He was just 27 at the time of his death and was probably the first of their friends to die.

After fewer than five weeks in London, by 5 May Mansfield was on her way back to Carco's flat, where she carried on working on the first draft of 'The Aloe'. From there she wrote to Murry: 'I did not tell you that I dreamed all night of Rupert Brooke. And today as I left the house he was standing at the door – with a ruck sack on his back & his broad hat shading his face.'[32] On this particular trip, her return to Murry was precipitated by the fact that the other residents of the building were now calling her 'Carco's mistress' behind her back. It was necessary to call time on the affair once and for all, and so by 19 May she was back at Elgin Crescent – this time for good. Wood notes that her experiences of these trips were written into a little prose piece, a notebook – 'Femme Seule':

> The bell jangles. Ah, at last. I leap out of bed and run to the door in my chemise. 'Voici votre lait Madame' says the concierge gazing severely at my knees.
>
> 'Merci bien Madame' I cry, smiling gayly & swinging the milk bottle.
>
> 'Pas de poste pour moi.'
>
> 'Rien Madame.'
>
> Shut the door, stand in the hall a moment & listen listen for her hated twanging. I implore her once again to play you that charming little thing for one note only – coax her – court her
>
> Ninon de Long Clothes.[33]

That 'femme seule' motif was to crop up regularly in her writing and nowhere more so than in the story 'The Little Governess', also written at this time. The name 'Ninon de Long Clothes' is a popular pun on the name Ninon de l'Enclos (1620–1705), a well-known courtesan, writer and patron of the arts. In 1915 several pieces were published in the *New Age* under this pseudonym; Wood claims they were written by Mansfield and not Beatrice Hastings, the only other possibility, especially since Hastings never attributed them to herself.[34] But Mansfield was still outwardly denigrating Orage to Murry, and lying about her involvement with the *New Age*: 'No, you won't find anything of mine in the New Age because I won't send them a line. I think Orage is too ugly.'[35]

In June 1915 Mansfield and Murry took out a lease on their first proper house together, at 5 Acacia Road, St John's Wood, a large, white-stuccoed house on three floors, with a garden at the back in which stood a beautiful pear tree. With the Lawrences now moving to nearby Hampstead, the two couples saw a good deal of each other at this time, with Lawrence even introducing Mansfield to Bertrand Russell. Murry recorded how

> At the top of the gabled house was a beautiful attic-room which Katherine made her own. From its window we saw the first Zeppelin sailing over London; it so excited us that we forgot to put out the lights behind us, and were harried by special constables, doubly suspicious of us because the innocent Koteliansky was our frequent visitor.[36]

Now it was that her brother Leslie started spending time with Mansfield when he was on leave, with the two siblings reminiscing about their childhood. Mansfield's story 'Autumns: I', written at this time and situated in the very windy Wellington of her childhood, is a tender portrayal of the affection between the older sister and the younger brother. There was news of yet another death – this time Henri Gaudier-Brzeska, killed on 5 June at Neuville-Saint-Vaast, just north of Arras, ending a complicated and painful friendship that had engendered hurt on both sides. When Leslie, as a bombing officer, undertook special training on Clapham Common from 19 to 24 August, he was able to visit his sister more regularly. Indeed, he spent his final leave with Mansfield and Murry at Acacia Road, before his battalion of '30 officers and 920 other ranks', as Mitchell's detailed research reveals,

> finally left barracks in two trains at 6:45 pm on 26 September 1915 via Boulogne. Leslie managed to send a telegram to Kathleen: 'Off at last – the goodbye would have been too awful. Au revoir. Leslie'. They arrived at their final destination, Haute Farm, Ploegsteert, on 3 October 1915 to relieve the 16th Canadians in the fire trenches of Ploegsteert Wood.[37]

Murry and Lawrence, who had been hatching plans for their new magazine venture while Mansfield had been occupied with her brother, announced in a press leaflet the forthcoming publication of their new little magazine, *The Signature*. For Malcolm Bradbury, it was 'Perhaps the most significant wartime magazine [. . .] which essentially represented D. H. Lawrence's bitter, apocalyptic response to the conflict [. . .] "The persistent nothingness of the war makes me feel like a paralytic convulsed with rage"'.[38] The hope was that friends like Bertrand Russell and Gilbert Cannan would contribute and that rich acquaintances such as Lady Ottoline Morrell would help them garner subscribers; early on, Lawrence noted proudly that they had the grand total of 27 subscriptions, but as Bradbury notes, 'there were probably never many more.'[39] There were just three issues, dated 4 October, 18 October and 1 November, and only ever three contributors: Lawrence, Murry and Mansfield, the latter using the pseudonym 'Matilda Berry'. Two of Mansfield's contributions in the first issue were 'Autumns: I' and 'Autumns: II', both stories featuring a beloved younger brother called 'Bogey', one of Leslie's nicknames. Much later, she revised 'Autumns: II',

Leslie Beauchamp's grave marker, Ploegsteert Wood, Belgium, 1915.

transcribing it into the third person, and changing its title to 'The Wind Blows'; it would be published in the *Athenaeum* on 27 August 1920.

One of the greatest tragedies of Mansfield's life now occurred when on 11 October, three days before her 27th birthday, she received news in a telegram from Mr Kay at the Bank of New Zealand that Leslie, aged just 21, had been killed at Ploegsteert Wood on 6 October (just two days after her stories were published in the first issue of *The Signature*), blown to pieces by his own hand grenade during a military training exercise. Murry recorded his response at the moment Mansfield heard the news: 'Three minutes ago Tig had a telegram to say her brother is dead [...] I cannot believe it yet; and she cannot. That is the most terrible of all. She did not cry. She was white and said: "I don't believe it; he was not the kind to die".'[40]

An apocryphal story now ensued, used by several biographers since (even the most recent), with Mansfield herself as the originator in a letter to Kot, when she wrote, referring to a letter she had received from an officer friend of Leslie's, James E. Hibbert, 'He told me that after it happened he [Leslie] said over and over – "God forgive me for all I have done" and just before he died he said "Lift my head, Katy, I can't breathe".'[41] Whatever her reasons might have been for making the claim that Leslie called for her as he lay dying, it was, in fact, a lie. Hibbert's two letters to Mansfield, presumed lost, were eventually discovered among the Mansfield manuscripts acquired from Murry's estate by the ATL in Wellington. Murry had had them all along – and known the truth about their contents, though as Mitchell notes, 'he evidently did not want them made public in his lifetime.'[42] Hibbert recorded that Leslie 'was heard to say several times "God forgive me for all I have done", and then just before he died, he asked that his head might be raised as he could not breathe'.[43] Mitchell observes, 'Clearly, she very much needed to believe that she had a role in the final drama of her brother's life – that *she* was in Chummie's thoughts even as he lay dying.'[44]

Distancing herself from Murry, Mansfield now plunged headlong into her personal grief, from which he was wholly excluded: 'Here was a grief in Katherine', he wrote, 'which was beyond my power to assuage, a whole world of memory and experience which I had no power to enter, and I felt outcast.'[45] Mansfield needed a man's shoulder to cry on – someone dependable, someone who would understand. She didn't even have Ida to turn to – she had been away in Rhodesia with her father since March 1914 and wouldn't return until September 1916. Is it any surprise, then, that in her despair Mansfield now turned to support from Orage? He published 'Stay-Laces', her harsh satire on the war in the form of a dialogue, in the *New Age* on 4 November, her first overt publication in the paper for some time. For Wood, a hidden poignancy within 'Stay-Laces', which a reader wouldn't necessarily appreciate, appears in the conductor's calling out 'Selfridges! Sel-fridges', for it was from the Selfridges reading room that she had written her last letter to Leslie.[46] In addition, both the 'corset department' and 'palm court' restaurant were at Selfridges, the main setting for the story.

As Wood further notes, Orage's one constant influence throughout his life was the Bhagavad Gita, which he had studied in Leeds as a young man. In thinking what he might say to console Mansfield on her brother's death, he might well have referred to the following words, which would eventually be engraved on his tombstone:

> Thou grievest for those that should not be grieved for.
> The wise grieve neither for the living nor for the dead.
> Never at any time was I not nor thou these princes of men.
> Nor shall we cease to be hereafter.
> The unreal has no being.
> The real never ceaseth to be. (2.11)

That notion of being 'real' would resonate constantly with Mansfield from this point onwards, as did her newfound desire to commemorate and celebrate Leslie's life in her writing, her attempt, following Orage's advice, to 'make it "real"' (and of course, this is exactly what would draw her to Ouspensky and Gurdjieff in 1922).

By mid-November 1915 *The Signature* was good as dead in the water and so, unable to cope with the memories of living in a house in London where her brother had been such a recent visitor, Mansfield set off for France, initially accompanied by a rather bewildered Murry, whose supposed ill health (an army medical officer had queried his lungs as being possibly tubercular) prevented him from signing up. As she said in a letter to Kot on 19 November, 'Acacia Road and all that it implied is over – for ever.'[47] At the suggestion of Kot, they sublet the house in which they had been so happy, and which promised so much, to a Russian journalist, Michael Farbman, and his wife Sonia, fully furnished, for seven pounds and ten shillings per month. Kot rented a room from the Farbmans and eventually took over the whole house, living there until his death in 1955. In the same letter to Kot as above, Mansfield continued:

> I left one of my brother's caps in a drawer upstairs in his room. Would you get it and keep it safely for me – Also, I meant to give you for your room the fur rug in my sitting room – you know the one. I don't want the Farbmans' to use it – and I do want you to keep it for me. Put it on your bed. It is so warm and it looks and feels so lovely.[48]

Kot chose as his bedroom the room that used to be Mansfield's bedroom. As Galya Diment notes in her biography of Kot,

> Her blanket was on his bed; her chair was at his desk in the study; 'a little blue-green bowl' she once gave him occupied a place of honour on a small table in a sitting room. After Mansfield's death, her carved walking stick, which she bequeathed him because he liked it so much, found its special niche as well.[49]

Now installed in Bandol in the south of France, Mansfield, for the first time since leaving New Zealand in 1908, was able to enjoy prolonged proximity to the sea, which, as well as helping her through the grief she was experiencing, must have aided her memories of her homeland, which now came flooding back. She wrote to Kot: 'For one thing, and its awfully important, the sea is here – very clear and very blue. The sound of it after such a long silence is almost unbearable – a sweet agony, you know – – – like moonlight is sometimes.'[50] Murry, leaving Mansfield at the Hôtel Beau Rivage in Bandol, returned to England on 7 December, renting a small furnished room near the Lawrences in Hampstead and feeling utterly sorry for himself.

Mansfield's letters to Murry were initially all vivacious and colourful, although it was now that her so-called rheumatism returned to plague her – the symptoms of her gonorrhoea manifesting itself once more, though she, of course, still had no idea of their origin. She was also suffering from tuberculosis, but those symptoms were being masked by her other current maladies. Soon, loneliness and ill health got the better of her, and when Murry's letters did not arrive daily (there was, after all, a war on), Mansfield's unreasonable distress manifested itself in anguished letters to him, including one to Lawrence bemoaning her relationship with Murry. Sadly, this letter no longer exists, but according to Murry in a reply to her, as a result,

> Lawrence went for me, about you, terribly [. . .] He said that it was all my fault, that I was a coward, that I never offered you a new life [. . .] that your illness was all due to your misery and that I had made you miserable, by always whining & never making a decision.[51]

It seems inconceivable that Mansfield would not also have been writing to Orage at this time, especially given the recent publication of her story in the *New Age*. What he must have made of Murry's weak-willed dilly-dallying and self-absorption is anyone's guess. But it seems that whatever response Orage gave was not what Mansfield was expecting. So she reverted back to the safer bet, Murry, and now pounded him with protestations of love, leading him to acknowledge, 'This Katherine I had never known. [. . .] Always between us there had been, in each, something that did not yield, something that claimed its freedom, and refused to say "TOUJOURS".'[52] Something had now changed – for both of them.

Thanks to Lawrence, Murry managed to engineer himself an invitation to Garsington for Christmas, a treat he was not likely to forego for Mansfield – or anyone else. Ottoline Morrell, as Frances Wilson tells us, 'otherwise known as Lady Utterly Immoral or Lady Omega Muddle [. . .] was a six-feet-tall redhead with the face of a handsome horse', who nevertheless got the best of Lawrence during their brief friendship, and who now befriended Murry and would soon do the same for Mansfield herself.[53] After spending Christmas at Garsington with the Morrells' various guests, including Lawrence and Frieda, Murry, all puffed up, travelled back to Bandol on 31 December to a little house Mansfield had found for them, the Villa Pauline, on the outskirts of the little town, forever associated with one of the happiest and most creative periods of her life. As she was to write two years later,

> Ive two 'kick offs' in the writing game. <u>One</u> is joy – real joy – the thing that made me write when we lived at Pauline, and that sort of writing I could only do in just that state of being in some perfectly blissful way <u>at</u> <u>peace</u>. Then something delicate and

> lovely seems to open before my eyes, like a flower without thought of a frost or a cold breath – knowing that all about it is warm and tender and 'steady' – And that I try, ever so humbly to express.[54]

Her happiness and contentment during this stay in France was reiterated many years after her death by Murry, for as he said, in Bandol, 'she had been happier than she had ever been before or was ever to be again.'[55] Mantz noted, 'As to Murry's personal life with Katherine, he admitted candidly: "We had some terrible times, the only happy time we had was at Bandol".'[56] Here it was, in Bandol, that Mansfield now picked up 'The Aloe' again, first started in Paris that spring, and completed the first draft. It was also at this time that she started writing to Ottoline Morrell herself, her first letter dating from 21 January 1916, whose rather sycophantic contents end, 'I long to meet you. Will you write to us again? But until we do see you – will you remember that you are real and lovely to us both and that we are ever grateful to you because you are.'[57]

In the meantime, Lawrence had now been offered the use of a little cottage in Porthcothan, Cornwall, and he began again to think of setting up a little community – his 'Rananim' – in what was then still a remote corner of England. He and Frieda arrived in Cornwall at the end of December 1915, the year which, for him, marked the end of 'the old world'. Aside from the effects of the war, his latest novel, *The Rainbow*, had been banned on grounds of obscenity, leaving him deeply depressed, in dire financial straits and desperately seeking an escape. Cornwall had long existed as a liminal, otherworldly space in which England seemed remote, and it now seemed to offer some sort of spiritual escape for Lawrence.

After staying in Porthcothan, where they were briefly joined by the young writers Philip Heseltine and Michael Arlen, Lawrence and Frieda moved to a remote little hamlet called Higher Tregerthen, near Zennor, and Lawrence started bombarding Mansfield and Murry with letters begging them to come and join him and Frieda in their new community. Thus Mansfield and Murry's idyllic sojourn at the Villa Pauline in Bandol came to an end on 7 April 1916, having been browbeaten by Lawrence into returning to England, his enthusiasm for the project was so overwhelming.

Of the grey granite cottage at Higher Tregerthen, near Zennor, just outside St Ives, rent £16 per annum, into which Mansfield and Murry moved in April 1916, Lawrence had written, 'It is only twelve strides from our house to yours: we can talk from the windows: and besides us, only the gorse and the fields, the lambs skipping and hopping like anything, and sea-gulls fighting with the ravens, and sometimes a fox, and a ship on the sea.'[58] As Murry wrote to Ottoline from Bandol, 'We are going to stay with the Lawrences for ever and ever as perhaps you know; I daresay eternity will last the whole of the summer.'[59] This early Rananim was a huge disaster, and, as Murry correctly guessed, eternity lasted barely two months; yet the coming together of the two couples in Cornwall in 1916 remains one of the most celebrated episodes in twentieth-century English literary history. So many people have written about it, analysed it, fictionalized it and even staged it.

Here is Mansfield's own take on one day's traumatic events in a famous letter to who else but Kot, on 11 May 1916:

> You may laugh as much as you like at this letter, darling, all about the COMMUNITY. It <u>is</u> rather funny.
>
> Frieda and I do not even speak to each other at present. Lawrence is about one million miles away, although he lives next door. He and I still speak but his very voice is faint like a voice coming over a telephone wire. It is all because I cannot stand the situation between those two, for one thing. It is degrading – it offends ones soul beyond words. I don't know which disgusts one worse – when they are very loving and playing with each other or when they are roaring at each other and he is pulling out Frieda's hair and saying 'I'll cut your bloody throat, you bitch' and Frieda is running up and down the road screaming for 'Jack' to save her!! This is only a half of what literally happened last Friday night. [. . .] Lawrence isn't healthy anymore; he has gone a little bit out of his mind. [. . .] It is like sitting on a railway station with Lawrence's temper like a big black engine puffing and snorting [. . .] When he is in a rage with Frieda he says it is she who has done this to him and that she is 'a bug who has fed on my life'. I think that is true. I think he is suffering from quite genuine monomania at present, through having endured so much from her. Let me tell you what happened on Friday. I went across to them for tea. Frieda said Shelleys Ode to a Skylark was false. Lawrence said: 'you are showing off; you don't know anything about it.' Then she began. '<u>Now</u> I have

> had enough. Out of my house – you little God Almighty you. Ive had enough of you. Are you going to keep your mouth shut or aren't you.' Said Lawrence: 'I'll give you a dab on the cheek to quiet you, you dirty hussy'. Etc. Etc. So I left the house. At dinner time Frieda appeared. 'I have finally done with him. It is all over for ever.' She then went out of the kitchen & began to walk round and round the house in the dark. Suddenly Lawrence appeared and made a kind of horrible blind rush at her and they began to scream and scuffle [. . .] All the while she screamed for Murry to help her. Finally they dashed into the kitchen and round and round the table. I shall never forget how L. looked. He was so white – almost green [. . .]. Then he fell into one chair and she into another. No one said a word. A silence fell except for Frieda's sobs and snifs. [. . .] L. sat staring at the floor, biting his nails. Frieda sobbed . . Suddenly, after a long time – about a quarter of an hour – L. looked up and asked Murry a question about French literature. Murry replied . . Little by little, the three drew up to the table . . Then F. poured herself out some coffee. Then she and L. glided into talk, began to discuss some 'very rich but very good macaroni cheese'. And next day, whipped himself, and far more thoroughly than he had ever beaten Frieda, he was running about taking her up her breakfast to her bed and trimming her a hat.[60]

Mansfield and Murry left a month later; the relationship between the two couples was never the same again. The paradoxes and mysteries of Lawrence's life, which exasperated his friends while he was alive, and which have perplexed his biographers since his death, are explained thus by Wilson:

> For all his claims to prophetic vision, Lawrence had little idea what was going on in the room let alone in the world. His fidelity as a writer was not to the truth but to his own contradictions, and reading him today is like tuning into a radio station whose frequency keeps changing. He was a modernist with an aching nostalgia for the past, a sexually repressed Priest of Love, a passionately religious non-believer, a critic of genius who invested in his own worst writing.[61]

As for Frieda, Wilson has some admiration for what she had to put up with in her marriage to Lawrence, not least of which was the contempt of nearly every single one of his friends: '[I]n life Frieda was an essentially comic figure, the kind of bawdy, red-cheeked matron found in the art of Otto Dix and in German expressionist theatre. [...] Without goal or ambition, Frieda's one achievement (not inconsiderable) was in putting up with Lawrence.'[62] Their marriage was nothing short of a theatrical performance that required a constant – and changing – audience in order to validate itself, which even extended to Lawrence's public beatings of Frieda, since he was only affectionate to her 'when he thought no one was looking'.[63]

Lawrence and Frieda stayed on at Higher Tregerthen and made the best of things. But soon, the problem of Frieda being German compounded the couple's problems. Fearing they were spies, in mid-October 1917 the authorities gave them just three days to pack up and leave Cornwall. It was a bitter blow from which Lawrence never truly recovered. Returning to London marked the nadir of the couple's peripatetic existence, where, in extreme poverty, they were reliant on the generosity of friends until they were finally able to travel abroad in 1919, and where ultimately Rananim proved as much of a chimera as it had been in Cornwall. As far as posterity was concerned, one good thing came out of this car-crash period of their lives: Lawrence's novel *Women in Love*, which he had started writing, and where in the characters of Gerald and Gudrun can be found traces of Murry and Mansfield.

Mansfield was now deeply disillusioned with Murry – again. Nevertheless, he had found a little cottage for them in Mylor, on the other side of Cornwall, to which they moved in the middle of June, and although outwardly all seemed fine, the charms of this new rural idyll failed to appeal. By the end of the month, Mansfield was writing to Ottoline Morrell, with whom she had kept up a sporadic epistolary relationship since the beginning of the year:

> May I come and stay with you on the 13th of July for a few days? I have to go to London on the 8th and I should so love to come to you. Only I don't know whether you will have me – for I'll be alone – Murry can't be with me. I feel as though I have so much to tell you and to talk over – Even though we have barely met – its strange –[64]

In the meantime, there was a brief visit from Frederick Goodyear, on leave from France, who would soon be on his way to the Somme – and annihilation – which afterwards affected Mansfield very much, for she had always held a candle for Murry's old friend, and he for her. She now started telling people that she considered herself 'free', whatever that meant, and Lawrence soon surmised that she especially meant 'free' from Murry.

Garsington Manor, just outside Oxford, the home of Philip and Lady Ottoline Morrell, had become a wartime refuge for all types of conscientious objectors – such as Clive Bell, Virginia Woolf's brother-in-law – who worked the land as farm labourers. It was also a magnet for artists and writers, drawn to the endless generosity of its owners, and who were frequent visitors: Leonard and Virginia Woolf, Mark Gertler, Dora Carrington, Lytton Strachey, Bertrand Russell and, of course Lawrence and Frieda, to name but a few. Early Garsington regulars were keen for Mansfield to be invited. Bertrand Russell even wrote to Ottoline: 'I want to get to know Katherine Mansfield really well. She interests me mentally very much indeed – I think she has a very good mind, & I like her boundless curiosity.'[65] Murry had already spent the previous Christmas there while Mansfield had been in Bandol in the South of France, and Garsington curiosity about Mansfield herself was evident: 'her exact relationship to the wispy figure of Middleton Murry was something one had to establish by tactful enquiry.'[66] Ottoline recorded Mansfield's first visit to Garsington in July 1916, noting how she was 'strangely dark in her black and white clothes'. Her impression was that she regarded them all with a 'novelist's eye, as potential material, and that she herself was being recorded as "a grand lady patronizing artists for my own glory"'.[67] She was fascinated by Mansfield's past – no doubt enhanced by the latter's infamous ability to embellish the truth – be it about her colonial upbringing in New Zealand, her education at Queen's College in Harley Street (where Ottoline's old friend and suitor John Cramb had been one of her tutors), or the few weeks she spent with the Moody Manners Opera Company in the north of England in the early part of 1909.

The long, hectic weekend that Mansfield spent at Garsington from 13 to 17 July included many visitors, including Dora Carrington, David Garnett, Aldous Huxley and Lytton Strachey himself, who, as noted in the Introduction, wrote the following to his Bloomsbury friend Virginia Woolf from Garsington on 17 July:

> There were 16 souls here for the week-end that's just over: from Friday onwards the door seemed to open every two hours and new arrivals appeared in batches of five or seven. I at last lost count and consciousness, going off into a cosmic trance, from which I was only awakened by the frenzied strains of the pianola playing desperate rag-time, to which thirty feet were executing a frantic concatenation of thuds.
>
> Among the rout was 'Katherine Mansfield' – if that's her real name – I could never quite make sure. Have you ever heard of her? Or read any of her productions? She wrote some rather – in fact distinctly – bright storyettes in a wretched little thing called the Signature, which you may have seen, under the name of Matilda Berry. She was decidedly an interesting creature, I thought – very amusing and sufficiently mysterious. She spoke with great enthusiasm about the Voyage Out, and said she wanted to make your acquaintance more than anyone else's. So I said I thought it might be managed. Was I rash? I really believe you'll find her entertaining. But just now she's in the recesses of Cornwall, so it must be later on, if at all. I may add that she has an ugly impassive mask of a face – cut in wood, with brown hair and brown eyes very far apart; and a sharp and slightly vulgarly-fanciful intellect sitting behind it.[68]

The letter is worth quoting from at length, since it was the first time Mansfield, as mentioned earlier, was discussed by Bloomsbury proper, and the portrait cannot be called a flattering one. Mansfield, of course, was enacting her normal levels of dissembling and pretending, while deciding who was worth cultivating. In that sense, Strachey's portrait of her as amusing, mysterious and sharp is quite accurate, and Beatrice Hastings would certainly have approved of his deciding she had a 'vulgarly-fanciful intellect'. Mansfield may well have spoken enthusiastically about Woolf's first novel, *The Voyage Out*, but the truth was she hadn't actually read it, for she borrowed Ottoline's copy, sending it back in mid-August, with apologies for having kept it for so long.

Murry had finally been called up for service and now travelled to London, where he eventually got a job as a translator for the War Office at Watergate House. On 26 August both he and Mansfield were at Garsington together as a couple for the first time, before they both returned to London. With most of their belongings still at the Mylor

Mansfield at Garsington, *c.* 1916.

cottage in Cornwall, they now split up, Mansfield staying temporarily with Dorothy Brett in Earl's Court, and Murry lodging at a shabby little hotel in Bloomsbury. By late autumn of 1915, again through the Lawrences, Mansfield and Murry had met Dorothy Brett, known to everyone simply as 'Brett'. She was the hard-of-hearing daughter of Lord Esher, and had had a problematic childhood, leaving her as a somewhat emotionally stunted adult. She became devoted to Mansfield, especially towards the end of the writer's life, and indeed Mansfield dedicated her last short story, 'The Canary', to her, although their relationship was a complex one. She also became very close to Murry, as we shall see in later chapters. After Mansfield's death, she had an exceedingly brief physical affair with him, which she found overwhelming and confusing, and an equally brief physical affair with Lawrence.

Meanwhile, the 'Murrys' were leading a miserable separate existence. Mansfield had, by now, almost had enough, writing to Murry on 20 August, 'Are we never to be happy – never never? We haven't had any "life" together at all yet – in fact its only on the rarest occasion that we have any confidential intercourse [...] If it goes on like this I'll make an end to it in October – I can bear no more.'[69] It was also at this time that a rift opened up between the Lawrences, Kot and Mansfield and Murry following some sort of intervention by Frieda, which has never been fully understood, but that affected them all and stunted their friendship for the ensuing two years.

Ida Baker in uniform, 1917.

Mansfield and Murry's housing woes finally came to an end, thanks to Bloomsbury Group member John Maynard Keynes, who was renting out rooms in his house at 3 Gower Street, which subsequently became known as 'The Ark'. During a short-lived period from September 1916 to February 1917, Mansfield and Murry occupied the ground floor, next to the front door and the telephone, Brett was on the first floor and Dora Carrington on the second. Callers now included Lytton Strachey and Bertrand Russell, with Mansfield starting a serious flirtation with the latter. Ida finally returned from Rhodesia that autumn, and Mansfield helped to find her lodgings in Hampstead. She soon found work in a munitions factory, and saw Mansfield as often as she could.

In spite of the brief happiness and supposed creativity at the Villa Pauline, 1916 was Mansfield's barren year as far as her stories were concerned. There would not be a single story published and only three unfinished fragments composed. But at least she completed her first draft of 'The Aloe', though as yet she had no idea what to do with it. Poems were a different matter – there were eleven in total, most of them a dichotomous mix of either war, death and Leslie, or being happy in the south of France. The many moves and peripatetic living arrangements left her unsettled and unable to commit words to paper.

Christmas 1916 saw a large gathering at Garsington; a letter from Dora Carrington to her soldier brother in France listed the company:

> the lady of Gower Street Katherine Mansfield and her melancholy spouse, Lytton, Brett, Aldous Huxley of Balliol (attached to Maria Nys and she to him) a lanky youth with one eye gamey who writes poetry, and is well versed in the literary accomplishments which the lads of Balliol do acquire.[70]

Mansfield was tasked with writing a play, which the guests performed on Boxing Day. It was called *The Laurels*, and a fragment still exists. The cast list reads as follows:

> Lytton – – – – Dr Keit
> Carrington – – his grandchild, Muriel Dash
> Mansfield – – Florence Kaziany
> Aldous – – – – Balliol Dodd
> Maria – – – – Jane
> Murry – – – – Ivan Tchek[71]

It was a 'kind of Ibsen-Russian play', as Carrington told her brother, 'marvellously witty and good'.[72] Or as Huxley told his brother Julian, 'We performed a superb play invented by Katherine, improvising as we went along. It was a huge success, with Murry as a Dostoevsky character and Lytton as an incredibly wicked old grandfather.'[73]

The year 1917 was to be another nomadic one for Mansfield and Murry, with much of it spent apart. The comings and goings at the Ark, together with the lack of privacy – something Mansfield craved all her life – meant that she now started looking for accommodation elsewhere, without Murry. On 1 February she moved into a studio at 141A Old Church Street, Chelsea, and by the end of the month, Murry was installed in a little flat nearby at 47 Redcliffe Road.

It was now that George Bowden re-entered Mansfield's life, via some new documents. As was made clear in earlier chapters, Bowden openly affirmed to anyone who asked that all initiatives towards a divorce from Mansfield came from him, and that at no time did Mansfield or Murry ever suggest expediting it. But he also openly affirmed that there was seemingly never any rancour or bitterness between him and Mansfield – in fact, quite the reverse. As he himself wrote in a letter to researcher O'Brien in 1947, 'K.M. and I enjoyed a happy if short intellectual comradeship.'[74] However, much of this is directly controverted by new documents released by the National Archives in London – the original divorce file and an affidavit sworn by Bowden on 3 January 1917, in support of his divorce petition, which had first been filed on 20 May 1913. The file had been closed in the National Archives for a hundred years until 2019. In the sworn affidavit, Bowden explains his reasons for wanting to seek a divorce from his wife Kathleen Bowden (that is, Mansfield). He asserts that following the marriage, 'I lived and cohabited with my said wife at divers places and at No 62 Gloucester Place Marylebone in the County of London,' thus directly contravening his later account that said Mansfield left him the day after the wedding. What then follows is nothing short of astonishing:

> Shortly after our marriage, in fact from the date of our marriage, my wife had an insatiable desire for sexual intercourse. I was very much attached to her and exerted myself to my utmost to gratify her. When I failed she told me that she would go elsewhere. Against my remonstrances and entreaties she left me,

> and finally abandoned my home. From information I was able to obtain I caused these proceedings to be brought.[75]

This completely contradicts the explanation that Bowden had originally given Mansfield's mother in 1909 and his subsequent American father-in-law, which is that Mansfield had been unable to consummate the marriage because she was a lesbian, and that it was only the lesbianism that had ended the relationship. Apparently, Bowden now suggested in early 1917 that it was only Mansfield's excessive and constant lasciviousness (her 'insatiable desires') that had made the relationship unworkable, a very different 'truth' to his later fourteen-page account from the 1940s, as explained earlier. No rebuttal was filed by Mansfield or Murry, and Bowden's suit was not defended. In fact, there is no record of the affidavit in any of Mansfield's or Murry's extant papers. In the affidavit, Bowden made no mention of that convivial meeting with Mansfield and Murry in mid-1912 at which they all seemed so jolly, and where he even sang a song or two. However, what the affidavit does record is a second, apparently much less friendly visit in 1912, as noted in a previous chapter, in the account of which Bowden was clearly trying to convey the impression that Mansfield was now co-habiting (whether with or without 'insatiable desires') with her latest conquest – Murry. He then went on to claim that his

> domestic troubles impaired my ability to make a living at my profession and in the hope of bettering my financial position in a community where I was a stranger I took the advice of friends and came to California arriving in San Francisco towards the end of 1912. I have since supported myself by teaching music and voice culture.[76]

Mansfield's excessive sexual expectations, he seemed to be suggesting, were to blame for his inability to make a living and the root cause of his abandoning his life in England, making for California instead. He concluded by stating, 'My straightened means have compelled me to delay these proceedings. I have not sooner been able to save sufficient money to pay the necessary costs and have now only managed to lay aside the requisite sum with the strictest economy.'[77] The affidavit was sworn at the British Consulate in San Francisco in the presence of the Acting British Vice Consul.

It is hard to reconcile these nasty, vindictive claims with the apparently warm and intellectual friendship detailed in his later account. On 19 February 1947, in response to a letter of O'Brien's requesting more information on Bowden, Murry had replied thus:

> I know extremely little about the man to whom Katherine Mansfield was married. The few facts I do know are these: His name was Bowden, he had been a choral scholar of King's College Cambridge [. . .] and he was a professional teacher of singing when Katherine met him.

He then tantalizingly added, 'I do in fact know a little more about him, but that I must not divulge to anybody. However, it is quite immaterial.'[78] Murry almost certainly would have been referring to the affidavit, which he and Mansfield would have seen in early 1917 as the respondent and co-respondent in the proceedings. Mansfield was promiscuous during 1910–11, but only *after* she had left Bowden. And even assuming that a short sexual relationship occurred during Mansfield's second attempt at living with Bowden in early 1910, it was in fact *she* who left *him*, and not the other way around. We will possibly never truly know why Bowden made such extreme and shocking accusations in the affidavit, but what is clear is that forever afterwards all three parties made sure that no one would find out – for one hundred years.

Mansfield and Murry's relationship hit a rocky patch at the time of the affidavit, which may not be mere coincidence. By February 1917, as noted earlier, the couple were living apart and remained so for the whole of that year. John Carswell believed this separation was for purely legal reasons: 'At last Katherine was managing to obtain a divorce from Bowden, and all could have been ruined, as the law then stood, if the King's Proctor had been able to show that she was living with Murry.'[79] Given the contents of Bowden's affidavit, this does rather seem a case of locking the stable door after the horse has bolted. And in any case, it was not Mansfield seeking the divorce. Wood observes,

> We have no evidence as to Mansfield's reaction to the affidavit. However, Mansfield published 'Mr Reginald Peacock's Day' in the *New Age* on 14 June 1917. Her depiction of the protagonist (clearly meant to be Bowden), was of a vain and self-centred man who found that the constraints of living with a young wife

> were restricting his professional career and social ambition: 'The truth was that once you married a woman she became insatiable and the truth was that nothing was more fatal for an artist than marriage, at any rate until he was well over forty .... Why had he married her?' Here we see Mansfield, picking up the word 'insatiable' from the affidavit and mockingly repeating the word 'truth'. 'Mr Reginald Peacock's Day' was not the truth either, but Mansfield had clearly read the affidavit and this was her response.[80]

As if life wasn't now complicated enough, Tomalin notes a curious brief reappearance by Sobieniowski in 1917, Mansfield's year for 'old flames'. In February she moved to a studio flat in Chelsea – 'the first studio flat she found was "snatched" from her by a "perfidious Pole", according to a letter she sent to Ottoline; one can't help speculating that it may have been Floryan.'[81] Tomalin then goes on to reveal, 'Her old incubus Sobieniowski leaves his trace in another way about this time, for there are fragments of translation from the Polish playwright Wyspianski in her hand and his; but she told no one about this' – another example of Mansfield compartmentalizing again.[82]

It was now, alone (well, not quite), that Mansfield tried to reinvigorate her stalled writing career, which had seemingly been on hold for so long; it's not hard to guess to whom she now turned. Though there were epistolary remonstrances of love between Mansfield and Murry during this period of physical separation, the truth was that she also now rekindled her close relationship with Orage, for she started publishing in the *New Age* once more: during the course of 1917 five stories and pastiches appeared in the paper, including 'Mr Reginald Peacock's Day'. Orage's former lover Beatrice Hastings was no longer on the scene, and, given that Mansfield was living alone, it would have been easy for her and Orage to meet up, as they now surely did. Having enjoyed a sexual relationship from 1910 to 1912 and possibly beyond, at this new low point in her life – with Murry distanced and totally submerged in his work at the War Office almost to the exclusion of all else – for the next few months at least, Mansfield and Orage were free to enjoy each other's company. They could well have gone on holiday together: there is evidence, as Wood has uncovered.[83] Orage (using the pseudonym R.H.C.) sometimes used his 'Readers and Writers' column in the *New Age* to record some personal activities. For example, on 10 May 1917, he wrote of having 'been away on a moment or two's holiday', which may well have been with Mansfield; her story 'Late at Night' was published in the same issue.[84] Wood has also uncovered another exciting possibility: that Mansfield shared with Orage at this time some of her juvenile stories (perhaps while on that holiday), one of which he then playfully reprinted in the 'Readers and Writers' column the following week, on 17 May (in the same issue as Mansfield's dialogue 'The Black Cap'). Here is what Orage wrote:

> Here, by the way, is a little sketch sent me by a correspondent who assures me that it was written without premeditation by a girl of eight. Surely, where it comes from is a source with which we older people have lost touch. Otherwise, would not the world be listening to us as we shall listen to this with pleasure and wonder?
>
> THE YELLOW WOLF.
>
> All night long the yellow wolves were howling in the silent wood. The trees were rustling and shaking, and footsteps were about. And still the wolves were howling more and more, and came nearer and nearer.
>
> Now little Betty was lying down beside a tree, and Jane came to the wood and Tom to the hill to see if they could find her. Jane came right into the wood, and then she saw Betty, not with the yellow wolf, but with the yellow silk handkerchief which her father had brought from the fair, and which she had got out of Jane's drawer because she liked it so. Now then Jane was carrying Betty home to the house, and nothing else happened like that.[85]

Any reader of Mansfield's juvenilia will immediately recognize the influence of one of her favourite childhood books, *Christmas-Tree Land* by Mrs Molesworth, with its fantasy forests, magical incidents and a duplicitous little girl.[86] Mansfield even mentions a character called Betty in her 1911 story 'Being a Truthful Adventure' (coincidentally also published in the *New Age* in 1911): 'Of course, she was Betty Sinclair; I'd been to school with her.'[87] It's easy to imagine the amusement this would have engendered between the couple, who were now seemingly as close as they had ever been. In addition, if 'The Yellow Wolf' is by Mansfield, it would, as Wood notes, represent her most youthful professional publication, albeit long after it was written.

It's also curious, notes Wood, that during the period when Mansfield had rekindled her relationship with Orage (who now helped reignite her stalled writing career), she was also polishing 'The Aloe' for the Hogarth Press: is his experienced and sure editor's hand to be seen in its final version? We can be sure that any traces of his involvement would have been destroyed either by Mansfield – or more probably by Murry after her death, when all Mansfield's papers came into his possession. It's an enticing thought and, of course, makes complete sense. Here was the man, notes Wood, that Mansfield turned to in every single one of her greatest moments of difficulty or despair, something which Ida, too, recognized.[88] Indeed, John Carswell acknowledged that Orage was 'one of the greatest "ghosts" that ever wielded a pen.'[89] That is not to suggest he rewrote material, but his skills as an editor were legendary.

Talking of the Hogarth Press, of course, the other important relationship that developed during the course of this year was that between Mansfield and Virginia Woolf. Having initially met at Garsington, the two writers now started meeting regularly, and talked of writing and of each other's work. Many factors underlie the intense, strangely ambivalent relationship that developed between them. It continued all through Mansfield's writing life up to her death, in January 1923. It puzzled and haunted her rival up to within two months of her suicide, on 28 March 1941, when she recalled Mansfield's enlightened attitude (compared to her own) to the manuscript copy of James Joyce's *Ulysses*: 'There's something in this: a scene that should figure I suppose in the history of literature,' Mansfield had so astutely observed.[90] We have Virginia's famous 'civet cat' reaction to Mansfield after dinner one night in October 1917, quoted in the Introduction and reproduced again here:

> The dinner last night went off: the delicate things were discussed. We could both wish that one's first impression of K. M. was not that she stinks like a – well civet cat that had taken to street walking. In truth, I'm a little shocked by her commonness at first sight; lines so hard & cheap. However, when this diminishes, she is so intelligent & inscrutable that she repays friendship.[91]

Mansfield was, as noted previously, rather fond of the French perfume 'Genêt Fleurie' or 'Flowering Broom', but scent was not approved of in the rarefied air of Bloomsbury, and Mansfield could not have known that a little spray of perfume would so upset the delicate olfactory balance of the woman who would famously become her literary sparring partner. Snobbery? Perhaps. Leonard was more pragmatic, writing of Mansfield long after her death:

> By nature, I think, she was gay, cynical, amoral, ribald, witty. When we first knew her she was extraordinarily amusing. I don't think anyone has ever made me laugh more than she did in those days. She would sit very upright on the edge of a chair or sofa and tell at immense length a kind of saga, of her experiences as an actress [. . .] [T]he extraordinary funniness of the story was increased by the flashes of her astringent wit. I think that in some abstruse way Murry corrupted and perverted and destroyed Katherine both as a person and a writer [. . .] Her gifts were those of an intense realist, with a superb sense of ironic humour and fundamental cynicism.[92]

This description of Mansfield, by a contemporary who knew her well, underlines how her humour attracted Virginia's husband and how this, in turn, must have led to insecurity and jealousy on the part of Virginia herself, at the very mention of her name, not just as a writer, but as a woman and a potential rival. Despite this, the Woolfs were both taken with her – it was obvious that Mansfield had an extraordinary talent for writing, which manifested itself in the now pitch-perfect version of 'The Aloe', renamed 'Prelude' (possibly with Orage's editorial help). Having recently set up the Hogarth Press, they now offered to print the long story as their second publication.

Wood records a curious publication in the *New Age* on 30 August 1917: a playlet by William Margrie called 'The House Hunters; or, Multum in Parvo', featuring a 'John Clifton' and a 'Kate Mansfield', who are planning to get married but cannot decide where to live, causing a rift in their relationship. 'They must be a couple of loonies', says another character, 'if they break off their engagement over the question of living in one part of London or another.' 'But, my dear John,' says another, 'surely you are not going to break off an engagement of five years' standing?' 'It is quite evident now', says Kate, 'that John thinks more about his business than he does about me.' Eventually the problem is solved. 'Why not [. . .] get married at once and then go for a long honeymoon in a caravan? Then you could live where you liked.' It was to be no ordinary caravan but 'a splendid, slap-up twentieth century motor caravan a sort of hotel on wheels'.[93] William Margrie (1877–1960) is nowadays referred to as an 'eccentric philosopher', known as the 'sage of Peckham'; a socialist by background like Orage, he had joined the Independent Labour Party in about 1907. As Wood observes,

> There is no recorded connection between Margrie and Katherine. Why he should now attempt to ridicule her marriage plans is unclear. Possibly Orage had invited the contribution and then, disingenuously, suggested to Margrie that he change the names of the principal characters. It seems that Orage was going through another bout of jealousy, because Mansfield was progressively re-uniting with Murry, and the Bowden divorce was imminent.[94]

In fact, the decree nisi was issued on 17 October 1917, on the grounds that the respondent, Kathleen Bowden, had been guilty of adultery with the co-respondent, John Middleton Murry. And that seemed to be the end of that.

The Woolfs' typesetting of 'Prelude' began on 4 October with a few hiccups along the way. (It would not be published until 11 July 1918, in a print run of about three hundred copies.) The *New Age* may have ridiculed their situation, but Murry and Mansfield were still living apart, and their relationship had rarely been so strained. Murry now believed himself to be in love with Ottoline; overworked at the War Office and spiralling into depression, he was taken in by her at Garsington, where he arrived on 24 November. Mansfield visited him there a week later for a couple of days, when she herself caught a chill. On her return to London, she became so ill that even Aunt Belle thought it prudent to visit with Chaddie – probably the last thing Mansfield wanted. Murry was therefore left at Garsington without her while she recuperated back at her studio in Chelsea. Mansfield's health remained so precarious that a few days before Christmas, Murry briefly made the trip down from Garsington to see her. It was clear from the doctor's reports that her left lung was seriously infected and that unless she now avoided English winters, consumption would take hold. Thus it was that the pair, miserable and both suffering from ill health, spent Christmas apart, their relationship as uncertain as ever as the new year beckoned.

6

Marriage and Discontentment, 1918–20

The year 1918 was to prove as tumultuous as any other in the never-ending saga that was Mansfield's life. The chill that she had caught before Christmas turned into pleurisy; by early January 1918, her health had deteriorated significantly, since together with her ongoing severe 'rheumatism' (in fact, the symptoms of the gonorrhoea she didn't know she had), a 'spot' had been discovered on her right lung. Her doctor therefore offered the advice given to all potentially tubercular patients living in a cold climate at that time: to travel to a warmer one.

There were other more personal difficulties, too. In the autumn of 1917 Murry's relationship with Ottoline Morrell had taken a more intimate turn; in fact, he now claimed that Ottoline had fallen deeply in love with him (which she hadn't), and thus Mansfield was forced into a false relationship with her, outwardly friendly, inwardly wary, which Ottoline had astutely picked up on. From this point onwards, Mansfield's relationships with people like Ottoline and Virginia could be likened to flickering candles that one by one were extinguished, mainly because she would spend less and less time in England, but also because of other acquaintances' growing dislike of Murry. On 7 January 1918, therefore, heeding her doctor's advice, Mansfield set off for Bandol once more, on her own this time, since Murry's work at the War Office meant he could not get leave and even Ida had been refused permission to accompany her. It does also seem that for some reason, by the end of 1917, she had turned her back on Orage – again, favouring the safety of Murry and marriage. Perhaps her worrying ill health and the insecurity it engendered led her to seek respectability and safety. In fact, it explains why she would stay with Murry until the last months of her life, when, having nothing left to lose, she found herself willing to break free.

It is quite astonishing to note that during those incredibly difficult and complex war years of 1914–18, when hardly anyone was travelling for pleasure, if all her various sojourns are added together, Mansfield spent almost twelve months in France. This latest journey, however, proved horrendous. With no one to help her, and weak from her recent severe illness, she arrived in Bandol traumatized (there were particularly ugly scenes on the train from Marseilles) and more ill than ever. Arriving at the Hôtel Beau Rivage on 11 January, she learnt there had been a change of owner and, much to her disappointment, no one remembered her from her earlier, happy visit in 1915. Nevertheless, she stayed at the hotel for over two months.

It was in Bandol, on 19 February 1918, that Mansfield suffered her first haemorrhage of the lungs, coughing and spitting blood. She tried to make light of the episode but was clearly frightened. On that day she wrote in a notebook,

> I woke up early this morning and when I opened the shutters the flail round sun was just risen. I began to repeat that verse of Shakespeare's: 'Lo here the gentle lark weary of rest' and bounded back into bed. The bound made me cough. I spat – it tasted strange – it was bright red blood. Since then I've gone on spitting each time I cough a little more.[1]

To Murry in a letter written on the same day, she wrote:

> I want to tell you some things which are a bit awful – so hold me <u>hard</u>. I have not been so well these last few days. [. . .] I have been spitting a bit of blood. See? Of course I'll tell you? But if you worry [. . .] I can't tell you [. . .] and after all Lawrence often used to. [. . .]
>
> Before the doctor came (you can imagine) I was so frightened – Now I'm confiding . . . its not serious. But when I saw the bright red arterial blood I nearly had a fit.[2]

Discussing the fact that Lawrence had often coughed blood somehow gave her comfort, since he always appeared so vigorous and full of life, even if miserably poor and down-at-heel. Indeed, Frances Wilson's account of the Lawrences' utter poverty in 1918 reveals the almost-abject destitution in which they now found themselves:

> Here, between a wood and a railway, they reached the fag-end of their poverty. Lawrence, in shoes without socks, was down to one set of clothes – a green- and red-striped blazer and a pair of grey flannel trousers. Because he washed them every night, the sleeves of his blazer and the hems of his trousers had shrunk so that his wrists and ankles protruded.[3]

With little else to do except sit out her time in Bandol, Mansfield now experienced a few weeks of extraordinary creativity. By the end of January, she had begun 'Je ne parle pas français' and had sent Murry the first part by 4 February. He professed to be overwhelmed by its contents, but she carried on writing anyway. On 10 February she almost hallucinated a complete story while sleeping – 'Sun and Moon' – which she wrote down as soon as she woke up. By 10 February 'Je ne parle pas français', a story that she knew was good, was finished. Mansfield's moment of satisfaction, however, was marred by the arrival of Ida just two days later; she had worked tirelessly to obtain a travel permit, but Mansfield had, in the meantime, decided she had no need of her.

Still flushed with creative inspiration, Mansfield continued writing. Recalling weekends at Garsington, she wrote one of her most celebrated stories, 'Bliss', during the second half of February 1918, telling Murry on 26 February, 'You will again "recognize" some of the people. Eddie of course is a fish out of the Garsington pond (which gives me joy) and Henry is touched with W.L.G. [the novelist W. L. George]'.[4] As Alpers remarks, 'The satire of arty London drawing-rooms is as clever and thin as that of Aldous Huxley, himself the model for Eddie.'[5] Indeed, a diary entry of Virginia Woolf from 9 March 1918 describes Huxley at this time: 'We had tea at the 17 Club. One room was crowded, & silent; at the end of the other Aldous Huxley & a young woman in grey velvet held what should have been a private conversation. A. has a deliberate & rather dandified way of speaking.'[6] Mansfield mimics this dandified tone perfectly in 'Bliss':

> The bell rang. It was lean, pale Eddie Warren (as usual) in a state of acute distress.

> 'It is the right house, *isn't* it?' he pleaded.
>
> 'Oh, I think so – I hope so,' said Bertha brightly.
>
> 'I have had such a *dreadful* experience with a taxi-man; he was *most* sinister. I couldn't get him to *stop*. The *more* I knocked and called the *faster* he went. And *in* the moonlight this *bizarre* figure with the *flattened* head *crouching* over the *lit-tle* wheel. . . .'
>
> He shuddered, taking off an immense white silk scarf. Bertha noticed that his socks were white, too – most charming.
>
> 'But how dreadful!' she cried.
>
> 'Yes, it really was,' said Eddie, following her into the drawing-room. 'I saw myself *driving* through Eternity in a *timeless* taxi.'[7]

In 'Bliss', Mansfield also brings to life the pear tree in the garden of 5 Acacia Road: 'The windows of the drawing-room opened on to a balcony overlooking the garden. At the far end, against the wall, there was a tall, slender pear tree in fullest, richest bloom; it stood perfect, as though becalmed against the jade-green sky.'[8] In the story, the protagonist Bertha Young experiences two epiphanic moments: first, in a sexually charged moment looking at the pear tree with the enigmatic Pearl Fulton, and at the end of the story, when Bertha sees her own husband share a furtive moment of affection with the same character. The story concludes with Bertha exclaiming, 'Oh what is going to happen now?', as Mansfield reintroduces for the last time the image of the pear tree, which was 'as lovely as ever and as full of flower and as still'.[9] The implication is that once these impermanent moments of 'bliss' have passed, the tree will go on existing, flowering, in all its beauty.

With her health rapidly deteriorating and her tuberculosis now confirmed, on 21 March Mansfield, along with Ida, made the difficult journey from Bandol in the south of France to Paris, desperate to return to England. On arrival in Paris, they found themselves unable to travel any further – the bombardment of the city by the Germans with their huge, new long-range gun had begun, and there were strict regulations regarding foreigners crossing the Channel. Even finding a hotel proved a difficult and demoralizing business. Mansfield had never witnessed anything like it – the true horrors of the war were now all around her. At times the bombardment was taking place every eighteen minutes, making any semblance of normal life impossible. On 11 April 1918 the two women were finally able to cross the Channel back to England, these experiences indelibly printed on Mansfield's mind and inevitably colouring all her future responses to the war.

Now back in London and staying at Murry's bachelor lodgings on the Redcliffe Road, Mansfield received confirmation from her English doctor that she had tuberculosis. The only bright moment came on 29 April, following the decree absolute of the divorce proceedings; on 3 May she and Murry were finally able to marry at the Kensington Register Office. Given the gossipy nature of literary London, it would seem highly unlikely that Orage would have been in the dark. (In addition, he and Mansfield had been in close contact for much of 1917.) Ida was not invited, the Lawrences were sitting out the remainder of the war in deepest Derbyshire and the rapprochement with Kot had not yet taken place. The only witnesses were, therefore, Brett and J. D. Fergusson. It was clear that Mansfield was ill, and her newly married state was not going to change that, but at least her name changed, from the hateful and embarrassing 'Kathleen Mansfield Bowden' to its legal substitute 'Kathleen Mansfield Middleton Murry'.

The typesetting of 'Prelude', begun all the way back in October the previous year, was still ongoing, much to Mansfield's frustration. With Murry working late hours at the War Office (and coming home exhausted), on 9 May she went alone for lunch with the Woolfs. Even they noticed how ill she looked, Virginia writing to Ottoline a few days later: 'I saw Katherine Middleton Murry the other day – very ill, I thought, but very inscrutable and fascinating... She confessed that she was immensely happy married to Murry, though for some reason she makes out that marriage is of no more importance than engaging a charwoman.'[10] Why did Mansfield always feel the need to feign such indifference regarding Murry to everyone except Murry himself (and to any female who for one reason or another might be perceived a threat)? Marriage to Murry appeased her parents and the rest of her family, and gave her respectability and stability, but not much else. For even in what should have been this proud moment of officially becoming man and wife, Murry was unable to step up to Mansfield's vision of how he should behave. They had been married for less than two weeks when he suggested that, for the good of her health, she should probably leave London for the summer. Mansfield was left aghast that he could even suggest such a thing – she had only recently come back from France, when they had been apart for over three months. She had also caught him more than once holding a handkerchief to his lips when she coughed. His distaste – and fear

Mansfield, 1917.

– was obvious, but then tuberculosis at that time was claiming 50,000 deaths a year, and roughly 50 per cent of people admitted to sanitoria were dead within five years.

Anne Estelle Rice (now Drey) suggested that Mansfield join her in Cornwall at the well-appointed (and expensive) Headland Hotel in Looe. Angry with Murry, but also sensing that it was probably the most sensible thing for her health, on 17 May Mansfield travelled to Cornwall. A little over five weeks since her arrival back in London from war-torn Paris, the couple were separated – again. In Murry's defence, he had recently been appointed Chief Censor, a prestigious (and time-consuming) post carrying a salary of £500 per annum, which left little time for nursing a sickly wife. Before Mansfield's departure, the couple had registered interest with an agent for a house in Hampstead, but it would not be available until August, and Murry now used this as an excuse to compel Mansfield to recuperate and grow strong again away from London until then. But all of Mansfield's frustration and bitterness over Murry's behaviour and attitude since her return from Paris now manifested themselves in a letter to him less than a week after her arrival in Looe:

> You see, I was in the S. of F. from December till April. What was it like on the whole – just HELL. As you know it nearly killed me. Then I came back to rest with you. All my longings all my desires – all my dreams & hopes had been just to be with you amen – to come back to my home. Bien! I came. Heard how ill I was, scarcely seem to have seen you – except through a mist of anxious – felt that all your idea was for me to get away into the country again – Well I understand that – although please try & realise the appaling blow it was to me to uproot again – & so soon – with hardly a word spoken – Please do try & realise that. [. . .]
>
> Our marriage – You cannot imagine what that was to have meant to me. Its fantastic – I suppose – It was to have shone – apart from all else in my life – And it really was only part of the nightmare, after all. You never once held me in your arms & called me your wife. In fact the whole affair was like my silly birthday. I had to keep on making you remember it – – – – –[11]

Anyone seeking evidence of Murry's insensitivity to the needs of others and his incompatibility with Mansfield need look no further than this letter. Even though subsequent letters feigned happiness, the truth was that Murry was not the right man for Mansfield, and had she not been beleaguered with illness, the marriage would never have taken place. She was scared and ill; he was not exactly her 'rock' (Murry was genetically incapable of being anyone's 'rock') – but he offered some sort of security, which, given that she was now coughing up blood, she had never needed as much as she did now. And so she made the best of things, and Murry carried on being Murry. Cornwall wasn't all bad. There were trips out with Anne to savour, when Mansfield felt up to it, and the beauty of the Cornish coast reminded her of New Zealand, just as Bandol had done. It was in mid-June that Anne started to paint the famous portrait of Mansfield in a red dress, never finished during Mansfield's lifetime, which was rediscovered by Ruth Mantz: 'At the home of Anne Rice I discovered the unfinished portrait of K. M. which she had painted in Looe in May 1918. She "could not get the mouth right".'[12]

Murry arrived on 21 June for a short break with Mansfield, the latter trying to forget all the previous hurts and slights. In truth, Cornwall had helped her recuperate from her terrible experiences in Paris; the couple then returned to London, back to Redcliffe Road, on 29 June. 'Prelude' was finally published by the Woolfs on 11 July, followed by more good news: Mansfield's story 'Bliss', written in Bandol in February, was published in the August number of the *English Review*. Even though today it is recognized as one of Mansfield's masterpieces, Virginia was not impressed, writing in her diary on 7 August,

> I threw [it] down with the exclamation. 'She's done for!' Indeed I dont see how much faith in her as a woman or writer can survive that sort of story. I shall have to accept the fact, I'm afraid, that her mind is a very thin soil, laid an inch or two deep on very barren rock [. . .] the whole conception is poor, cheap, not the vision, however imperfect, of an interesting mind.

And then, as if she still needed to convince herself, she added, 'She writes badly too.'[13]

Mansfield's ill health continued to plague her, with her bad temper returning (Ida being her constant punch bag at this time) and a visit to the Woolfs cancelled. On 10 August she learnt that her mother had died two days previously, which brought to the fore so many mixed emotions. In public, of course, in letters to family and friends, she lauded her mother as 'the most exquisite, perfect little being – something between a star and a flower'.[14] In private, however, she must have run a gauntlet of emotions from sadness and guilt to anger and bitterness, for she was soon to discover that her mother had completely cut her out of her will in 1909 and had never reinstated her. No letters or notebook entries record what she felt on hearing this news – most likely they were all excised, either by Mansfield herself or by Murry after her death.

But life moved on, and finally, on 26 August, the couple were able to move into 2 Portland Villas, Hampstead, a tall house nicknamed 'The Elephant' on account of its 'towering greyness', where Mansfield would remain for twelve months – one of the most settled periods of her adult life.[15] It was to be the couple's first proper home together since the aborted attempt at 5 Acacia Road in St John's Wood, so cruelly terminated by the death of Leslie. Ida moved in with them as housekeeper, and they also employed two maids, Violet and Gertie. The couple were finally 'established' in the sort of home befitting their rising status in the literary world, where they could properly receive visitors. Friendships were now relaunched: with Kot, with Ottoline (who sent boxes and boxes of flowers from Garsington) and particularly with Lawrence, who would come to see them a few times, Mansfield more enthusiastic about his visits than Murry. With his younger brother Richard's help, Murry set up his own press to rival the Woolfs' in the basement, Mansfield naming it the 'Heron Press', after her brother Leslie's middle name.

Here it was, in Hampstead, that Mansfield first met Victor Sorapure (1874–1933), the doctor she came to trust and admire above all others. She was lucky to find in Sorapure an intellect coupled with a generosity of spirit, as well as a spiritual understanding of the world, that guided her health and tuberculosis treatment for the last four years of her life. It was now Sorapure who – finally – correctly diagnosed that the various aches and pains Mansfield had, for many years, referred to as her 'rheumatiz', were, in fact, caused by an old infection with gonorrhoea, possibly dating as far back as 1909 and her relationship with Floryan Sobieniowski, although any number of other candidates from her messy life during 1910–11 would seem as likely; when the disease is left untreated, arthritis-type pain occurs. It was Baker who first confirmed this when she wrote, 'the trouble was not correctly diagnosed nor was she fully cured until many years later in 1918 when Dr Sorapure took charge of her.'[16] Understanding that Mansfield would never be able to survive the constraints of living in a sanatorium, where writing would be forbidden, it was Sorapure who recommended beginning a regime at home, and when that eventually failed, suggested she travel south instead, to warmer climates. As Mansfield explained in a letter to Ottoline on 17 August 1919, stating that Sorapure's words were 'breath, life – healing, everything',

> My doctor strongly urges me not to put myself away – not to go into a sanatorium – he says I would be out of it in 24 hours and it would be a 'highly dangerous experiment'. 'You see', he explained, 'there is your work which I know is your Life. If they kept it from you you'd die – and they would keep it from you. This would sound absurd to a german specialist but I have attended you for a year and I know'.[17]

Two other doctors had also been consulted: her father's cousin, Sydney Beauchamp (brother of Elizabeth von Arnim), as well as a colleague of Murry's from the War Office. Both had been pessimistic regarding Mansfield's chances of survival – either a strict sanitorium regime, or she would not live beyond four years, advised the latter, presciently as it turned out. But Sorapure's understanding – not only of Mansfield's condition, but, more importantly, of her psyche – won the day.

And so, as 1918 drew to a close and with Ida carefully watching over her, Mansfield was to be found undertaking a 'cure' at home, with the fresh air of Hampstead Heath all around her. She now started typing out all the stories that were to feature in her next collection of short stories – her first since *In a German Pension* in 1911. It was almost certainly at this time that she now wrote 'Psychology', originally thought to have been written in 1920, because the first mention of it was in a list of stories sent in a letter to Murry on 26 January 1920. However, the story's setting is her studio in Chelsea in 1917, when she was living alone, and, John Wood suggests, recounts a visit from Orage, whom she was seeing regularly during that year of estrangement from Murry. Orage, of course, was still technically married to his wife, Jean, though they had been separated for many years, so there had been no question of him being able to marry Mansfield. Their relationship, as the female protagonist explains in the story, was on a deeper level. If anyone needs to understand the true depth of the relationship between Orage and Mansfield, they need look no further than this passage from 'Psychology':

> For the special thrilling quality of their friendship was in their complete surrender. Like two open cities in the midst of some vast plain their two minds lay open to each other. And it wasn't as if he rode into hers like a conqueror, armed to the eyebrows and seeing nothing but a gay silken flutter – nor did she enter his like a queen walking soft on petals. No, they were eager, serious travellers, absorbed in understanding what was to be seen and discovering what was hidden – making the most of this extraordinary absolute chance which made it possible for him to be utterly truthful to her and for her to be utterly sincere with him.
>
> And the best of it was they were both of them old enough to enjoy their adventure to the full without any stupid emotional complication. Passion would have ruined everything; they quite saw that. Besides, all that sort of thing was over and done with for both of them – he was thirty-one, she was thirty – they had had their experiences, and very rich and varied they had been, but now was the time for harvest – harvest.[18]

Ignoring the faked similarity in age, the above passage reads almost as a love letter to a soulmate – and perhaps an apology for marrying the wrong man. And the discussion on psychology in literature is a strange and prescient echo, according to Wood, of Orage's article 'Talks with Katherine Mansfield at Fontainebleau', written after her death. Here is the discussion in 'Psychology':

> He got up, knocked out his pipe, ran his hand through his hair and said: 'I have been wondering very much lately whether the novel of the future will be a psychological novel or not. How sure are you that psychology *qua* psychology has got anything to do with literature at all?'
>
> 'Do you mean you feel there's quite a chance that the mysterious non-existent creatures – the young writers of to-day – are trying simply to jump the psycho-analyst's claim?'
>
> 'Yes, I do. And I think it's because this generation is just wise enough to know that it is sick and to realize that its only chance of recovery is by going into its symptoms – making an exhaustive study of them – tracking them down – trying to get at the root of the trouble.'
>
> 'But oh,' she wailed. 'What a dreadfully dismal outlook.'
>
> 'Not at all,' said he. 'Look here. . . .' On the talk went.[19]

And here is Orage, remembering conversations with Mansfield in the autumn of 1922 in London, and during the few weeks when they were both at the Prieuré in Fontainebleau-Avon together, before Mansfield's death:

> 'I can see such a scope for subtlety of observation that Henry James might appear myopic. At the same time, no quality need necessarily remain unemployed; but every power of the artist might be brought into play.'
>
> 'You would not necessarily have a happy ending?' I asked.
>
> 'Not by any means. The problem might prove to be too big. Heroes and heroines are not measured either by what they passively endure or by what they actually achieve, but by the quantity and quality of the effort they put forth. The reader's sympathy would be maintained by the continuity and variety of the effort of one or both of the characters, by

> their indomitable renewal of the struggle with every fresh invention.[20]

In fact, according to Wood, written in between two diary entries dated 21 and 24 October 1918 are two alternative endings for 'Psychology':

> Again there came that silence that was a question – but this time she did not hesitate. She moved forward, very softly & gently, as though fearful of making a ripple in that boundless pool of quiet. She put her arm round her friend.
>
> The friend is astonished, murmurs it has been so nice. The other – Goodnight dear friend. A long tender embrace. Yes, that was it – of course that was what was wanting.
>
> ––––––––––––––––––––
>
> Like a blow on the heart.
> I – I have come – for –
> She leaned against the door, quite faint.
> Yes? said she.
> This. Tightly, quickly he caught her up into his arms.[21]

The above second ending is a much more romantic one than the first, or the one chosen in the final version. And here is Mansfield placing herself into the narrative, with her well-known look of a Far-Eastern doll: '"Oh, you." He thumped the Armenian cushion and flung on to the *sommier*. "You are a perfect little Chinee".'[22] Here is an even clearer indication of Orage as the male protagonist with his connection to Armenian Spiritualists – Gurdjieff and Ouspensky. In 'Psychology', Wood notes,

> the characters' 'thrilling quality of their friendship' was that 'their two minds lay open to each other [. . .] which made it possible for him to be utterly truthful to her and for her to be utterly sincere with him.' Later Katherine writes in a draft passage almost certainly intended for a story: 'Don't you think it would be marvellous [. . .] to have just one person in one's life to whom one could tell everything? [. . .] how wonderful it would be – how wonderful! to feel, from this person, this one person I really don't need to hide anything'. This person was certainly not Murry.[23]

That last quotation comes from a piece of prose written just above a notebook entry for 31 December 1918, a few weeks after the composition of 'Psychology'.[24] Face-to-face visits may have been impossible, but Orage was on Mansfield's mind. Even that use of the word 'Chinee', referencing Mansfield herself, is fascinating, since her nickname for him in 1922 when they were secretly corresponding would be 'China'.

Meanwhile, November brought visits from Virginia (indeed, she would visit Mansfield almost weekly until Christmas), who reported in a letter to her sister Vanessa that

> poor Katherine Mansfield seems very bad, though I dont like to ask her how bad, and she says she's going to Switzerland with Murry and will be cured. I cant help finding her interesting in spite of her story ['Bliss'] in the English Review; at least she cares about writing, which as I'm coming to think, is about the rarest and most desirable of gifts.[25]

That proposed trip to Switzerland would have been news to Murry, given he had spent literally every penny he had (and some he didn't have) on setting up 'The Elephant'. Hard to imagine, too, that any doctor would have told Mansfield she could expect a full cure, when indeed every single one had told her she was dying. However, it would have made for an interesting conversation, and Mansfield did love to appear interesting – especially to Virginia. But she didn't need to make up stuff and nonsense; when she talked about writing in that forthright way of hers, it was clear that Virginia was fascinated.

Peace was declared on 11 November: after more than four years of horrific fighting and the loss of millions of lives, the First World War was over. As the guns on the Western Front fell silent, they sounded jubilantly instead in London, and sirens could be heard echoing along the Thames. As Mansfield wrote to Ottoline, 'My thoughts <u>flew</u> to you immediately the guns sounded. [. . .] I thought of my brother and of you.'[26] December brought visits from Gertler and Lawrence, the latter lending her a book by Jung and ambitiously hoping she might soon be able to visit him and Frieda in Derbyshire. On Christmas Day, the last Christmas Mansfield would ever spend in England, the Murrys gave a party, attended by Kot, Gertler and the Campbells. Mansfield and Murry – the literary couple – were putting on a show.

The year 1919 marked the beginning of the last four years of Mansfield's life (though she didn't know it) – the most successful in terms of her professional career, the most harrowing in terms of her health and the most complex in terms of her relationship with Murry. The sheer number of letters sent attests to the long periods the couple were to spend apart during these last tumultuous years, as the two things Mansfield longed for more than anything (apart from good health) – a stable home life and her man by her side – drifted continually out of reach. Indeed, they were the things she most envied about her literary friend and rival, Virginia. In a letter to Virginia in April 1919 she had written, 'A husband, a home, a great many books & a passion for writing – are very nice things to possess all at once.'[27] But later that year she would write to Murry, 'Thats one thing I shall grudge Virginia all her days – that she & Leonard were together,' and ten days later, 'How I envy Virginia; no wonder she can write. There is always in her writing a calm freedom of expression as though she were at peace – her roof over her – her own possessions round her – and her man somewhere within call.'[28] Just two months later, remembering her utter distress a few weeks previously, she wrote again to Murry: 'I used to feel like Virginia but she had Leonard. I had no-one.'[29] And it is just this sense of isolation – a lone warrior battling ill-health – together with a complicated, frequently disappointing marriage, that are the overriding features of the remainder of this biography.

The year began so promisingly, when Murry was appointed editor of the prestigious literary weekly the *Athenaeum*, recruiting friends J.W.N. Sullivan and Aldous Huxley as his assistant editors (T. S. Eliot having decided at the last minute not to take up the role). With a salary of £800 per annum, Murry was able to leave his War Office post as Chief Censor and devote himself full-time to the editorship. Mansfield 'entered into the project enthusiastically', becoming a weekly reviewer on the paper, as well as contributing numerous stories and poems.[30] She also began collaborating with Kot on a translation of Chekhov's letters, which were eventually published as a series of thirteen articles in the paper over the course of several months. The Murrys even hosted an *Athenaeum* party at 'The Elephant', to which they invited many of the leading literary and artistic figures of the day, including St John Hutchinson, Frank Swinnerton, Roger Fry, Edward Dent, Clive Bell and Bertrand Russell.

After a silence of over two months, which had hurt and puzzled Virginia, on 24 February Mansfield now invited her to tea, apologizing and explaining how her worsening health had left her unable to see visitors. It's fair to say that thanks to Murry's editorship of the *Athenaeum*, the couple had now 'arrived'; Virginia forgave her. But there were a few sneers and jeers from Bloomsbury, as well as from a jealous Lawrence: 'I like Murry as the benevolent patron of us all: tra-la-la!' he wrote to Kot. Alpers notes how

> Murry invited Lawrence to contribute, and printed 'the Whistling of Birds', over the pseudonym, 'Grantorto', but he returned a short story about a rabbit called 'Adolf' which employs the French word *merde*, thus setting off once more all of Lawrence's hatred, which soon was transferred to Katherine as well.[31]

Mansfield now embraced her role as the wife of the editor of London's foremost literary paper. Only two complete stories would be written this year: 'A Suburban Fairytale' and 'Pictures'. Instead, her life, aside from advising Murry as to how best to run the paper (she was very forthright in her views on that), was now given over to weekly book reviewing, a task she initially relished and was supremely good at.

Eventually, though, as always, the 'snail under the leaf' – Mansfield's long-standing terminology for the way life's course never did run smoothly – yet again made its presence felt. The sheer pressure of her workload, coupled with her advancing illness (she had been coughing blood again), meant that by July she had come to the conclusion that the life she was leading was unsustainable. She was also increasingly distressed at Murry's perceived heartlessness towards her, as he lived and breathed the *Athenaeum* and was rarely at home. Murry, of course, was in his element, embracing his new role to the full; he knew his worth as an outstanding editor, and his burgeoning importance within London's literary world. This might explain what happened when, in mid-August, Mansfield's father Harold Beauchamp, now a widower, arrived in England and saw his daughter for the first time since 1912. He also met Murry, but, as Alpers explains,

> Murry that day was in 'one of his moods' [. . .]. When Beauchamp laughed, he looked the other way – 'never spoke *once* to him, paid him not a moment's attention. It could not have been more fatal'.
>
> This no doubt explains the tragic circumstances that while Katherine's £300 a year continued until her death, it was never

> again raised or supplemented, although her needs increased enormously.[32]

It has to be said that Murry's behaviour in general at this time hurt Mansfield; various notebook entries remark upon his indifference, absence of warmth and general selfishness:

> Often I reproach myself for my 'private' life – which after all, were I to die, would astonish even those nearest to me. Then, (as yesterday) I realise how little Jack shares with me. Last week I had no idea what was going in the paper, no copy of the paper and J. hadn't the smallest curiosity as to whether I had seen or had not seen it. He never even asked. It might have been a report for the Home Office. [. . .]
>
> All this hurts me horribly, but I like to face it and see all round it. He ought not to have married. There never was a creature less fitted by nature for life with a woman.[33]

In such circumstances, Mansfield did what she always did, and planned her escape – indeed, this became the overriding feature of her life during these final years, as we shall see – to the extent of wondering whether she should, after all, enter a sanatorium. Dr Sorapure, however, who almost understood her better than she understood herself, knew that this level of enforced confinement would distress her too much, since she would find it almost impossible to write; indeed, Murry himself, looking back at that time, noted how her doctor 'definitely advised her against it, on psychological grounds'.[34] Instead, Sorapure urged her to head to the Mediterranean and a warmer climate before the onset of winter, a plan she gladly accepted: memories of the preceding cold winter in Hampstead made the choice an easier one.

Before she left, another Beauchamp relative came to call on her briefly: Elizabeth von Arnim, born Mary Annette Beauchamp (the daughter of Mansfield's beloved great-uncle Henry Herron), and now officially Countess Russell, having married Bertrand Russell's older brother, from whom she was recently divorced. Mansfield hadn't seen her since a brief Beauchamp gathering for Mansfield's engagement to Bowden in March 1910, and the two cousins would eventually become close friends before Mansfield's death. But for now, on 11 September, Mansfield, together with Murry and Ida, left Hampstead, travelling to a hotel in San Remo on the Italian Riviera. Because of Mansfield's obvious symptoms of tuberculosis, the hotel complained and asked them to leave. There were few people willing to house them, but, finally, the owners of the Casetta Deerholm in nearby Ospedaletti agreed to rent them the small villa, which was perched on an isolated hillside outside the town, overlooking the sea. After seeing his wife installed at the Casetta, Murry returned to London and the *Athenaeum* at the end of September, later recording how 'In her new hope Katherine had entirely forgotten her past experiences of the horror of separation.'[35] If he himself remembered those same horrors as he travelled back to England, he put them to the back of his mind; the *Athenaeum* beckoned.

Initially, Mansfield settled happily back into her routine of reviewing for the *Athenaeum*, though she wrote to Murry saying that the insects were plaguing her. However, her obsession with receiving letters from him, evidenced on previous separations, now reared its head, a factor which would become a tangible – and frustrating – feature of this eight-month separation: 'I live for letters when I am away from you – for them – on them – with them.'[36] Soon, her mood darkening, she began sending Murry letters expressing her loneliness and depression. As early as 20 October, just three weeks after Murry's departure, she was writing, 'Shall I send this letter? Or write another one – a gay one? No, youll understand. There is a little boat – far out – moving along, inevitable – it looks & dead silent – a little black spot like the spot on a lung – – – – – –'.[37] And as her mental health deteriorated, so her physical ailments became more pronounced. Murry responded: 'I feel so utterly helpless. [...] You say that the depression keeps your cough going & keeps you weak. And this depression is just an invisible enemy to me. I can't even approach it; all that there is is to get depressed myself,' which is hardly the response to revive someone as low in spirits as Mansfield was at this time.[38]

On 9 November Mansfield received word that Murry's brother Richard had completed the typesetting of *Je ne parle pas français* for the Heron Press. This was the full, unexpurgated edition – the version later published in *Bliss and Other Stories* would have the more salacious elements culled by her publisher, Michael Sadleir, much to Mansfield's annoyance. Murry now sent Mansfield Virginia's new novel, *Night and Day*, and her review of it appeared in the *Athenaeum* on 21 November. It has become possibly Mansfield's most famous review – because of the author she was reviewing as much as for her caustic, no-holds-barred comments, which hurt Virginia deeply, and from which their relationship never recovered. To Murry, she wrote on 10 November, as she began her review,

> I am doing Virginia for this week's novel. I don't like it, Boge. My private opinion is that it is a lie in the soul. The war never has been; that is what its message is. I dont want G. forbid mobilisation and the violation of Belgium – but the novel cant just leave the war out. There must have been a change of heart. It is really fearful to me the 'settling down' of human beings. I feel in the profoundest sense that nothing can ever be the same that as artists we are traitors if we feel otherwise; we have to take it into account and find new expressions new moulds for our new thoughts & feelings.[39]

The absence in Woolf's novel, as Mansfield perceived it, of any sense of a literary response to the recent, catastrophic four years of war, with its devastating loss of life and hardship for millions, was, she believed, unpardonable. Indeed, Mansfield ended her review with the following devastating critique:

> We had thought that this world was vanished for ever, that it was impossible to find on the great ocean of literature a ship that was unaware of what has been happening. Yet here is 'Night and Day' fresh, new, and exquisite, a novel in the tradition of the English novel. In the midst of our admiration it makes us feel old and chill: we had never thought to look upon its like again![40]

Virginia was naturally hurt by such a harsh review. Sadly, Mansfield died at the beginning of 1923 and so never read Virginia's 'war' novel, *Jacob's Room* (published on 26 October 1922, after she had entered Gurdjieff's Institute in Fontainebleau), or *Mrs Dalloway* (1925), in which Virginia, perhaps as a result of Mansfield's critique, found those 'new expressions new moulds for our new thoughts & feelings'. In a diary entry for 28 November, Virginia wrote,

> K. M. wrote a review which irritated me – I thought I saw spite in it. A decorous elderly dullard she describes me; Jane Austen up to date. Leonard supposes that she let her wish for my failure have its way with her pen. He could see her looking about for

> a loophole of escape. 'I'm not going to call this a success – or if I must, I'll call it the wrong kind of success'. I need now not spread my charity so wide, since Murry tells me she is practically cured.[41]

Why Murry would say such a thing, knowing Mansfield was as ill as she had ever been, and was indeed now experiencing extreme depression and loneliness, is a complete mystery.

Harold Beauchamp, having left England, was now motoring through the south of France with his Māori chauffeur and called in to see Mansfield and Ida at the Casetta on 12 November, together with his rich cousin Connie and her companion Jinnie Fullerton, who both lived in Menton, just a few miles away across the French border. The visit left Mansfield feeling wistful and even more depressed. Connie and Jinnie suggested to her that the villa in Ospedaletti was too isolated and that it would be better if she moved to Menton instead, where they would be happy to look after her. Instead, Mansfield, seeking an outlet for her terrible mood-swings and vicious bouts of bad temper, now blamed much of her depression on Ida, claiming in a letter to Murry that she could not live with her anymore:

> weve got to wait our six months but when they are up I WILL not have L.M. near – I shall rather commit suicide – That is dead earnest. In fact, I have made up my mind I shall commit suicide if I dont tear her up by the roots then. It would be kinder for us both – for you and for me of course I mean. We'd have no love otherwise – you'd only slowly grow to think I was first wicked and then mad. Youd be quite right. Im both with her – mad – really mad like Lawrence was only worse. I leaned over the gate today and dreamed she'd die of heart failure and I heard myself cry out 'oh what heaven what heaven'.[42]

Poor Ida. Yet, in spite of all the insults and bad temper directed at her, she never once failed her friend, and remained constant in her attentions, to the unhappy end.

During this period of severe depression and loneliness, on 4 December 1919, Mansfield also directed her rage at Murry, sending him three poems – 'Et Après', 'He wrote' and 'The New Husband' – the latter a bitter and caustic commentary on their relationship and what she perceived as Murry's abandonment of her. Murry, whose work at the *Athenaeum* was all-consuming, was left aghast. His own anguished response – 'this can't go on – something must change' – catapulted him into action, and by mid-December he was to be found on holiday with Mansfield in Ospedaletti: a temporary plaster that did little to solve the actual problem.[43] In a notebook entry for 17 December, the day after Murry's arrival, Mansfield wrote,

> All these 2 years I've been obsessed by the fear of death. This grew & grew & grew gigantic & this it was that made me cling so, I think. Ten days ago – it went – I care no more. It leaves me perfectly cold. Well it was that & the letters perhaps. Gone is my childish love, gone my desire to live in England. I don't particularly want to live with him. [. . .]
>
> Something has stopped – a wall has been raised and its too recent for me to wish to go there even. [. . .]. I'm not in the least curious either – & not in the least inclined to lament.[44]

From now on, Mansfield's relationship with Murry mutated into something less romantic and more pragmatic. Some of her letters – and notebook/diary entries – clearly have an eye for posterity, since she also added in the same entry as above, 'If one wasn't so afraid – why should I be – these aren't going to be read by Bloomsbury et Cie', referencing the fact that she and Murry recognized that their letters and diaries might one day be published, and read by their enemies (such as members of the Bloomsbury Group). This is a factor that always has to be remembered, especially during these final years of Mansfield's life, the words on paper frequently belying her true feelings.

Despite her increasing ill health, 1920 was to prove the most productive of Mansfield's career as a writer. Indeed, looking back, it's hard to comprehend how she managed to accomplish so much: twenty stories (most of which would be published first in the *Athenaeum*, once the paper made the decision from June 1920 onwards to accept fiction), including a couple of fragments; three poems; and over eighty reviews – almost two a week. The year began with exciting news for Murry, at least: in the New Year's Honours List he was awarded an OBE for his work at MI7 during the war. Having arrived to spend Christmas and New Year with Mansfield in Ospedaletti, he left on 2 January to return to England and the *Athenaeum*.

Of course, inevitably, Mansfield's depression soon returned, and her health continued to deteriorate, exacerbated by the inclement winter weather; she described her life in Ospedaletti as hellish, with 'fearful fits of crying'.[45] To compound her depression, on 10 January she was shocked to learn that her father, having returned to New Zealand from Europe, had immediately married Laura Bright, his first wife Annie's best friend. Over the next two days, at one of the lowest points of her life, she wrote her excoriatingly bitter story 'The Man Without a Temperament' and sent it to Murry. For Kaplan,

> The story enacts the very dilemma she had described to Murry on 4 December 1919: 'It would spell failure for you to live abroad with me [. . .] I can imagine what hours we should spend when I realised and you realised the sacrifice'. The tedium and emptiness of those imagined hours shape the story of Robert and Jinny Salesby, who are living in a hotel on the riviera, listlessly passing the hours between meals and bedtime in a state of either polite boredom or suppressed emotions of regret and anger.[46]

Mansfield's loneliness, isolation, illness and separation from Murry now combined into one anguished cry for help. The weather at Ospedaletti turned even worse in January 1920, with wild storms lashing the house on its exposed position on the side of a hill overlooking the sea. Her depression refused to lift and her physical health deteriorated rapidly; she took to writing distressing letters to Murry revealing her sense of isolation and abandonment, and in a notebook recorded that these were the worst days of her life. Gradually, her reliance on Ida grew and her attitude towards her old school friend softened as she realized how much she needed her, especially following a disturbed night when their doorbell was rung continuously. This frightening event was the final straw, precipitating the two women into abandoning the Casetta and moving to Menton on 21 January 1920. Mansfield moved into Connie and Jinnie's luxurious nursing home, L'Hermitage, while Ida found work nearby.

Now in Menton, a local French doctor's prognosis seemed more positive, and Mansfield's spirits started to lift until she received what she perceived to be yet another extraordinarily selfish letter from Murry about her financial state, which brought her spirits crashing down again. She replied to him:

> Curse money! Its not really a question of money. It was the question of sympathy, of understanding, of being in the least interested of asking just once how I was – what I thought about & felt – what I did – if I was 'alright'? I cant get over the fact that it never occurred to you and it makes me feel you don't want my Love – not my living love – you only want an 'idea' –[47]

Mansfield's relationship with Murry, especially concerning their finances, became deeply troubled during this period. He seemed unable to provide her with the emotional and financial support she craved, and her anxiety was exacerbated by the fact that Connie and Jinnie had indicated that Mansfield's father paid her allowance (now £300 a year) only grudgingly. This eventually turned out to be a false claim, but at the time left Mansfield feeling hurt and even more insecure.

Murry, fielding ever more distressing letters from the south of France, nevertheless remained busy in London during the week and spent most weekends at Garsington. He had recently fallen out with Lawrence (again), over some articles the latter had submitted to the *Athenaeum*, and Lawrence now directed his rage at both Murry and Mansfield as a result, sending her a particularly vicious letter on 6 February, in which he wrote, 'You revolt me, stewing in your consumption.'[48] Many years later, in an unpublished journal entry of 7 November 1932, recalling those events, Murry noted how Lawrence had gone even further, addressing Mansfield thus: 'You are a loathsome reptile – I hope you will die.'[49] Less than three years later, in January 1923, Mansfield would die of the disease that in 1930 would also kill Lawrence. Alpers pronounced Lawrence's letter 'a vile attack which seemed to end forever the personal friendship which had meant so much', and even Lawrence biographer Mark Kinkead-Weekes deemed it 'inexcusable [. . .] perhaps the nastiest of all his outbursts of rage'.[50]

Meanwhile, with his literary editor's hat on, Murry was keen for Mansfield to republish her first collection of stories, *In a German Pension*, which had been out of print since its first publication in 1911. Mansfield, however, refused, claiming it was not good enough. Murry disagreed; he believed that the stories were excellent, but Mansfield would not back down. At this time, he was negotiating with various publishers regarding a new collection of her short stories, finally settling on Constable and its publisher, Michael Sadleir, who offered her an advance of £40 for her new collection. Mansfield had firm views on which stories the new volume should contain, refusing, for example, to allow 'The Woman at the Store' to be republished. She also initially refused any excisions in 'Je ne parle pas français', eventually capitulating, but forever afterwards regretting her decision.

Wood's research records that on 5 February 1920, Orage mentioned Mansfield in the *New Age*:

> I have only just got to the autumn issue of 'Art and Letters.' [. . .] Miss Katherine Mansfield's name attracted me – as it always would – but only, I discovered, to the thrush's second song. In actual fact her sketch, 'The Pictures,' appeared in a slightly different form in THE NEW AGE of May 31, 1917.[51]

'The Pictures' had first been composed in dialogue form as 'The Common Round' for the *New Age* in May 1917, and Mansfield had then rewritten it in narrative form as 'The Pictures', published in *Art and Letters* in the autumn of 1919. (It would be further revised before being included in *Bliss and Other Stories* later in 1920 simply as 'Pictures'.) There is no record of what Mansfield's response was to Orage's comments, but the phrase 'Miss Katherine Mansfield's name attracted me – as it always would' would surely have brought her a little pleasure at this time and may well have engendered some correspondence, subsequently destroyed.

In mid-February 1920, with Mansfield finding the Hermitage nursing home too noisy, Connie and Jinnie moved her into their private residence, the Villa Flora, where they tried to convert her to Catholicism. For a short period, she dallied with the idea of becoming a Roman Catholic, but ultimately turned away from such a commitment. Unfortunately, privacy and peace and quiet – essentials for Mansfield – were equally hard to come by at the Villa Flora. In desperation, after a few more weeks Mansfield finally decided to return home to London to be with Murry at 'The Elephant'. However, seeking a more permanent base in Menton, and recognizing that she would have to return in a few months, since her lungs would not stand a damp English autumn and cold winter, she now put down a deposit on the Villa Isola Bella, an empty villa belonging to cousin Connie in Garavan, a suburb of Menton on the Italian border, before returning with Ida to London and 'The Elephant' at the end of April. Before leaving, Mansfield had made the acquaintance of Sydney and Violet Schiff, a rich literary couple and patrons of the arts, who divided their time between their homes in

London and the Riviera; she now briefly enjoyed their lavish hospitality, and they would remain friends until the end of her life.

Before Mansfield returned to England, Beatrice Hastings made a brief epistolary appearance in their lives. She no longer worked for the *New Age*, and having heard of Murry's illustrious appointment as editor of the *Athenaeum*, she now, as Gray explains, 'made a formal application to the editor, so that her services could be accepted in a strictly businesslike manner, or be rejected without feelings being hurt'.[52] Murry, having no idea what to do, wrote to Mansfield on 22 March – Beatrice had always made him feel uncomfortable, and Mansfield had never shied away from giving him details of their previous relationship (though by no means all of them). Mansfield was horrified. She immediately rushed off a telegram (which no longer exists) and then wrote a letter:

> Darling, your memory is very short lived. Yes, it is true, I did love B. H. but have you utterly forgotten what I told you of her behaviour in Paris – of the last time I saw her and how because I refused to stay the night with her she bawled at me and called me a femme publique in front of those filthy Frenchmen? She is loathesome & corrupt & I remember very very well telling you I had done with her, explaining why & recounting to you how she had insulted and abused me – I should have thought you could not have forgotten those things – [. . .] Remember that B. H. is bad, has insulted us – insults us worse by thinking she has only to write to you for you to wag your tail.
>
> [. . .] I solemnly warn you that if you stir B. H. you will discover such a nest of serpents that you will repent it. Dont forget Our Pride. Not that shes so important in herself; its what she stands for. Dont you see?[53]

Naturally, Murry acquiesced to Mansfield's demands:

> I had absolutely forgotten what she did in Paris; and I'm wondering whether I ever knew, really. I think you must be under the impression that you told me more than you actually did [. . .] I shall simply send her an official letter saying that the Editor regrets.[54]

Here was yet further evidence of Mansfield concealing so much of her 'real' life from Murry.

That minor crisis out of the way, Mansfield and Ida returned to England and 'The Elephant' at the end of April 1920, and within a couple of days Mansfield called in at the *Athenaeum* offices. Her description of what she saw, written in a letter to Sydney and Violet Schiff, was scathing:

> The untidiness of John's desk [. . .] was my first crushing blow. There was over all the office a smell of stone and dust. Unthinkable disorder and ugliness. Old Massingham like a cat dipped in dough blinking in the doorway & asking whether the French were furious with [Lloyd] 'George' – Huxley wavering like a candle who expected to go out with the next open door, poor silly old men with pins in their coat lapels, Tomlinson harking back to the mud in Flanders, Sullivan and E. M. Forster very vague, very frightened.[55]

The impression given was that of a poorly run, down-at-heel gentlemen's club, where a fastidious woman such as Mansfield would have been very much a fish out of water. However, despite her reservations, it was not long before she found herself back in the swing of London literary life. She had been away for about eight months, having spent five tortuous months in Ospedaletti and about three months in Menton. Still unwell, she hoped that late spring and summer in England, in her own home and with her husband, would boost her morale. Certainly, there were trips to the theatre, dinners at home (Eliot and his wife Vivienne came on 14 May – Mansfield disliked her immensely), and she now renewed a wary friendship with Virginia, the latter still smarting from that review of *Night and Day* and whom she saw on 28 May and again on 2 June. On 1 July Mansfield attended the first *Athenaeum* literary lunch, organized by Murry. Virginia's own comments on the occasion in her diary were not exactly favourable:

> We were at the first Athenaeum lunch – a long single file of insignificant brain workers eating bad courses. [. . .] This lunch was [. . .] a glimpse into the scullery where the Sullivans & Pounds & Murrys & Huxleys stand stripped with their arms in wash tubs. [. . .] But I'm rather acid about Murry, on account

> of his writing I think, & Heaven knows, a story by Katherine always manages to put my teeth on edge.[56]

Well, at least she was being honest. Less honest was Brett, who at this time – and during Mansfield's eight-month absence – had become close to Murry; when he wasn't slaving away at the *Athenaeum*, he could be found partnering Brett in frequent games of tennis, and generally spending much of his free time with her. He and Brett wrote letters to each other, even though she was also living in Hampstead; Mansfield, ever suspicious, read some of them. In one, Murry had written, 'You know I love you just as I know you love me. And your tenderness during a time when I was going to pieces through strain and anxiety has done more than anything else to help me pull myself together.'[57] This was written in March while Mansfield was in Menton, having recently suffered the worst bouts of depression and illness of her entire life. Somehow, Murry made the suffering all about him, and Brett became his willing confidante. Mansfield's notebooks now revealed her own suffering, her understanding of Murry's true nature, their incompatibility and her disgust at what she perceived as Brett's betrayal. Here is an example from 12 August:

> I cough and cough and at each breath a dragging boiling bubbling sound is heard. I feel that my whole chest is boiling. I sip water, spit, sip, spit. I feel I must break my heart. And I can't expand my chest – it's as though the chest had collapsed. Life is – getting a new breath. Nothing else counts. And Murry is silent, hangs his head, hides his face with his fingers as though it were unendurable. 'This is what she is doing to me! Every fresh sound makes my nerves wince.' I know he can't help these feelings. But oh God! how wrong they are. If he could only, for a minute, serve me, help me, give himself up! [...] At such times I feel I never could get well with him. It's like having a cannon ball tied to one's feet when one is trying not to drown. It is just like that.[58]

And later, having secretly read some of Brett's letters to Murry, Mansfield wrote:

> Brett in her letters to Murry is unbalanced. This morning when she wrote how she wanted to rush into the cornfield

> – horrified me. And then he must smack her hand and she threatens to cry over him until he's all wet. Poor wretch! She's 37, hysterical, unbalanced, with a ghastly family tradition – and he had 'awakened' her. Her face is entirely changed: the mouth hangs open, the eyes are very wide, there is something silly and meaning in her smile which makes me cold. And then the bitten nails – the dirty neck – the film on the teeth! Whatever he may feel about it now the truth is she flattered him and got him! She listened and didn't criticise & sat at his feet and worshipped and asked for the prophet's help and he told her the old old tragedy. If Murry hadn't met me which would have won? His vanity & self absorption would have delivered him into the arms of countless INFERIOR females (it's always the 5th rate who play this 'game'.) [. . .] I wonder if the whole thing will be repeated this winter. I suppose so . . . .[59]

A few days later, Murry let slip that he had discussed the possibility of moving in with Brett once Mansfield had gone back to Menton for the winter. How on earth did he think Mansfield would react to such news? It's hard to comprehend the insensitivity of such a plan, and Mansfield now stored it away with all her other grudges. Ultimately, it would lead to a final parting of the ways – but not just yet. As Mansfield now wrote,

> I suppose one always thinks the latest shock is the worst shock. This is quite unlike any other I've ever suffered. The lack of sensitiveness as far as I am concerned – the selfishness of this staggers me. This is what I must remember when I am away. Murry thinks no more of me than of anybody else. I mean I am the same: the degree of his feeling is different but it's the same feeling. I must remember he's one of my friends – no more. Who could count on such a man! To plan all this at such a time and then on my return the first words I must be nice to Brett. How disgustingly indecent. I am simply disgusted to my very soul![60]

Even though Mansfield remained with Murry, most of the time outwardly happy and also stayed friends with Brett, it was realizations such as the above that ultimately turned her away from her marriage, to find joy elsewhere.

By the end of August, Mansfield's health had once more deteriorated, together with her mood. She was now confined to bed. On 23 August Virginia visited for what would turn out to be the final time, both promising to write to each other, and Mansfield to send her diary. The diary was never sent, and their correspondence did not survive beyond 1920. Mansfield and Ida returned to Menton and the Villa Isola Bella on 13 September. Although the difficult journey had left her suffering from fever and dysentery, Mansfield's stay in Menton from September 1920 to the beginning of May 1921 was to be one of the most productive periods of her entire writing career.

Enter Sobieniowski, who, short of money again, now wrote to Murry and asked for recompense to return love letters written by Mansfield to him in 1909. His letter must also have made some reference to the Chelsea episode from 1917 (when he and Mansfield had seen each other and for a while collaborated on a translation of Wyspiański's play *The Judges*), but she, dissembling as always, claimed to know nothing about *that*. She wrote to Murry from Menton on 16 September 1920: 'It is imbecile and odious that you should be so troubled. What F. refers to as the Chelsea period and good received beats me.' Nevertheless, she

Mansfield and John Middleton Murry, 1920.

proposed offering Sobieniowski £40 (her entire advance on *Bliss and Other Stories*): 'I want you to go with F. to a solicitor receive the letters get his sworn statement and hand him my cheque for the amount.'[61] And then a week later, on 23 September, she wrote 'Burn all he gives you – won't you? A bon fire.'[62] But Murry did not burn them. The whole business involving Sobieniowski and the solicitors must have taken around five weeks to complete, whereupon he then sent the letters to her in France. Mansfield's letter of 2 November records, almost as an aside, 'Floryan's letters came – thank you darling.'[63] She must have burnt them herself – or got Ida to do it.

Could Murry's affair with Princess Elizabeth Bibesco, begun around this time, have been a knee-jerk reaction to the revelations he had discovered in the letters between Mansfield and Sobieniowski? Cherry Hankin, the editor of Murry's letters to Mansfield, notes that 'between September 1920 and 11 January 1921, only one letter from Murry survives. One can only conjecture as to why the bulk of Murry's letters from this period were destroyed, and by whom.'[64] The above complications and ensuing correspondence may offer an explanation. And as if there weren't enough difficulties at this time, Beatrice Hastings now made a reappearance, extremely impoverished and unwell, managing her life, as Gray tells us, 'on a mere £10 a month, with no margin for hospital expenses':

> She had for several years been suffering from a fibrous growth in her womb, which now needed excision [...] Once she could lie sideways under her clean sheets, the first writing Beatrice did was of a letter, describing her dire circumstances to KM (then still at the Villa Isola Bella). Presumably she had to appeal once again for some urgent debt-reclamation.[65]

Beatrice had helped Mansfield financially in the past – it was time to call in the debt. Mansfield's reaction to Murry showed no compassion: 'Did I tell you I had another letter from Beatrice H? A hateful sniggering letter – a hiccup of a thing.'[66] Presumably no money was sent. And yet, Beatrice remained firmly in her psyche: just a week later, she became the subject of a nightmarish dream that Mansfield wrote down and sent to Murry:

> I was living at home again in the room with the fire escape. It was night: Father & Mother in bed. Vile people came into my

> room. They were drunk. Beatrice Hastings led them. 'You dont take me in old dear' said she. 'Youve played the Lady once too often, Miss – coming it over me.' And she shouted, screamed Femme marqué [branded woman] and banged the table. I rushed away.[67]

In November Mansfield wrote the short story 'Poison', in which Beatrice is portrayed as Mansfield remembered her, without even changing the name. However, entwined with her portrayal of Beatrice is the depiction of another woman who had been troubling Mansfield at this time: Princess Elizabeth Bibesco. Mansfield, bitter and deeply hurt by Murry's affair with Bibesco, had invested some of her own emotions in this depiction of what she calls the 'promiscuous love' of an older, more experienced woman for a younger man, echoing, of course, Hastings and the artist Modigliani, but far more deftly capturing what had been going on behind her back at home – no wonder that Murry initially disliked the story and chose not to publish it in the *Athenaeum*. Her letter to him explaining her rationale behind the story's composition must have made Murry blush with embarrassment and shame. No other story she wrote was ever unpicked in such detail as this:

> And about Poison. I could write about that for pages. But Ill try & condense what Ive got to say. The story is told by (evidently) a worldly, rather cynical (not wholly cynical) man against himself (but not altogether) when he was so absurdly young. You know how young by his idea of what woman is. She has been up till now, only the vision only she who passes. You realise that? And here he has put all his passion into this Beatrice. It's promiscuous love not understood as such by him; perfectly understood as such by her. But you realise the vie de luxe they are living – the very table, sweets, liqueurs, lilies, pearls – And you realise? she expects a letter from some one calling her away? Fully expects it? which accounts for her farewell & her declaration. And when it doesn't come even her commonness peeps out – the newspaper touch of such a woman. She can't disguise her chagrin. She gives herself away – – – He of course, laughs at it now, & laughs at her. Take what he says about her 'sense of order' & the crocodile. But he also regrets the self who dead privately would have been young enough to have actually wanted

> to Marry such a woman. But I meant it to be light – tossed off – & yet through it – oh – subtly – the lament for youthful belief. These are the rapid confessions one receives sometimes from a glove or a cigarette or a hat.
>
> I suppose I haven't brought it off in 'Poison'. It wanted a light, light hand – and then with that newspaper a sudden . . . let me see lowering of it all – just what happens in promiscuous love after passion. A glimpse of staleness.
>
> And the story is told by the man who gives himself away & hides his traces at the same moment.[68]

The fact that Mansfield gives this woman the name of Beatrice would also have been quite triggering for Murry. As Gray notes,

> This recurring Beatrice must have become a sore point with Murry, for long after his wife was deceased he deleted most references to her in the sparse journal he concocted out of Katherine's papers in 1927, where she appears merely as an uncharacterised 'B.' In the two volumes of KM's letters Murry put out in 1928 there is no mention of any BH at all.[69]

Perhaps the most celebrated story written during Mansfield's time in Menton is the long, episodic 'The Daughters of the Late Colonel', begun in late November 1920 and completed through the course of one exhausting day on 13 December, with Ida staying up until 3 a.m. to provide a celebratory cup of tea once the story was completed. As Mansfield later explained in a diary entry for 17 January 1922, 'The only occasion when I ever felt at leisure was while writing The Daughters of the Late Col. And then at the end I was so terribly unhappy that I wrote as fast as possible for fear of dying before the story was sent.'[70]

The first mention of the story came on 27 November in a letter to Murry: 'I have a long story here – very long which I want to get published serially. Its supremely suitable for such a purpose. And it would bring me in money. Its form is the form of The Prelude BUT written today – not then. The Prelude is a child's story.'[71] As she subsequently explained to Murry's brother Richard a few weeks later on 1 January 1921, 'Its the outcome of the Prelude method – it just unfolds and opens. But I hope its an advance on Prelude. In fact I know its that because the technique is stronger.'[72] In the story Mansfield affectionately immortalizes Ida and

Mansfield at her worktable, Villa Isola Bella, Menton, France, 1920.

her cousin Sylvia Payne, all of whom had attended the same school – Queen's College in Harley Street. The protagonists Constantia (Con) and Josephine (Jug) are two middle-aged spinster sisters who have had their wants and desires so subjugated by those of their domineering father (the late Colonel) that, after his death, they find themselves unable to make the simplest decision for themselves. Ida's middle name was Constance and 'Jug' was the nickname for Sylvia. The story also preserves something of the Baker family circumstances while growing up, when Ida and her sister, May (together with their brother Waldo), lived with their widowed and domineering father, Colonel Baker. The first seven years of Ida's life had been spent in Burma. Her mother died in 1903, and Ida was sent to board at Queen's College, where she met and befriended Mansfield. The first tentative title of the story was 'Non-Compounders', a term used at Queen's College for girls who attended only some of the college's courses, or those who were not boarders but lived at home, such as Sylvia.

On 2 December 1920 *Bliss and Other Stories* was published by Constable, to overwhelmingly positive reviews, including a brief note from Virginia: 'My dear Katherine, I wish you were here to enjoy your triumph – still more that we may talk about your book – For what's the use of telling you how glad and indeed proud I am?'[73] There was another, much longer letter sent, but it no longer exists. Mansfield's response was a deliberate final farewell to her literary friend:

> Please don't talk of a triumph, even in jest. It makes me hang my head. I wish some day I might deserve your long generous letter – but the day is far off, I realise that. Thank you for it all the same. It came on Xmas day too, and so was a two-fold gift.
>
> I think of you often – very often. I long to talk to you. Here, at last there is time to talk .. If Virginia were to come through the gate & were to say 'Well – Katherine' – oh, there are a thousand things Id like to discuss.
>
> I wonder if you know what your visits were to me – or how much I miss them. You are the only woman with whom I long to talk work. There will never be another. [...]
>
> Farewell dear friend. (May I call you that)[74]

There has been much speculation as to why Mansfield so deliberately chose to end the relationship with Woolf in this way, that final 'Farewell dear friend' sealing its demise. Perhaps the rivalry and the false notes of praise it engendered were no longer how Mansfield wished to live her life. The tension and competition had to go, and so Mansfield cut herself free.

In the meantime, Mansfield's local French doctor, Bouchage, had made it clear that the level of effort Mansfield was putting into her reviewing could not be sustained without seriously affecting her health – something had to give. She therefore announced to Murry her decision to stop reviewing: her last review for the *Athenaeum* appeared on 10 December. Once more, it appears from her letters that do survive that Murry's selfish letters in response to her own, detailing his close relationships with other women – in particular, Elizabeth Bibesco – had left her reeling. In a now-famous telegram, she told him to stop sending her 'false depressing letters'.[75] The telegram precipitated Murry into joining her in Menton, arriving on 20 December – evidence yet again of his 'reacting' rather than 'acting'. Their marital situation was becoming unsustainable.

7

Endgame, 1921–3

Positive reviews for *Bliss and Other Stories* continued to appear as the new year dawned, notably by Walter de la Mare and J. C. Squire. Murry went back briefly to England on 11 January, returning to Menton just over a week later on 19 January, his marital woes due to his own thoughtless behaviour having reached a make-or-break point. He now understood that the serious state of Mansfield's health, together with her severe depression, required him to be near her. Needing to extricate himself from Brett, Princess Elizabeth Bibesco and others, he finally made a bold decision, returning once more to London on 3 February for a few days to resign his editorship of the *Athenaeum*, which on 19 February was merged with another paper to become the *Nation and Athenaeum*.

There was some regret in literary circles at Murry's announcement of the ending of the *Athenaeum*; as Lea reports, 'Only Lawrence as usual struck a discordant note. "I hear the Athenaeum lost £5,000 a year under our friend the mud-worm"' (his favourite name for Murry during their numerous feuds).[1] It also meant, as Alpers notes, 'the parting of the ways between the Murrys and Bloomsbury as a whole'.[2] Now Murry was no longer in a position of power, 'their barely submerged hostility need no longer be held in check.'[3] Although Mansfield was relieved to finally have Murry with her permanently, she continued to be hurt by his insensitivity and meanness about money, as we shall see. Yet outwardly, all seemed well with the couple as they set about the business of being 'literary' together.

'Life of Ma Parker' was one of the last stories Mansfield wrote at the Villa Isola Bella and remains one of her most celebrated. Yet even in a story as outwardly bleak as this one, a comedic element is present in the preposterous 'literary gentleman', who, as Mansfield indicates precisely through the use of humour, is neither literary, nor a gentleman. An outwardly heartrending story of female working-class misery is made all the more poignant as a result of the biting and sarcastic humour directed at Ma Parker's employer:

> 'A baker, Mrs Parker!' the literary gentleman would say. For occasionally he laid aside his tomes and leant an ear, at least, to this product called Life. 'It must be rather nice to be married to a baker!'
>
> Mrs Parker didn't look so sure.
>
> 'Such a clean trade', said the gentleman.
>
> Mrs Parker didn't look convinced.
>
> 'And didn't you like handing the new loaves to the customers?'
>
> 'Well, sir', said Mrs Parker, 'I wasn't in the shop above a great deal. We had thirteen little ones and buried seven of them. If it wasn't the 'ospital it was the infirmary, you might say!'
>
> 'You might, *indeed*, Mrs Parker!' said the gentleman, shuddering, and taking up his pen again.[4]

Mansfield feels no need to give this character a name. He is representative of a type who considers himself better than others, when he is obviously no such thing. Through the use of incisive wit, the mean-mindedness of the 'literary gentleman' spreads like moral eczema through the story.

Every Mansfield story – without exception – concerns, to a greater or lesser extent, two issues in particular – love and/or money. In 'Life of Ma Parker', lack of money has contributed to the harshness of Ma Parker's life – without it, she has no freedom:

> It was cold in the street. There was a wind like ice. People were flitting by, very fast; the men walked like scissors; the women trod like cats. And nobody knew – nobody cared. Even if she broke down, if at last, after all these years, she were to cry, she'd find herself in the lock-up like as not.
>
> [. . .]
>
> She couldn't go home; Ethel was there. It would frighten Ethel out of her life. She couldn't sit on a bench anywhere;

> people would come arsking her questions. She couldn't possibly go back to the gentleman's flat; she had no right to cry in strangers' houses. If she sat on some steps a policeman would speak to her.
>
> Oh, wasn't there anywhere where she could hide and keep herself to herself and stay as long as she liked, not disturbing anybody, and nobody worrying her? Wasn't there anywhere in the world where she could have her cry out – at last?
>
> Ma Parker stood, looking up and down. The icy wind blew out her apron into a balloon. And now it began to rain. There was nowhere.[5]

This is one of Mansfield's bleakest polemics against the lot of women in society and demonstrates how some of her characters are present to cast light on the fundamentally isolated, frightening nature of the human condition. For Mansfield, money equals independence. Ma Parker has virtually no money and therefore no independence; her life has been one of constant self-sacrifice, her own needs subjugated to those of her family, to the extent that she no longer has a first name – she is simply 'Ma'. Her role as a mother has superseded her role as an individual. The passage above is made all the more poignant since it is written in Ma Parker's own voice, her own idiolect through the use of free indirect discourse; the reader is inside her mind as she goes about the drudgery of her daily life. The death of her beloved grandson is the final straw in Ma Parker's bleak life. We see the story moving powerfully towards its epiphanic moment – Ma Parker's overwhelming need to grieve in private, without holding back, for her grandson's death and finally for herself and the harshness of the life that has been allotted to her, with the final, terrible revelation that even this simple, cathartic act will be denied her, because of her lot in life, because she is poor, because she has nowhere private to go that will not arouse suspicion in one of her class.

Writing aside, Mansfield had someone else on her mind apart from Murry. The success of *Bliss and Other Stories* together with the continuing disappointments in her relationship with Murry now prompted her to write to Orage on 9 February. Tellingly, the letter to Orage was sent while Murry was away in London, publishing the final edition of the *Athenaeum* on 11 February, and hosting a farewell dinner attended by former contributors, including Virginia, who afterwards wrote

Mansfield a letter to which she never responded. This is what Mansfield wrote to Orage:

> Dear Orage,
> This letter has been on the tip of my pen for many months.
>
> I want to tell you how sensible I am of your wonderful unfailing kindness to me in the 'old days'. And to thank you for all you let me learn from you. I am still – more shame to me – very low down in the school. But you taught me to write, you taught me to think; you showed me what there was to be done and what not to do.
>
> My dear Orage, I cannot tell you how often I call to mind your conversation or how often, in writing, I remember my master. Does that sound impertinent? Forgive me if it does.
>
> But let me thank you, Orage – Thank you for everything. If only one day I might write a book of stories good enough to 'offer' you . . . If I don't succeed in keeping the coffin from the door you will know this was my ambition.
>
> Yours in admiration and gratitude
> Katherine Mansfield
>
> I haven't said a bit of what I wanted to say. This letter sounds as if it was written by a screw driver, and I wanted it to sound like an admiring, respectful, but warm piping beneath your windows. I'd like to send my love, too, if I wasn't so frightened
>
> K.M.[6]

Alpers notes that 'Orage, on his death, was found to have kept very few personal papers, but this letter was among them, suggesting that for him, as well, it possessed a special significance.'[7] It stands out as Mansfield looking back from her present unhappy life, alone, sick and disillusioned with Murry. It was a letter written from a place of complete despair and a desire to reconnect and to perhaps forge a new direction for herself. It would take another year or so, but eventually this is exactly what would happen. As the letter also makes clear, it was prompted by her realization that she owed much of her literary success to Orage's early guidance (and 'Prelude' was in this new collection). As Wood observes,

> Much of Orage's critical writing is concerned with prose style. His search for purity of style seems to be related to his ambition for a classless culture reflecting his ambition for a classless society: 'a pure style in writing reveals nothing but the thoughts and the pure individuality of the writer. His idiosyncrasies, his class, his education, his reading should all be kept out of sight. [. . .] Pure style is pure mind'.[8]

Mansfield's achievements in her prose echo Orage's dictum. Her own deceptively simple stories are easy to read, while hiding multiple layers of meaning, exactly what, according to Wood, Orage felt was needed. Mansfield, it seems, had turned out to be Orage's most promising and successful student. Wood believes that Mansfield wanted to dedicate *Bliss and Other Stories* to Orage,

> but being married to Murry had felt obliged to dedicate it to him instead, even though his mind was on his affairs with other women. Instead, her letter to him took the place of a dedication – her personal way of thanking – and recording her debt to – her mentor, who had taught her so much, and who, on more than one occasion, she had loved. We know that Orage would, years later, tell Frieda that Katherine was the only woman he had truly loved, and to Mantz he recounted his regret at the way he had ultimately stood by Beatrice Hastings instead of Katherine during those early years of intense friendship – and more. Even Ida recognised that he was the one constant love of Katherine's life, to whom she turned in moments of difficulty and despair.[9]

As if Mansfield's life wasn't troubled enough, Lawrence now re-entered the picture. A year earlier, having called her 'revolting', 'stewing in your consumption', and Murry 'a dirty little worm', now, in Sicily with Frieda, *still* stewing in his own anger and jealousy over the Murrys, he resurrected the muddy, wormy analogies in two letters. To Mary Cannan, who was also on her way to Menton that February, he wrote of Mansfield, 'Spit on her for me, when you see her. She's a liar, out and out,' and to Kot, 'I hear the Athenaeum lost £5,000 a year under our friend the mud-worm. [. . .] I hear he is – or was – on the Riviera with K. – who is doing the last gasp touch, in order to impose on people. [. . .] Two mudworms they are, playing into each other's long mud-bellies.'[10] That's a lot of worms – and mud.

Murry was back in Menton before the end of February and Ida was now sent back to London to remove their belongings from 'The Elephant' in Hampstead, their one proper home now as disintegrated as Mansfield's tubercular lungs. For Mansfield, close, continued proximity to Murry now became a blessing as well as a curse, as his many faults manifested themselves on an almost-daily basis. On 13 March she wrote a letter to Ida, marking it 'Confidential':

> Just now – making out the weeks bills he asked me for 11 francs for the carriage – half, plus a 2 franc tip! I think its awful to have to say it. But fancy not paying for your wifes carriage to & from the surgery! Is that simply extraordinary or am I? I really am staggered. I think it is the meanest thing I ever heard of.[11]

She tried to make light of Murry's stinginess, but it would become a festering sore as time went on. Meanwhile, Murry's affairs with Princess Bibesco and Brett rumbled on; Mansfield wrote to Ida:

> Elizabeth Bibesco has shown signs of life again. A letter yesterday begging him to resist Katherine. 'You have withstood her so gallantly so far how can you give way now'. And 'you swore nothing on earth should ever come between us'. From the letter I feel they are wonderfully suited and I hope he will go on with the affair. He wants to. 'How can I exist without your literary advice', she asks. That is a very fascinating question. I shall write to the silly little creature & tell her I have no desire to come between them only she must not make love to him while he is living with me, because that is undignified. He'll never break off these affairs, tho', and I dont see why he should. I wish hed take one on really seriously – and leave me. Every day I long more to be alone.[12]

The princess's letters to Murry now forced Mansfield to take matters into her own hands, writing one of the most effective slap-down letters in twentieth-century literary history:

Dear Princess Bibesco

I am afraid you must stop writing these little love letters to my husband while he and I live together. It is one of the things which is not done in our world.

You are very young. Wont you ask your husband to explain to you the impossibility of such a situation.

Please do not make me have to write to you again. I do not like scolding people and I simply hate having to teach them manners.

Yours sincerely
Katherine Mansfield.[13]

Aside from all the marital debacles, Mansfield's health was deteriorating rapidly, and it was clear that she could not spend the summer in the heat of the Riviera. Murry recorded how 'A gland in her throat became tubercular and very painful and had to be drained.'[14] She had heard of a treatment for tuberculosis by a Swiss doctor, Dr Spahlinger, and decided to travel to Switzerland to meet him, asking Ida to

Elizabeth Bibesco, 1921.

accompany her as she was uncertain of Murry's intentions, given the Bibesco fiasco. As ill as ever, Mansfield now looked to Switzerland as a place where she might find respite from her symptoms, and possibly even a cure, as well as time away from the other malady in her life – Murry himself.

In early May 1921 Mansfield and Ida travelled to Montreux in Switzerland, while Murry returned to England to deliver a series of lectures at Oxford, which he would later publish in a successful volume called *The Problem of Style*. In the letters they exchanged while he was in Oxford, it is clear that from Murry's rather blinkered point of view, the couple had now reached a pinnacle of happiness, as here, in a letter he wrote on 19 May 1921: 'Well, darling – we've had a strangely mixed time together – but if it had been a time of unmixed suffering it would still have been worth the price to get to the condition we're in now.'[15] Mansfield, as always, responded by hiding her true feelings under an outwardly loving exterior. But her reservations remained.

From Montreux, Mansfield travelled alone to Sierre to visit a Dr Stephani, who confirmed the serious nature of her tuberculosis, but who also believed she might yet have a chance of survival, if she were to follow a regimented cure. Murry travelled to Switzerland from England in early May, and together they moved to the Hôtel Château Bellevue in Sierre. By the end of the month, they had moved further up the mountain to the nearby Palace Hôtel in Montana, with Ida as companion to Mansfield. Mansfield's father Harold's cousin, the writer Elizabeth von Arnim, had a grand house, the Chalet Soleil, at nearby Randogne-sur-Sierre. Having met briefly in Hampstead in 1919, she and Mansfield now started meeting regularly, especially when the Murrys rented the Chalet des Sapins, in nearby Montana-sur-Sierre. Indeed, Mansfield's friendship with her cousin Elizabeth would go on to become one of the defining relationships of the last eighteen months of her life.

As Murry was later to write of this time in Switzerland, 'the peace of the Chalet des Sapins was the peace of the Villa Pauline in a new dimension.'[16] Lea records how

> The chalet was heated and comfortable, their daily routine unvarying. From breakfast till lunch, and from tea till supper, they worked. In the afternoons he went skiing or skating, or, if she was feeling strong enough to accompany him, collecting wild flowers and mushrooms. At night they read to each other

> – poems, novels, plays. Katherine 'Came nearer to following a regime than ever before or after'; and, rightly or wrongly, Murry believed that if only they had stayed, her life might have been prolonged by years.[17]

There now followed yet another intense period of creativity that saw Mansfield write more stories (and fragments of stories) than at any other time in her life. During 1921, 31 stories, complete and partially complete, were written, including some of her most famous, such as 'At the Bay' and 'The Doll's House'. The culmination of all this story-writing was another collection – sent to her new agent in London, J. B. Pinker, as well as to Michael Sadleir at her publishing house, Constable – and which she initially decided to call *At the Bay and Other Stories*. However, by early October, having just finished writing 'The Garden Party', she immediately decided not only to add it to the collection, but to name the collection after it.

'The Garden Party' remains one of the most celebrated and discussed of all Mansfield's stories. As we have already discerned, all of Mansfield's mature fiction writing has a sociological basis. Nowhere is this emphasis more clearly demonstrated, especially with reference to children, than in 'The Garden Party'. Here is the 'Burnell' family from 'Prelude' and 'At the Bay' under a different name – the 'Sheridans' – and slightly older; gone are the young children, the ubiquitous Stanley Burnell and the sensual Beryl. Instead, Mansfield presents us with the development of the teenage mind and its gradual succumbing to adult values and morals. On the surface, the story reads as a homely vision of youthful femininity and middle-class values, set within the picturesque New Zealand landscape. Yet these values, these notions, are the backdrop for a discourse on the plight of the working classes, the presentation of staid, middle-class reaction to social inferiors, a child's last attempt to understand the world naturally and simplistically, without the need for a social mask, though this mask becomes more stiflingly present each time Laura, the protagonist, at the onset of adulthood, tries to shy away from it. In addition, and most importantly, it is a war story.

In a story sixteen pages long, the garden party itself occupies a mere half-page of narrative. The first four pages focus attention on the workmen as much as on any other characters. There are then three pages of pre-garden party preparations, followed by the first mention of the death that permeates the remaining nine pages of narrative. Yet, reading

Elizabeth von Arnim, Countess Russell, studio portrait, 1924.

the story, one is not aware that the garden party takes up so little space; the title 'Death of a Carter' would be much more appropriate. Mansfield uses the garden party as an excuse, a shroud, within which are encapsulated her myriad themes. Its false importance symbolizes the way adults tend to gloss over everything ugly, to deny ugliness an entry into the common round of life.

The only character developed in any detail is Laura. The reader barely becomes acquainted with the other children, Jose, Meg and Laurie – names deliberately taken from the pages of Louisa May Alcott's *Little Women* (since that is what they are becoming) – or the father or mother. They are stereotypes, predictable in their behaviour and actions and used as vehicles for the expression of social rules and behaviour. Laura is a misfit who has to learn to toe the line, to recognize her position in society and that of others, and not to flout any of the rules. Laura's journey can be seen not so much as a coming-of-age narrative, but rather as 'a reversal ritual [where] the accidental death of the carter allows Mrs. Sheridan to turn it into a status elevation for Laura'.[18]

And this ultimately false status is symbolized through daisies: initially present in the grass in the early morning, but mowed away by the gardener during the preparations for the garden party, they mutate into brassy-gold false flowers decorating a black hat given to Laura by her mother, a bribe to enable her to forget the accident in the street below the house: 'this charming girl in the mirror, in her black hat trimmed with gold daisies, and a long black velvet ribbon. Never had she imagined she could look like that. Is mother right? she thought. And now she hoped her mother was right.'[19] The use of free indirect discourse here, as so often with Mansfield, reveals dilemma, though not always resolution (as, for example, in the case of Ma Parker). Laura's epiphanic moment after she has seen the dead carter reveals how innocence has not yet mutated into cynical experience.

Mansfield has a specific agenda in portraying the death of a carter in 'The Garden Party'; she explained her philosophy behind the story in a letter:

> That is what I tried to convey in The Garden Party. The diversity of life and how we try to fit in everything, Death included. That is bewildering for a person Laura's age. She feels things ought to happen differently. First one and then another. But life isn't like that. We haven't the ordering of it. Laura says 'But all these things must not happen at once'. And Life answers 'Why not? How are they divided from each other'. And they do all happen, it is inevitable. And it seems to me there is beauty in that inevitability.[20]

Yet, in spite of all this literary activity – and outward happiness – Mansfield now recognized the false notes in her life and in particular in her relationship with Murry. Together with her ingrained restlessness, these factors compounded her desire to seek new avenues for treatment, both spiritual and physical. In October 1921 Kot sent her a letter informing her of a revolutionary new treatment for tuberculosis, practised by a Russian called Dr Manoukhin in Paris, which involved the radiation of the spleen. She was immediately interested and asked for more information. In early December Mansfield herself wrote to Manoukhin in Paris, asking him if he would take her on as a patient. She admitted to Kot that she had become a true invalid, barely able to walk for the past year. In her mind, she now found herself turning away from what she perceived as her dull life in Switzerland, believing in the potential for Manoukhin to effect in her a complete cure. Her decision was also compounded by reading a book entitled *Cosmic Anatomy and the Structure of the Ego* (1921), whose Eastern mystic philosophy she wholeheartedly embraced; the book made her all the more determined to seek a spiritual cure for her diseased body since physical cures had proved worthless. In January 1922, from Switzerland, she wrote in her notebook:

> I have read a good deal of Cosmic Anatomy – understood it far better. Yes, such a book does fascinate me. [. . .] To get even a glimpse of the relation of things, to follow that relation & find it remains true through the ages enlarges my little mind as nothing else does.[21]

The book, by 'M. B. Oxon', had, in fact, been sent to Murry by Orage. Mansfield's letter to Orage from 9 February 1921, thanking him for being her mentor and friend, was almost certainly the catalyst for Orage sending Wallace's book to Switzerland a few months later, knowing Mansfield would read it – which she did. On finishing the book, she wrote to her friend Violet Schiff that she had 'passed through a state of <u>awful</u> depression. [. . .] But I see my way now, I think. What saved me finally was reading a book called Cosmic Anatomy – and reflecting on it.'[22]

Orage had been a theosophist for many years, with interests also in mystical literature, Nietzsche and the insights of the *Mahabharata*. One of his earliest publications was *Consciousness: Animal, Human and Superhuman*, published by the Theosophical Society in 1907. 'M. B. Oxon' was, in fact, the pseudonym of Dr Lewis Alexander Richard Wallace, a Scottish theosophist who had made a good deal of money sheep farming in New Zealand and who went on to fund Orage by giving him half the amount needed (£500) to purchase the *New Age* in 1907 (with Bernard Shaw volunteering the other £500). In return, Orage indulged Wallace and allowed him to publish his theosophical articles in the magazine. In addition, Beatrice Hastings, Orage's partner at this time, was also a theosophist. Therefore, as well as immersing herself in all things Eastern, from her first meeting with Orage in February 1910, Mansfield became part of the close-knit theosophical community at the *New Age*. Thus the author of *Cosmic Anatomy*, as well as the book's contents, would have been well known to her, as noted in Chapter Four, though of course not to Murry: much of the book's contents had been serialized in the *New Age*, when Mansfield was closely allied to the paper. It also seems entirely possible that Orage deliberately sent the book to Murry, knowing that he would hate it, and that, understanding Mansfield's contrary nature, this would immediately make her curious to read it. James Moore concurs with this opinion:

> But why of all reviewers to Murry? Murry with his entrenched hostility to occult ideas? And if Katherine were the intended recipient, why not simply send it to her in the first place? Murry said he found the book's gnostic speculations positively repellent mumbo jumbo. His scepticism only accentuated her enthusiasm.[23]

Orage played this point well. Keen for Mansfield to read the book, he nevertheless did not wish to be seen sending her things directly. Mansfield and Orage now kept up a secretive correspondence, with Mansfield giving him the code name 'China'; for example, on Saturday, 14 January 1922, she wrote in her notebook: 'Posted my story to Pinker. Heard from China.'[24] Mantz notes of this period that 'There had been a quickening of emotion for each of them since she wrote her letter of gratitude and they corresponded over the renewal of friendship in the world of mysticism.'[25]

As was expected, Murry himself disliked the occult teachings in the book and voiced his scepticism over it as well as of Manoukhin's X-ray treatment of the spleen, but to no avail. In his 1951 edition of Mansfield's letters, he penned a long editorial note about her decision to leave Switzerland and travel to Paris, which clearly, thirty years on, still troubled him greatly, leaving him with the feeling of needing to justify what subsequently happened and Mansfield's ensuing death:

> I have regretted nothing more bitterly than that, when Katherine discovered that the Manoukhin treatment required a consultation with the inventor in Paris, I did not resolutely oppose her going. [. . . I]t was the slippery slope which led to Katherine's confinement in Paris, her abandonment of the Swiss mountains, and a disillusion the more shattering because her hopes had been set so high. And it had for me the peculiarly dismal consequence that it set a barrier between Katherine

> and myself. I was required 'to have faith' in the Manoukhin treatment. I had little.[26]

In early January 1922, before leaving for Paris, Mansfield sent Orage another letter, of which only a partial draft survives:

> My dear Orage
> Whether I shall ever be able to say I have read your new book I do not know. I can foresee no change in my present condition of reading it and reading it.[27]

As Wood notes, 'your new book' refers to Orage's volume *Readers and Writers (1917–1921)*, published in early 1922, which he may well have sent her in advance of publication. The book's preface was dated 'December 1921'. For Wood,

> her comment is clearly complimentary. It is a book to dip in and out of; a collection of some of his 'Readers and Writers' columns from the *New Age*; many of his observations about the evolving literary landscape and new works are profound even today. He also set out his views about how modern English literature should be written; with which views, of course, Mansfield would have been familiar.[28]

Wood also observes that all references to Hastings had been removed from the excerpts, which would have pleased Mansfield but disgusted Hastings, who, even though she had long parted from Orage by 1917, had still been a contributor, though no longer an editor.

Meanwhile, Mansfield's mind was now set firm on the treatment being offered by Dr Manoukhin. Thus it was that on 30 January she and Ida left Switzerland for Paris, leaving Murry behind at the Chalet des Sapins. He, as seemingly oblivious as ever to Mansfield's true feelings, wrote jocularly in his diary for 1922: 'Tig left by the 2 p.m. funicular. Bless her!'[29] In Paris the next day, Mansfield and Ida took rooms at the Victoria Palace Hôtel and Mansfield immediately went to Manoukhin's clinic, where she was examined and told that treatment could begin immediately. She wrote to Murry, outlining the treatment and her main reservation, which was financial, since it would cost 4,500 francs (about £3,000 today) for the first fifteen sessions. The very next day she was back at the clinic, where she was given assurances as to the efficacy of the treatment, although she still remained in two minds as to whether she might be being duped. Murry however, responded positively – he was having a grand time in Switzerland, his writing was going well, and he was enjoying spending time with Elizabeth von Arnim in her luxurious chalet and with her glamorous friends. So the treatment began, with Manoukhin assuring Mansfield that he could cure her completely. The treatment was, of course, not only pointless, but positively harmful. By the end of it she would be as ill as ever.

Murry, happily writing and skiing, was once again insensitive to Mansfield's feelings of unhappiness and hopelessness and fears over her health. She had had enough: yet another bitter exchange of letters resulted in Murry arriving in Paris on 11 February. As Lea notes, Murry had characteristically left it 'to her to decide whether he should join her or finish his novel. Naturally, she told him to finish it, but with such "an obvious 'oh!'" that he was filled with shame and set off for Paris there and then.'[30] Even in his diary, his indecision is plain to see, as here in the entry for 2 February: 'The question is: what shall I do? If I go to Paris it will be very hard for me to do any real work; I don't find it easy precisely, even here. I suggested by letter that I should stay as I am.' Three days later, on 6 February, nothing has changed: 'I wrote to say that whatever she wd. like me to do – go to Paris and live or stay here – I wd. do like a shot.' Finally, on 8 February, he writes: 'Finally made up my mind to leave Montana for Paris.'[31] Mansfield's frustration was palpable, as in this extract from a letter sent on the same day, in which she crystallized months – years – of frustration with him:

> It is no good. I now know that I must grow a shell away from you. I want – 'I ask' for my independence. At any moment in the future you may suddenly leave me in the lurch if it pleases you. It is a part of your nature. I thought that it was almost the condition of your working that we were together. Not a bit of it! Well, darling Boge, for various reasons I cant accept this. And now that I am making a bid for health – my final bid – I want to grow strong in another way, too.[32]

Yet once Murry arrived, all frustrations – as had happened time and again – were superficially buried. Ida, inevitably, was dispatched back to Switzerland to sort out their day-to-day affairs. *The Garden Party and Other Stories* had been published at the end of February to glowing reviews. The couple now settled down into a similar routine of working that they had undertaken at the Chalet des Sapins, although Mansfield's health remained poor, and she was barely able to leave the hotel, unless it was to go to the clinic. Murry's diary for 20 April, for example, records, 'A bloody depressing day [. . .] Tig has been really ill this week – pains in her lungs continually – intense pains in the abdomen. She says she feels weaker than she has felt for months – and her cough to my ear seems to have taken on the deep lung-tearing sound.'[33] Despite her health, Mansfield still managed to write a few stories during this period, and several more incomplete stories, but with nothing like the intensity and polish of her year in Switzerland. She also worked on some translations of Tolstoy and Dostoevsky with Kot, while lying on her hotel bed.

Murry, however, was under no such physical constraints and enjoyed being in Paris. As a couple, and through Manoukhin, they came to know several members of the Russian colony then in Paris, including Ivan Bunin and Dmitri Merezhkovsky. On his own, however, Murry was now received by some of the leading French men of letters at that time, including Paul Valéry and Charles du Bos. Another famous meeting occurred on 29 March, facilitated by their English friends Sydney and Violet Schiff, also in Paris at this time, when Mansfield and Murry met James Joyce in the lobby of their hotel and discussed *Ulysses*. Violet Schiff famously revealed afterwards that Joyce felt that Mansfield understood the book far better than Murry.

During April, Mansfield's health appeared to improve, which, of course, renewed her faith in the potential success of Manoukhin's treatment, but by the end of the course of treatments, it was distressingly clear that she was as ill as ever. Their residence in the Victoria Palace Hôtel was over; it marked the last time she and Murry would reside in the same place together for more than a few days at a time. Forlornly, therefore, on 4 June, the couple rather aimlessly retraced their steps back to Randogne in Switzerland, this time staying at the Hôtel d'Angleterre. The journey, without Ida's careful assistance, proved horrendous, and Mansfield quickly developed pleurisy. Ida now gladly rejoined Mansfield as her companion secretary, and the two women moved down the mountain to the Hôtel Château Bellevue in Sierre, where they were soon accompanied by Brett, leaving Murry at the Hôtel d'Angleterre. While in Sierre, on 7 July, Mansfield wrote 'The Canary', her last complete story. It was also during her stay in Sierre, on 7 August, that she wrote a letter to Murry – a sort of informal will – to be opened after her death. Murry knew nothing of the letter – she sent it directly to her bank in London, where it was forwarded to him after her death:

> Dearest Bogey
> I have been on the point of writing this letter for days. My heart has been behaving in such a curious fashion that I cant imagine it means nothing. So, as I should hate to leave you unprepared, I'll just try & jot down what comes into my mind. All my manuscripts I leave entirely to you to do what you like with. Go through them one day, dear love, and destroy all you do not use. Please destroy all letters you do not wish to keep & all papers. You know my love of tidiness. Have a clean sweep, Bogey, and leave all fair – will you?
>
> [. . .]
>
> Monies, of course, are all yours. In fact, my dearest dear, I leave everything to you – to the secret you whose lips I kissed this morning. In spite of everything – how happy we have been! I feel no other lovers have walked the earth together more joyfully – in spite of all.
>
> Farewell, my precious love.
> I am for ever and ever
> Your
> WIG.[34]

There is, of course, a good deal of dissembling in this celebrated letter. In one sense, at the time of its composition, the couple had never been further apart in their thinking and their future desires and plans. They were leading separate lives. But as her husband, Murry would legally be the main beneficiary of her will, as well as the future guardian of her literary estate. It was, therefore, time to be canny. Mansfield's will, drafted a week later, on 14 August, emphasized even more prominently her desire for Murry to publish as little as possible: 'All manuscripts notebooks papers letters I leave to John Middleton Murry likewise I should like him to publish as little as possible and to tear up and burn as much as possible He will understand that I desire to leave as few traces of my camping ground as possible.'[35] It's clear that Mansfield finally understood how desperately ill she was, and that her affairs needed to be put in order. The professions of love and joy in the above letter were most certainly for posterity, rather than reflecting the couple's current, difficult, conjugal state; Murry, of all people, would have known that.

The next day, together with Murry and Ida, Mansfield left Switzerland and returned to London, ostensibly for Mansfield to consult with Dr Sorapure but, in fact, to reconnect with Orage and to find out more information regarding the circle of philosopher P. D. Ouspensky that Orage had been discussing with her. During this period in London, Mansfield stayed with Brett at her house in Hampstead, with Murry lodging next door with the Russian artist Boris Anrep. It was to be the couple's final parting of the ways. Finally, Mansfield and Orage were now able to meet in person again, after rekindling their deep friendship. Mantz records, 'In conversation, Orage described how he had gone to meet Katherine at her invitation. For a moment at the door they simply stood and regarded each other with delight from long acquaintance, deep-rooted and proved by maturity.'[36] Ida, too, recalled Mansfield's happiness at meeting up with Orage:

> She had always been fond of him, and when she got back after her first visit to him she was happier than I had expected. She said it had been wonderful, he had been so affectionate, embracing her and calling her 'darling', as though in a return to earlier, happier days.[37]

While in London, Mansfield also continued Manoukhin's expensive X-ray treatment of the spleen with a London radiologist, Dr Webster. However, her confidence in his treatment being as effective as that of Manoukhin's was not high, and she realized that, at some point, she would have to return to Paris in order to continue the treatment with Manoukhin himself. But there was now another, more compelling reason to return to Paris.

During the month of September 1922, Mansfield and Orage became fascinated with the esoteric theories of G. I. Gurdjieff, on which they attended lectures by Ouspensky. Mansfield's secret intention – kept from Murry – was to return to Paris, not just to continue her treatment with Manoukhin, but with a notion of perhaps entering the community near Fontainebleau that Gurdjieff was just then setting up – the Institute for the Harmonious Development of Man – whose philosophy decreed that a cure for physical ailments such as tuberculosis depended first upon a healing of the inner spirit. Two days earlier, on 28 September, Orage had resigned his editorship of the *New Age* in preparation for a similar move. For Mansfield, now gravely ill, this spiritual approach seemed to offer a real possibility of an alternative cure from her tuberculosis, in addition to her radiation treatment. It also meant that she and Orage would be together again.

As for Murry, Lea records, 'the teachings of Ouspensky and Gurdjieff, which had come to mean everything to her, not merely meant nothing to him, but were positively repugnant. Although in Hampstead, they occupied adjoining houses [. . .] there was little or no communication between them.'[38] Murry soon escaped to Vivian Locke-Ellis's house in Sussex, now creating a physical – as well as spiritual – distance between them.

In the unpublished second part of his biography, Murry wrote of this moment in his life:

> The pattern repeated itself to the end. When we were finally in Switzerland, I felt I ought not to have allowed her to go in pursuit of health from Dr Manoukhin in Paris; still more, towards the very end, I felt I ought not to have allowed her to go to the Gurdjieff Institute in Fontainebleau, where she died. But, as always, I numbly acquiesced, and eventually accompanied her, from England to the South of France, from the South of France to Switzerland, from Switzerland to Paris, from Paris to London. But not from London to Fontainebleau. For in that journey a different issue was involved. To have entered the Gurdjieff Institute would have meant, for me, the violation of my own spiritual, or intellectual integrity. Not that Katherine demanded, or expected, that I should go with her. There was not even the mute appeal that I should do so. We had come, at last, to a parting of the ways, and we both acknowledged it.[39]

Orage, who had been introduced to the ideas of Ouspensky by the poet F. S. Flint in 1911, had actually met the philosopher in 1913, and the two men corresponded thereafter. In 1919 Orage published Ouspensky's 'Letters from Russia' in the *New Age*.[40] As Louise Welch notes, 'As late as 1919, Orage was unaware that his friend, Ouspensky, had found someone who "knew"' (that is, Gurdjieff).[41] Indeed, Orage had been attending Ouspensky's talks for over a year by the time Mansfield met him; in the

G. I. Gurdjieff arriving in New York, January 1924.

spring of 1921, Ouspensky had written to Orage telling of his intention to move to London and share, as Welch records, '"fragments of an unknown teaching". This was the first indication to Orage that Ouspensky had found what they were both seeking.'[42] Indeed, 'Many years later Orage said that when he listened to the Gurdjieff-inspired Ouspensky he felt like a medieval alchemist in search of gold. But when Gurdjieff himself visited the group in London one cold February evening in 1922, he felt that he had at last found the gold itself.'[43] Thus Orage felt compelled to resign his editorship of the *New Age*, and follow Gurdjieff to Fontainebleau, a move that shocked and stunned people close to him, including his faithful secretary Alice Marks, who had worked for him for ten years. When she queried his decision, he simply replied, 'I am going to find God.'[44] He was also going to find Mansfield.

For Mansfield herself, now gravely ill, such a spiritual approach seemed to offer a real possibility of an alternative cure from her tuberculosis, in addition to her radiation treatment. And so she travelled alone to Paris, where, on 3 October, on the advice of Orage, she consulted with Dr James Carruthers Young, a medical doctor and Gurdjieff adherent who was also an advocate of holistic medicine, and 'who gave her permission to apply to the Institute'.[45] On 16 October 1922 Mansfield entered Gurdjieff's Institute, initially on a fortnight's trial, but soon becoming a permanent resident. Back in London, on 17 October, Murry, slightly bewildered, but doing his best to play the role of a dutiful brother-in-law, attended on her behalf the wedding of Mansfield's youngest sister, Jeanne, to Charles Renshaw. More of him in the next chapter.

After her death, Orage analysed the impetus for Mansfield joining the Fontainebleau community:

> The real reason, and the only reason that lead [*sic*] Katherine Mansfield to the Gurdjieff Institute was less dissatisfaction with her craftsmanship than dissatisfaction with herself; less dissatisfaction with her stories than with the attitude toward life implied in them; less dissatisfaction with her own and contemporary literature than with literature.
>
> [. . .]
>
> For she realized that it is not writing as writing that needs criticism, correction, and perfection, so much as the mind, character, and personality of the writer. One must become more to write better.[46]

For Mansfield, an entire attitude change towards her craft – a complete transformation – was needed. Orage recorded her conversations on this very subject:

> 'I have not been able to think', she said, 'that I should not have made such observations as I have made of people, however cruel they may seem. After all, I did observe those things, and I had to set them down. I've been a camera. But that's just the point. I've been a selective camera, and it has been my attitude that has determined the selection; with the result that my slices

> of life (thank you, Mr. Phillpotts!) have been partial, misleading, and a little malicious. Further, they have had no other purpose than to record my attitude, which in itself stood in need of change if it was to become active instead of passive. Altogether, I've been not only a mere camera, but I've been a selective camera, and a selective camera without a creative principle. And, like everything unconscious, the result has been evil.'
>
> 'Well, what is your new plan?'
>
> 'To widen first the scope of my camera, and then to employ it for a conscious purpose – that of representing life not merely as it appears to a certain attitude, but as it appears to another and different attitude, a creative attitude'.[47]

Murry, who in 1922 had not yet entered his own mystical phase, admitted, 'I could scarcely bear to discuss the doctrines of Ouspensky with Katherine. The gulf between us was painful to us both; and living under the same roof became a kind of torture. I could not bear it.'[48] And Mansfield wrote in a similar vein to Murry from Paris on 11 October, just before entering the Prieuré, thinking back to their time together in Menton: 'I remember what we really felt there. The blanks, the silences, the anguish of continual misunderstanding. Were we positive, eager, real – alive? No, we were not. We were a nothingness shot with gleams of what might be.'[49]

Gurdjieff was 56 when Mansfield arrived at the Prieuré in October 1922. He had been born in 1866 in Alexandropol, on the Russian–Turkish border. The experiences and special education to which he was exposed, as James Moore explains, imbued him with an irrepressible striving to understand clearly the precise significance of the life process on earth, of all the outward forms of breathing creatures and, in particular, of the aim of human life in the light of this interpretation.[50] Gurdjieff believed that civilization had thrown men and women out of balance, so that the physical, the emotional and the intellectual parts had ceased to work in accord. Twenty years of his life, from 1887 to 1911, were spent in Central Asia, dedicated to a search for traditional knowledge. He started teaching in Moscow in 1912, but this work was disrupted by the First World War and the Russian Revolution. Together with the followers he had gathered over these years who had somehow managed to leave Bolshevik Russia, he arrived, eventually, in Paris. There had been plans to set up his Institute in London, but these had been cut short by the British authorities, who suspected him of being a Russian spy. He arrived in Paris on 1 October 1922, having leased the Prieuré at Fontainebleau-Avon sight unseen.

What precisely was Gurdjieff's teaching? Moore sums it up thus: '"I teach," he said gnomically, "that when it rains, the pavements get wet." [. . .] His one constant demand is Know thyself [. . . his] one master-idea: that Man is called to strive for self-perfection, in service to our sacred living Universe.'[51] Copying from *Cosmic Anatomy*, Mansfield had written in her notebook at the end of February 1922:

> Do you know what individuality is?
>
> No.
>
> Consciousness of will. Conscious that you have a will and can act.[52]

Okakura, in the *Book of Tea*, which, as we saw in a previous chapter, had been a favourite of Mansfield's since 1910, had written, 'We nurse a conscience because we are afraid to tell the truth to others; we take refuge in pride because we are afraid to tell the truth to ourselves.'[53] Reaffirming this premise, in October 1922, she now wrote in her notebook: 'Therefore if the Grand Lhama of Thibet promised to help you – how can you hesitate! Risk! Risk anything! Care no more for the opinion of others, for those voices. Do the hardest thing on earth for you. Act for yourself. Face the truth.'[54]

Olga Hinzenberg (known as Olgivanna), in her article recollecting Mansfield's time in Fontainebleau, recorded Mansfield's arrival at the Prieuré:

> She stood in the doorway of our main dining-room and looked at all and at each with sharp, intense dark eyes. They burned with the desire and hunger for impressions. She wanted to sit down and eat with all the students, but someone called her to a different dining-room. [. . .] I told Gurdjieff what a lovely face she had and how much I liked her.[55]

Gurdjieff spoke very little English or French, and his initial contact with Mansfield was limited. Nevertheless, as Moore states, she, like many others, 'was magnetised not by a system of self-supportive notional abstractions, but by a human being of Rabelaisian stature, by the fine energies at his disposition, and by this empathy, his vision, his humour, and by his sheer quality of "being"'.[56] The recollections of another resident, Tcheslaw Tchekhovitch, offer a revealing insight into how Mansfield was perceived by the Russian community there. Of her first few days at the Prieuré, he recorded,

> During the following days, she went from one group to another, apparently fascinated by our activities. Everywhere, her graciousness elicited the same welcoming response. She was often to be found in the kitchen when it was at its busiest, in the cowshed when the cows were being milked, and each morning in the barnyard scattering the grain with a delicate hand. We bent over backwards to please her and make her life easier. Often it was my job to carry wood up to her room, where we kept a fire burning day and night. Not to make her feel a burden, we were careful to bring the wood when she was not there. Her room was on the second floor, next to Mr. Gurdjieff's. An especially peaceful atmosphere suffused this beautiful room, with its large window looking out over the gardens.[57]

There has always been speculation as to the reason why Gurdjieff allowed Mansfield to join his Institute when it was obvious she was dying. In the end, it was probably an act of charity for which he received little recognition. There is no other reason to account for his choice in allowing someone with only weeks to live to enter the Prieuré, knowing that the death of a famous English writer at his Institute, so soon after its opening, would certainly not aid his cause in any way – indeed, would lay himself and his institution open to denigration. As Ouspensky said, many years later,

> I remember one talk with Miss Katherine Mansfield who was living there. This was not more than three weeks before her death. I had given her G's address myself. She had been to two or three of my lectures and then come to me to say that she was going to Paris [. . .]. She already seemed to me to be halfway to death. And I thought she was fully aware of it. But with all this one was struck by the striving in her to make the best use even of these last days, to find the truth whose presence she clearly

> felt but which she was unable to touch. [. . .] Soon after my return to London I heard of her death. G. was very good to her, he did not insist upon her going although it was clear that she could not live. For this in the course of time he received the due amount of lies and slanders.[58]

Two of Gurdjieff's followers were medically qualified doctors, so there could be no doubt as to the true state of Mansfield's health. However, Tchekhovitch offers a startling revelation in his recollections that Gurdjieff, fearing for the reputation of his newly founded Institute, had initially wanted Mansfield to leave:

> One day, after Mr. Gurdjieff had just left for Paris, as he did regularly, I noticed that Katherine's demeanour had changed: she looked overwhelmed, as if everything in her had slowed down. 'Bonjour, Katya. How are you?' 'Bonjour, Tchekhovitch.' Her voice was subdued; its tone had changed. She took her usual place and watched us working with a far-away look in her eyes. Suddenly, she put her head in her hands and began to weep. I went over to her and put my hand on her shoulder. 'What's wrong, Katya?' 'It's nothing.' Then she added, 'I'm very unhappy.' I insisted on knowing what was tormenting her. 'Well,' she said sorrowfully, 'Gyorgi Ivanovitch doesn't want me to stay here any longer. He's asked me to leave.' 'And what about you? What do you want?' 'I want to stay here. I'm so happy among all of you.' 'Then why is Gyorgi Ivanovitch asking you to leave?' 'He wants me to go to a sanatorium. I'm quite ill, you see. I have tuberculosis and I don't have much longer to live. I want so much to stay here until the end. Here, I've found what I've been seeking for a long time. I don't want to be anywhere else, with people I don't know. I want to stay here with all of you. But I think that he doesn't want me to die here.' I was so taken aback by this unexpected confession that, at first, I could not think of anything to say to her. But I could not keep silent. A strange determination came over me on her behalf: not to give up, not to lose hope. I could not believe Gyorgi Ivanovitch would refuse to let her stay at the Prieuré if she expressed her wish sincerely, from the depths of her being. Gently, I spoke my mind. 'You know as well as I that Gyorgi Ivanovitch is a good man. He won't refuse, if

> you speak to him frankly.' Then, wanting to provide her with a request he could not turn down, I added, 'Don't just ask to stay. Tell him it's the only way for you to find true happiness.' [. . .] I learned later that Katherine Mansfield's request had put Mr Gurdjieff in a very difficult position. At first he had been reluctant. 'If she dies here, just imagine what malicious gossip will ensue – another pretext for slander. They are bound to say that we were the cause of her premature death.' This was the essence of Mr Gurdjieff's realistic and somewhat bitter remarks with Mme de Salzmann, Mrs Frank Lloyd Wright, and Mme Chaverdian had begged him to agree to Katherine's request. These women were not easily put off. 'Gyorgi Ivanovitch, people have already said plenty of scandalous things about you, so one more isn't going to make much difference! We'll share that burden with you.' 'All right, then,' he said, looking at them intently. 'So be it. We'll all bear it together!'[59]

Thus it was that Gurdjieff and his followers, having accepted that the terminally ill Mansfield would die at the Institute, went out of their way to help her; two women, Olgivanna, and a young Lithuanian girl, Adele Kafian, who spoke no English, were tasked with looking after her. In her own personal recollections of Mansfield, Adele described the cowshed balcony expressly made for the writer, on Gurdjieff's orders, since the exhalations of cows were believed to aid tuberculosis sufferers:

> On the leader's instructions, a balcony was constructed for her in the cowshed, for rest, or, perhaps, to renew her strength through the radiation of animal magnetism, or perhaps simply for the healthy smell of fresh manure.
>
> It was a tiny wooden balcony, artistically designed, with a small staircase of five or six steps, surrounded by a balustrade gilded in Eastern style. The floor was covered with mattresses and real Eastern rugs. Cushions and round pouffes, covered with coloured tapestry, invited one to rest and gaze at the ceiling, cleverly painted by our talented artist with all kinds of birds, insects and little animals hiding among fanciful branches. Among them one could detect caricatures of all the inmates of the house. Under the balcony stood our three cows and the mule, Drafit.

> When my turn came to work for a week in the cowshed, I gave special care to the little balcony; I decorated the staircase with leaves and branches, and used to sit and wait for Mrs. Murry.[60]

The artist in question was Alexandre de Salzmann; in the mural, Orage was depicted as an elephant.[61]

Mansfield's initial impressions of Gurdjieff were mixed: 'Mr Gurdjieff is not in the least like what I expected. Hes what one wants to find him, really. But I do feel absolutely confident he can put me on the right track in every way.'[62] Indeed, by 12 November she was writing,

> Here, I confess, after only five weeks, there are things I long to write! Oh, how I long to! But I shall not for a long time. Nothing is ready. I must wait until la maison est pleine. I must say the dancing here has given me quite a different approach to writing. I mean some of the very ancient oriental dances. There is one which takes about 7 minutes and it contains the whole life of woman – but everything! Nothing is left out. It taught me, it gave me more of woman's life than any book or poem. There was even room for Flaubert's Cœur Simple in it.[63]

Bells rang continuously, announcing the various stages of the day. At 6 a.m., a little bell would sound, announcing breakfast – just coffee and bread. Then a long day's work began, with a variety of tasks including farming, meal preparation, laundry and housework. In the evening, another bell called them to the grand dinner, at which they would feast, and then either participate in or watch the sacred dances. Although Orage was kept busy with manual labour tasks, he nevertheless sought out Mansfield's company whenever he could:

> I saw Katherine Mansfield almost every day in the institute, and we had many long talks together. For months she was quite content not to be writing or even reading. We had a common surprise in contrasting our current attitude towards literature with the craze we had both experienced for many years. What has come over us? she would ask whimsically. Are we dead? Or was our love of literature an affectation, which had now dropped off like a mask? Every now and then, on the other

> hand, a return of the old enthusiasm would be experienced. She would begin a story and confide to me that she was rather enjoying the thrill of writing again. The following day she had torn it up, quite cheerfully, and with a grimace of humour. Premature delivery![64]

Ouspensky, too, was touched 'by the striving in her to make the best use of even of these last days, to find the truth whose presence she clearly felt but which she was unable to touch'.[65] Mansfield told him,

> I know that this is true and that there is no other truth. You know that I have long since looked upon all of us without exception as people who have suffered shipwreck and have been cast upon an uninhabited island, but who do not yet know of it. But these people here know it. The others, there, in life, still think that a steamer will come for them tomorrow and that everything will go on in the old way. These already know that there will be no more of the old way. I am so glad that I can be here.[66]

Initially, although they corresponded, Mansfield had told Murry they should remain apart until at least Easter 1923, stating, 'I cannot see you until the old Wig has disappeared.'[67] But she clearly had a change of heart, writing to him on New Year's Eve, inviting him to come to Fontainebleau to see her on 9 January 1923, and to stay for a few days. Perhaps she had a foreboding feeling of how close she was to dying. The day before, two of the residents, Jessmin Howarth and her daughter, Dushka, helped her to get her room ready:

> We [. . .] had opportunities to talk with Katherine Mansfield who would sit on the stairs in her red jacket, and with wonder and laughter, go over some of the esoteric conversation that had taken place at [. . .] table. We were glad that we had gone into her room and had given it a 'spring cleaning' before her husband was to arrive from England. She died the next day.[68]

A handwritten note by another Gurdjieff disciple describes Mansfield's last few hours:

> Katherine Mansfield sat in the study-house for over an hour listening to the music, looking happier than I had ever remembered, holding her husband's hand. It was unusual for her to stay up so late, she was especially anxious to have J.M.M. hear the music which she enjoyed so much. We all felt she had used too much energy, was too excited and overtaxed her strength.[69]

On the evening of Murry's arrival, while excitedly climbing the wide wooden staircase up to her room accompanied by Murry, Mansfield suffered a massive lung haemorrhage and died. The morning after her death, on 10 January, Murry telegraphed Ida, who arrived late the same day, staying in Mansfield's room, her body by then having been transferred to a side chapel in the Protestant church in Fontainebleau. As she wrote the next day, 'I spent my day there, sorting and packing her things.'[70] That evening, guests who had arrived for the funeral dined at the Chalet de la Fôret. Afterwards, Ida wrote, 'I remember walking up and down the garden outside the hotel with Orage, up and down, up and down. I felt I wanted to stay with him, because of what he had been to Katherine.'[71]

The funeral took place in the afternoon of Friday, 12 January. Present at the funeral, in addition to Murry, were his brother Richard, his close friend H. M. Tomlinson, Ida and Brett, Mansfield's sisters Chaddie and Jeanne, and Jeanne's husband Charles Renshaw, together with a large cohort of mourners from the Institute itself, including, of course, Gurdjieff and his brother Dimitri, as well as Orage. The cortège was described thus: 'First the big hearse drawn by black horses sagely nodding their black plumes: then the attenuated crocodile of carriages and cars, twisting in and out of the narrow streets, winding by the longest route and the most grudging pace to the municipal cemetery.'[72] Mansfield was buried in the communal cemetery at Avon, near Fontainebleau, a few feet away from Gurdjieff's own eventual grave, and, in a strange twist of fate, next to the railway line carrying trains from Paris to the Mediterranean; how many times, unwittingly, Mansfield, comfortably sat in her train carriage and eagerly staring out at the French landscape, had sped past the graveyard where she would ultimately be laid to rest. That evening there was a huge feast in the Study House, followed by the sacred dancing and music – a fittingly exotic and spiritual end to Mansfield's brief life.

Brett's copy of the first edition of the *Journal of Katherine Mansfield* from 1927, edited by Murry, contains further fascinating information on Mansfield's last hours. On the last page, Murry provides a half-page description, briefly explaining Mansfield's reasons for going to Fontainebleau, and his visit there on 9 January. His published text ends with the words, 'As she came up the stairs to her room at 10 p.m. she was seized by a fit of coughing which culminated in a violent haemorrhage. At 10.30 p.m. she was dead.'[73] In the space below, in pencil, Brett gives her own description of what transpired that fateful night (presumably from asking those present), and also afterwards at the funeral – when she herself was present:

> K. coughed – the haemorrhage came on, she stood up & cried in a low deep voice slowly – 'I am dying, I am dying –' M. went downstairs for the Doctor – a Russian – he came up & did not know what to do – then the English doctor arrived & immediately sent for ice – M. was sent out of the room – and forgotten – alas – K. M. while still conscious kept darting anxious agonized looks at the door waiting, hoping for M. to return – he never did return, & she lost consciousness & died without seeing him again – she was soaked in blood – and was unhappy in her death.
>
> J. M. at her funeral was almost unconscious, he had to be held up by her sisters. He broke down completely on arriving home in England = When the shawl was taken off her coffin in the cold stark chapel I nearly screamed = the white wooden coffin – & K of all people shut up in it = I felt as if they were going to take the lid off & I couldn't bear it = An old priest with snow white hair preached = it was four oclock & cold = when I returned to Paris I took out the shawl K. had left me – there was straw in it from the stable where she used to sit at Fontainbleau – I felt her near me, cherishing me & telling me to have courage & 'go on' = It was as if she were in the room with me & her scent clung to the shawl.[74]

Many years later, in a letter, Murry confirmed some of the details in the above note: 'I was not actually in the room when Katherine died, I was outside in the corridor while two doctors – one my friend, Dr James Carruthers Young, – were trying to control the appalling violent haemorrhage.'[75] After her death, Tchekhovitch recorded that 'Her absence left a great emptiness, which was felt by us all. For a long time

I was haunted by the image of her face, especially her radiant expression as she sat, in perfect stillness, watching us practise the sacred dances.'[76]

Mansfield was happy at Fontainebleau: that much is clear from her letters, notebooks and the testimonials of many of the other inhabitants of the Prieuré. After her death, she was assigned, as Moore states, 'the sheepish role of wronged woman to Gurdjieff's predatory male'.[77] From all we know of Mansfield and her determined personality, together with the above recollections, this scenario is impossible to countenance. In fact, the precious few weeks Mansfield spent in Fontainebleau-Avon from October 1922 to January 1923 brought her back into the life of the living, from a place of wretched illness and desolation. Separated from Murry and the complications of their married life, her one final, courageous act was to find her tribe. In the company mostly of complete strangers, she now felt able to assess her old life, to renew herself and to prepare for her future, whatever that might comprise. Sadly, but inevitably, that future ended in her untimely death.

Mansfield's grave at the Avon cemetery near Fontainebleau, with G. I. Gurdjieff's at back right (two standing stones).

8

Afterlife

The probate record following Mansfield's death read as follows:

> MURRY Kathleen Mansfield of the Priory Fontainebleau near Paris France (wife of John Middleton Murry) died 9 January 1923
>
> Probate London 5 April to the said John Middleton Murry journalist. Effects £266 *6s. 4d.*[1]

This was not a huge sum, but as Mansfield's posthumous reputation increased, and sales of her books grew (in no small part due to Murry's own editorial endeavours), the royalties from her literary estate would leave Murry and his heirs comfortably off.

After Mansfield's death, many people who had known her were swift to condemn the Gurdjieff Institute and its adherents (some even while she was still there). For example, Vivienne Eliot wrote to Ezra Pound in Paris in reply to his request to know the whereabouts of Lady Rothermere, 'She is now in that asylum for the insane known as La Prieuré where she does religious dances naked with Katherine Mansfield.'[2] Lawrence's judgement on the affair sums up the general view of the literary establishment at that time: 'I have heard enough about that place at Fontainebleau where Katherine Mansfield died, to know it is a rotten, false, self-conscious place of people playing a sickly stunt.'[3] Beatrice Hastings called it that 'factory of magic at Fontainebleau'.[4] Mansfield's early biographers and critics were mystified by her decision; Ian Gordon, for example, claims that '[t]he final scenes of faith-healing under the guidance of a crazy Russian [...] can hardly be the basis of a fair judgement either of her real quality or of her view of life.'[5]

An intriguing footnote to Mansfield's connection with Gurdjieff concerns her old German teacher, Walter Rippmann. John Wood notes that Rippmann's second son, Hugh (1909–1980), who, following his father's lead, changed his name to the less Germanic 'Ripman', became a pupil of Ouspensky in 1933, and subsequently went on to study directly with Gurdjieff in 1948. He founded a group of Gurdjieff disciples in Washington, DC, and led them until his death in 1980. He would have been well aware of his father's connection to the famous author Katherine Mansfield and may have become fascinated by her spiritual journey at the end of her life.

On 24 February 1948 Charles Renshaw, husband of Mansfield's sister Jeanne, who had been present at the funeral alongside his wife, wrote the following account in order to correct the many falsehoods surrounding Mansfield's burial, as he perceived them, and in particular those by the French author Roland Merlin in his morbidly sentimental and sensational article 'Le Drame de Katherine Mansfield', which appeared in the magazine *France-Illustration* on 19 January 1946. Here is Renshaw's account:

> In May, 1926, KM's father, Sir Harold Beauchamp, of Wellington, New Zealand came to England to visit his two daughters, Chaddie Pickthall and Jeanne Renshaw (my wife). Following a short stay in London he decided to travel to France for the express purpose of seeing his son Leslie's grave in Flanders and KM.'s grave at Fontainebleau-Avon.
>
> Sir Harold was not away very long, & on his return to England came to stay with us at our country home in Hampshire.
>
> I could see that he had something which was weighing on his mind and one day he told me why.
>
> He was mortified at his discovery that KM had been buried in what he called the 'Common Ground' – an area which was likely to be dug up and used again as a burial ground when the cemetery became overcrowded.
>
> As far as Sir Harold knew, no provision had been made by Middleton-Murry with the Local Authorities to rectify this contingency. (It is possible, of course, that Murry never realized this position, otherwise I feel sure he would have taken the necessary steps to put this matter right.)

> Sooner than approach Murry, KM's father asked me if I would undertake arrangements with the Local Authorities at Fontainebleau to purchase a plot of ground for perpetuity in an adjoining section of the Avon Cemetery and furthermore undertake the somewhat grim commission for the exhumation and transfer.
>
> This request most certainly did not appeal to me, but I felt that it was a request which, under the distressing circumstances, was quite impossible for me to turn down, particularly as I had the greatest respect and affection for my father-in-law. [...]
>
> I cannot recall the exact date that I went over to Avon, but it must have been during the latter part of August, 1926.
>
> [...]
>
> Having broken the back of the business, I was informed that the necessary formalities would take some time – so I decided to visit Switzerland to await developments.
>
> I was away some ten days or so and was then informed that the formalities had been completed, the required permits obtained, title deeds ready to be signed & sealed & all was in readiness for the exhumation and transfer of KM's remains to the new grave. I returned to Fontainebleau forthwith.
>
> Proceeding to the Avon Cemetery, it was obvious that the work of exhumation had been completed and all that remained to be done was to recover over the coffin which was resting on a temporary platform just below the surface of the existing grave.
>
> I was not present at the time of the actual exhumation; this was perhaps unfortunate as I might have been in a position to confirm or otherwise M. Bontemp's statement reported in L'Illustration.
>
> M. Bontemps and his wife did, however, explain at great length & with the normal excitement, characteristic of the French, that from all appearances KM's features, after several years, appeared intact and in no way decomposed.[6]

The statement alluded to by Renshaw above concerns M. Bontemp's description of Mansfield's corpse on the day the coffin was exhumed and then reburied, which featured in Merlin's article:

> The coffin, quite deeply buried, had sagged slightly under the weight of the earth. Restoration was essential. I removed the split lid and replaced it with a new one. How can I describe my astonishment! Death had left Katherine Mansfield looking as she had six years earlier. The face bore no trace of decay, the body seemed untouched. Literally, she was at rest. [. . .] I ran to my wife to tell her of my discovery and to take her as witness: 'You must raise the lid so that Katherine "can be comfortable"', my wife advised. The work completed, I had Katherine Mansfield buried in the part of the cemetery where she belonged: close to a field that in spring blooms with daisies, in summer with heather here and there, and facing the forest.[7]

If only M. Bontemps had taken a photo of Mansfield's miraculously preserved body, we should have concrete evidence of his assertions, but alas it seems he did not. But three years is not so long, and if the lead lining had been solid enough, Mansfield's remains may well have been in a state of considerable preservation. Strangely, the *mairie* in Avon possesses a document, dated 9 June 1927, confirming the purchase, in perpetuity, of Mansfield's grave plot by Murry himself, and the subsequent burial of the body. It seems that Charles Renshaw was slightly mistaken in his dates, and that in the end, to save Murry's embarrassment, Murry's name was recorded on the official forms.

In 1947 a researcher working on Mansfield's time in Fontainebleau spoke with two sisters, Irene and Gisèle Marie, who had known Gurdjieff and often dined with him in Fontainebleau. Following a conversation with them, he wrote, 'The Marie sisters think it quite possible that he [Gurdjieff] may have paid for K. M's burial.'[8] This may go some way to explaining how Mansfield's remains were not immediately buried in the perpetual section of the graveyard, and why there is no name on the receipt from the undertakers. Indeed, the Gurdjieff brothers, leading the Russian contingent at the funeral, offered casual passers-by, in accordance with Russian pagan custom, horn-shaped paper bags containing *koutia*, a mixture of grains of corn and dried raisins, to throw into the grave.[9]

Another resident of Avon who apparently got to know Mansfield during her time at the Prieuré was a M. Clément Ballen de Guzman (1888–1968). Born in the same year as Mansfield, descended from a prominent Spanish family, he was the son of the then-Consul General of Ecuador in France and was educated at the Collège Carnot in Fontainebleau. A gifted artist in many fields and a talented lecturer, he was active in the Friends of the Fontainebleau Forest Association for over fifty years. A fixture of local society, he knew most people in Fontainebleau-Avon at the time of Mansfield's residency at the Institute, including Gurdjieff, and by extension got to know Mansfield herself. Interviewed in the late 1940s, he was able to provide some fascinating information.

Guzman first met Mansfield 'in connection with a plan for a hostel of some kind, to welcome Australian and New Zealand visitors in France. The Hostel was never founded, owing [. . .] to K. M.'s untimely death'. His impressions of her were as follows:

> K. M. had a very great charm, she was rather under the average size, pretty with auburn hair and the fringe we all know from her portraits. Her large and rather sad eyes were unforgettable. But her attire was shabby, not to say poverty-stricken and quite devoid of any elegance.

Guzman admitted that though her charm was undeniable, he was never sexually attracted to her: 'even when apparently in good health, she gave the impression of someone seriously ill.' He remembered Mansfield's 'room, with the ceiling painted blue and star-adorned'. He believed that Gurdjieff took Mansfield on, knowing how desperately ill she was, because he felt sorry for her. However, he also felt that the manual labour and general harsh treatment at the Institute 'hastened her end, which came very suddenly'. It seems that in conversations with Mansfield, she never once spoke of Murry. On the night of her haemorrhage, according to Guzman, 'I enquired whether, towards the end, she expressed a wish to see a clergyman (there is a Protestant Pastor at Fontainebleau), but apparently she was thoroughly irreligious.' Guzman said he used to see Mansfield at the local Café Henri II with the Gurdjieffs, although this establishment no longer exists. When the interview was conducted with Guzman in the late 1940s, he noted that as for her tomb, 'the upkeep is provided for by her friends; those who knew her and they are few, the many more who admire her.'[10]

In 1947, in reply to questions put to him, the then *pasteur* at the Protestant church in Fontainebleau, Henri Foulquier, wrote the following:

> I have learnt that after the death of K. M. at the Basses Loges, the management of the Priory, unwilling for the body to remain there, as happens usually in nursing homes and private hospitals, had the coffin removed to the church [...] to an adjoining room, which has since become the Sacristy, until the burial could take place at the Avon Cemetery.
>
> [...] When I arrived here in 42, I found the grave in a somewhat uncared for state and attempted, without success, to obtain information about K. M.'s end. The caretaker of the cemetery has described the circumstances of the exhumation, the state of conservation of the body etc in No 16 of France Illustration, of 19.1.46.[11]

So much misinformation has been spread regarding Mansfield's final resting place, including the number of times she was moved within the cemetery itself. Even very recent biographies seem to peddle the same false facts that her bones were more or less emptied into a pit containing other 'paupers', making it impossible to distinguish hers from any number of other bones, and that the current grave does not contain any remnants of Mansfield at all.

The facts indicate otherwise. Mansfield was simply buried in January 1923, in a grave plot that was not deemed 'perpetual'. That was all. It is likely that the funeral costs and the actual burial were paid for by Gurdjieff himself, Murry, apparently, too distraught to undertake such practical tasks. Following Harold Beauchamp's visit to his daughter's grave site in 1926 and being informed by the cemetery supervisor that the plot was not a perpetual one, he determined to make good this error and instructed his son-in-law Charles Renshaw to undertake the necessary work. No one bothered consulting Murry, for the simple reason that he himself seemed oblivious and possibly uninterested in the remains of his deceased wife, having now married again. Thus it was that Mansfield's white coffin was dug up – the same white coffin she had been buried in – and moved to the permanent site in the graveyard where she now lies buried.

What of Orage? He died in London on 6 November 1934, aged 61. Inscribed on his gravestone at St John-at-Hampstead churchyard are the following words from the Bhagavad Gita, which encapsulate some of his long-standing esoteric principles:

Thou grievest for those that should not be grieved for
The wise grieve neither for the living nor for the dead
Never at any time was I not nor thou nor these princes of men
Nor shall we ever cease to be hereafter
The unreal has no being
The real never ceases to be

The inscription on the original flat footstone of Mansfield's grave reads, 'Katherine Mansfield/ Wife of John Middleton Murry/ 1888–1923', followed by the Shakespeare quotation 'Out of this nettle, danger, we pluck this flower, safety,' from *Henry IV, Part 1* (II.3). As Wood notes,

> The inscription bears an uncanny resemblance to that proposed for his wife by Theobald Pontifex, the philistine vicar and father in Samuel Butler's *The Way of All Flesh*: 'I should give her name, the dates of her birth and death, and of course say she was my wife, and then I think I should wind up with a simple text – her favourite one for example.' To which the narrator responds: 'I said I thought this would be very nice, and it was settled.'[12]

In Chapter Four, we also discussed the possibility that the above Shakespeare quotation derives from Mansfield's story 'This Flower', which provides details of Mansfield and Murry's aborted child from 1912. As for Gurdjieff himself, eventually buried close to Mansfield in the graveyard at Avon, it would seem he never forgot his celebrated disciple. On 26 August 1949, in conversation with him just a few months before his death, Elizabeth Bennett recorded,

> When Mr G[urdjieff] was talking tonight about Katherine Mansfield, Mme de S[alzmann] told him that they have put up a plaque in her memory on the Prieuré wall, 'but not yet to M. Gurdjieff'. [...] There was one unexpected moment [during the toasts to the idiots, a ritual of sorts at Gurdjieff's table]. At Hopeless Idiots, Cathleen's was the only toast, and when I drank her health, Mr G. pricked his ears and said, 'Who? Where?' Mme de S. pointed to Cathleen and he said, 'Oh. I thought you said Katherine Mansfield. She my friend. But she die. So I astonished what you repeat that name. She my good friend.'[13]

In the aftermath of Mansfield's death, Lea records that 'during the second week of April Murry went over [to Fontainebleau-Avon] to consult with Orage, who was still at the Gurdjieff Institute.'[14] As Wood notes,

> Quite what Murry discussed with Orage is unclear. It may have been to discuss, following the grant of probate to Katherine's estate, his plans for marketing Katherine's unpublished work. It may have been to return Orage's letters to Katherine and to seek some agreement from Orage to suppress his extended relationship with Katherine, for the sake of her posthumous reputation. Murry subsequently suggested that Orage had proposed that he should take over the *New Age* from him. This seems unlikely as by then the *New Age* had been sold. In the event Murry, funded with money and royalties from Katherine's estate, started the *Adelphi*.[15]

Whatever the reason, it is clear that there was no love lost between the two men. It was under Orage's influence that Mansfield had gone to Fontainebleau-Avon and in whose company she had spent the last three months of her life. Murry, who clearly saw Orage as a rival, both personally and professionally, now did his best to write Orage out of the hagiographical narrative he immediately started to create around his dead wife, and Orage was too much of a gentleman to correct the facts for the sake of posterity. In addition, as Wood notes, 'Orage was remarkably reticent about his own life. Apart from his published writing, he left nothing by way of a personal memoir and he regularly destroyed his personal papers.'[16] After Orage's death in 1934, Murry did finally admit, 'I should have to say, in merest candor, that he, far more than many other men whom I knew far better, was an influence in my life; a queer kind of negative influence, no doubt, for I was always resisting Orage, but a very real one.'[17] Nevertheless, as Wood reveals, it was not just Mansfield's personal relationship with Orage that Murry sought to expunge. Her association with the *New Age* was also played down as far as possible:

> In 1931, Ruth Mantz published a bibliography of Katherine's work, which, Murry records in an introductory note, he had read in manuscript. In the foreword Mantz explains that with regard to each collected edition of Katherine's work, the 'date

> and place of first publication' of each story is also given. The stories which were included in Katherine's first book, *In a German Pension*, were correctly recorded as having been first published in the *New Age* in 1910. However, the first publication of those stories which appeared in the *New Age* in 1917 and which were subsequently included in Katherine's second collection, *Bliss and Other Stories* – 'A Dill Pickle' and 'Mr Reginald Peacock's Day' – were not attributed to the *New Age*. Likewise, in recording the publication of 'The Black Cap' as part of an anthology called *The New Keepsake for the Year 1921*, Mantz states that the story 'had never previously been printed'. It had, in fact, appeared in the *New Age* in May 1917. When *Something Childish and Other Stories*, Katherine's fourth collection, was published posthumously by Murry in 1924, it included two stories published in the *New Age* in 1910 – 'The Journey to Bruges' and 'A Truthful Adventure', first publication of which is acknowledged, and also 'Two Tuppenny Ones, Please', 'Late at Night' and 'The Black Cap', all of which were published in the *New Age* in May 1917, but where first publication is not acknowledged. In the 'Introduction' to the first version he published of her *Journal* in 1927, Murry wrote that after the demise of the *Signature*, 'Katherine Mansfield had nowhere to write, until I became editor of *The Athenaeum* in 1919. In the four years between 1915 and 1919, three stories of hers were published by English periodicals, all in 1918.' This was patently untrue.[18]

Stephen Gray also notes that in her bibliography, Mantz 'omitted any piece written anonymously by KM or in collaboration with BH, even when it had appeared initialled by them. Only Alpers in 1980 was to restore these to the reading list after half a century.'[19] It is impossible that Murry would not have known about these publications. The London literary world in the 1910s was a close-knit, incestuous one, and even if Mansfield herself had hidden her appearances in the *New Age*, they would have been noted by countless others, thus offering further evidence for Murry's deliberate erasure of Orage from Mansfield's life.

It is also clear to any biographer that Murry destroyed some of the records (as we know he did with the damning affidavit from 1917). The amount of roughly cut-out pages from any number of Mansfield's notebooks is proof enough. As Wood notes,

> Antony Alpers several times remarked that though he had collated the *Journal* with the *Letters*, he could not find material covering certain periods. Yet these were the three most vital periods of decision for Mansfield: when she frequented Garsington in 1917 and returned to Orage for counsel and to his *New Age* for publication; when she co-edited the *Athenaeum* at Hampstead in 1919; and when she returned to England for the last time in 1922, making her final decisions as to where she was going as a woman and a writer. These were periods that Murry ignored, for she had left him in 1917; she 'ghost-edited' for him in 1919; and she again – and finally – gave Murry up in 1922.[20]

Orage was in New York for ten years following Mansfield's death, leaving Murry to his own devices where Mansfield's memory was concerned; it was also during this time that Orage met and married Jessie Dwight. 'From then on,' Wood records, 'Orage himself had a personal reason for suppressing his relationship with Katherine.'[21] It's also no coincidence that Murry waited until 1936 (that is, *after* Orage's death in 1934) to publish his autobiography, *Between Two Worlds*, which ends with Mansfield's death in 1923:

> The review of the autobiography in *Time* magazine noted the omission of any record of Orage's relationship with Katherine. Murry, the 'most derided, most vilified man of letters in contemporary England,' completely fails, said the review, to mention Orage, one person who 'loomed large in Katherine Mansfield's life.'[22]

Orage's own personal response to the death of Mansfield was his essay *On Love, Freely Adapted from the Tibetan*, first published in the *New Republic* in New York in December 1924, and subsequently as a 24-page booklet by the Unicorn Press in 1932. It was in this essay that, according to Wood, 'Orage worked out his response to Katherine's death following a late-night conversation with Gurdjieff. Although subtitled "From the Tibetan," it is generally accepted as being by Orage alone.'[23] In the essay, Orage distinguishes between three types of love: instinctive love, emotional love and conscious love, with a focus on the purest and most divine of the three – conscious love:

The conscious love motive, in its developed state, is the wish that the object should arrive at its own native perfection, regardless of the consequences to the lover. 'So she become perfectly herself, what matter I?' says the conscious lover. 'I will go to hell if only she may go to heaven'. And the paradox of the attitude is that such love always evokes a similar attitude in its object. Conscious love begets conscious love. It is rare among humans because, in the first place, the vast majority are children who look to be loved but not to love; secondly, because perfection is seldom conceived as the proper end of human love – though it alone distinguishes adult human from infantile and animal love; thirdly, because humans do not know, even if they wish, what is good for those they love; and fourthly, because it never occurs by chance, but must be the subject of resolve, effort, self-conscious choice.

[. . .]

Meanwhile to study – what she is, and may become; what she needs, what her soul craves and cannot find a name, still less a thing, for. To anticipate today her needs of tomorrow. And without a thought all the while of what her needs may mean to me. You will see, sons and daughters, what self-discipline and self-education are demanded here. Enter these enchanted woods, ye who dare. The gods love each other consciously. Conscious lovers become gods.[24]

This was Orage's covert yet heartfelt declaration of what Mansfield had meant to him.

There is a good deal of evidence elsewhere to confirm Orage's deep feelings for Mansfield. When Frieda Lawrence died in 1956, she left extensive manuscripts recording her life and people she had known. These were collected and published posthumously. In one such manuscript, Frieda described a conversation with an unnamed man that took place at some point in 1932:

We sat in a corner after dinner, talking about Lawrence and Katherine, he coming out of himself, and I. Like old, old intimates, we both said nakedly much we had felt and not told before. [. . .] Next morning I thought, never can I meet this man again, we have come too close, he will want to retire into

> his reserve again. 'Your secrets are safe with me', I said to myself.[25]

Frieda's unnamed confidant that evening was Orage. They only met on this one occasion, and, according to Tomalin, 'while Frieda kept her word and said no more of what Orage had told her, her daughter, Barbara Barr, who overheard the conversation, subsequently disclosed to Tomalin that Orage had told Frieda that Katherine was "the only woman he had ever truly loved".'[26] However, Wood notes that Frieda was *not* the only person Orage told of his deep affection for Mansfield. Louise Welch, who in 1982 wrote about Orage's life in America, recounted an evening in a New York restaurant in the late 1920s: 'Sipping coffee until long after 3 am, Orage was in the mood that evening for the examination of his own past. He grew thoughtful. He spoke about his love affair with Katherine Mansfield as serious.'[27] Welch further recorded that Orage 'went so far to say that he preferred [Katherine] to Beatrice, but the latter, being more domineering and forceful had pushed Katherine aside. He now considered the episode a failure on his part.'[28]

Murry, who founded and became editor of the *Adelphi* in 1923, turned the journal into a hagiographical outpouring of unpublished Mansfield material, to the disgust of those who had known her. Lawrence, for example, was one of many who 'took Murry to task in his role of propagandist of Katherine Mansfield. [. . . He] had not shrunk from denouncing the whole policy and atmosphere of the *Adelphi* in this particular matter, which [. . .] he had found repugnant.'[29] Thus, generally unfavourable reviews of Murry's factory-like production of Mansfield volumes started the evolution of a dismissal of her work in general. As Jenny McDonnell notes, 'Sylvia Lynd described Murry's generation of a Mansfield industry as "boiling Katherine's bones to make soup", while Lawrence claimed he "made capital out of her death".'[30] Over time, Murry became progressively more disliked in English literary circles, scathingly caricatured, for example, as Denis Burlap in Aldous Huxley's novel *Point Counter Point* (1928).[31] The main reason for Murry's literary ostracization was precisely this over-exposure of his dead wife's work and his aim to publish as much of her literary remains as the public could stomach, while at the same time editing out any material that he felt did not correlate with the image of her he was trying to put across. This attitude was summed up by Katherine Anne Porter in 1937:

> The misplaced emphasis [. . .] [is perhaps owed] [. . .] to her literary executor [Murry], who has edited and published her letters and journals with a kind of merciless insistence, a professional anxiety for her fame on what seems to be the wrong grounds, and from which in any case his personal relation to her might have excused him for a time. Katherine Mansfield's work is the important fact about her, and she is in danger of the worst fate that an artist can suffer – to be overwhelmed by her own legend, to have her work neglected for an interest in her personality.[32]

A document purporting to be a 'biography' of Murry by Lawrence, under the pseudonym 'J. C.' (Jesus Christ), was privately printed in 1929.[33] This 'biography', entitled *The Life of J. Middleton Murry*, consists of one A4 sheet folded in half, with the title on the outside. Opening the page, one finds the following printed on the right-hand side:

> John Middleton was born in the year
> of the Lord 1891? It happened also
> to be the most lying year of the most
> lying century since time began, but what
> is that to an innocent babe![34]

Murry's new-found 'spirituality', together with the incessant promotion of his dead wife, was more than Lawrence and most of his literary friends and acquaintances could stomach, and they were determined to lampoon him for it. In spite of such criticism, however, Murry's editorial stance towards his first wife remained more or less the same until his death in 1957.

Someone who was happy to deliberately taint Mansfield's posthumous reputation before her own death in 1943 was Beatrice Hastings, even though Murry did his best to write her significance out of Mansfield's life as well. As Gray notes of Ruth Mantz's first approaches to Hastings when she had started writing her biography of Mansfield in the early 1930s, a project which was soon forcefully appropriated by Murry,

> Mantz had received a copy of the first *Straight-Thinker*, with a ratty note by Murry attached which reads: 'This from BH is

> horrible! Shows all that decay KM escaped!' But to Mantz Beatrice Hastings was as yet an unknown factor in KM's life, still objectively to be assessed. Now that she was in London collecting for a biography of Mansfield, would Hastings oblige with an interview?[35]

Beatrice obliged three times, noting how the boycott against her had been 'fairly effective', and suggesting that Mantz prepare some subject headings 'to see if I can help you clothe those dry bones?'[36] Gray acerbically notes how

> The 'dry bones' under discussion were of course the ones Katherine had instructed Murry not to boil. But Murry was relentless. Now Mantz's bibliography must be extended into *The Life of Katherine Mansfield*, which he would see to it was the sole authorized biography, concentrating essentially on the earlier life as the necessary companion volume to Katherine's own ones of letters and journals, as rejigged by him. When Mantz's work finally appeared from Constable in 1933, Murry had so controlled it on behalf of the estate that she had to put up with not only an introduction and a final chapter inserted by him, but his name on the title page as her co-author. As neither of them knew the first thing about life in New Zealand, that aspect of their joint effort is laughable. Murry could be recklessly censorious as well, because in Mantz's part of the text, after all those rounds of consultation, not one detail to do with any Beatrice Hastings is retained.[37]

In Frank Lea's 1959 biography of Murry, Hastings merits just one brief mention, referring to her letter asking for work on the *Athenaeum*, which, as we know, Murry turned down. Even Alpers dismissed Hastings in both his 1954 and 1980 biographies, omitting much of his research on her: 'For example, he leaves out the story that when Katherine Mansfield tried to seduce the hapless fifteen-year-old little Carl Bechhöfer, still in school, it was Beatrice who had had to mummy him through that shocking crisis.'[38]

Mantz eventually got her own back on Murry in her introduction to the catalogue for the Katherine Mansfield exhibition held at the Harry Ransom Humanities Research Center at Austin, Texas, in 1973, commemorating the fiftieth anniversary of Mansfield's death. Gray records how

> She explained how Jack Murry exerted a hold on her by persuading Stanford University to send her to England, via New Zealand, on a fellowship 'to finish editing the papers of KM'. With him the last of them all now dead, she was free to say that, from all her hard work, he had then produced KM's Journal, which was 'biographically inaccurate'. There was no trace in it 'of KM the mimic, the cynic, the mystic, the flirt who had to try her charm on every man'. In other words, the Beatrice side of her ended up deleted. Murry was not a professional censor for nothing.[39]

For Mantz, the collaboration with Murry was a frustrating and unhappy experience, and the rest of her life, until her death in 1979, was, to a large extent, taken up with the writing of numerous – unpublished – versions of her biography from 1933 as *she* would have written it, had he not taken it over.

Nevertheless, as Murry's star has waned, so Mansfield's star has risen. Her contribution to Modernist literature as an innovator of the short story is now widely recognized, and many of her stories are perceived as masterpieces of the genre. And finally, Mansfield's deep and long-standing relationship with her mentor, A. R. Orage, explored here in detail for the first time, thanks to the research of John Wood, has highlighted Orage's profound influence on both Mansfield's personal and professional life. As Beatrice Hastings so aptly noted, 'In a literary story, nothing can be hidden in the end; there is always a clue.'[40]

REFERENCES

Abbreviations

ATL Alexander Turnbull Library, Wellington, New Zealand

CL1 Claire Davison and Gerri Kimber, eds, *The Edinburgh Edition of the Collected Letters of Katherine Mansfield*, vol. I: *Letters to Correspondents A–J* (Edinburgh, 2020)

CL2 Claire Davison and Gerri Kimber, eds, *The Edinburgh Edition of the Collected Letters of Katherine Mansfield*, vol. II: *Letters to Correspondents K–Z* (Edinburgh, 2022)

CL3 Claire Davison and Gerri Kimber, eds, *The Edinburgh Edition of the Collected Letters of Katherine Mansfield*, vol. III: *Letters to John Middleton Murry, 1912–1918* (Edinburgh, 2023)

CL4 Claire Davison and Gerri Kimber, eds, *The Edinburgh Edition of the Collected Letters of Katherine Mansfield*, vol. IV: *Letters to John Middleton Murry, 1918–1923* (Edinburgh, 2025)

CP Gerri Kimber and Claire Davison, eds, *The Collected Poems of Katherine Mansfield* (Edinburgh, 2016)

CW1 Gerri Kimber and Vincent O'Sullivan, eds, *The Edinburgh Edition of the Collected Works of Katherine Mansfield*, vol. I: *The Collected Fiction, 1898–1915* (Edinburgh, 2012)

CW2 Gerri Kimber and Vincent O'Sullivan, eds, *The Edinburgh Edition of the Collected Works of Katherine Mansfield*, vol. II: *The Collected Fiction, 1916–1922* (Edinburgh, 2012)

CW3 Gerri Kimber and Angela Smith, eds, *The Edinburgh Edition of the Collected Works of Katherine Mansfield*, vol. III: *The Poetry and Critical Writings* (Edinburgh, 2014)

CW4 Gerri Kimber and Claire Davison, eds, *The Edinburgh Edition of the Collected Works of Katherine Mansfield*, vol. IV: *The Diaries of Katherine Mansfield, including Miscellaneous Works* (Edinburgh, 2016)

HRC Harry Ransom Humanities Research Center, The University of Texas at Austin

Introduction

1 Leonard Woolf and James Strachey, eds, *Virginia Woolf and Lytton Strachey: Letters* (London, 1956), pp. 60–61.

2 Anne Olivier Bell, ed., *The Diary of Virginia Woolf*, vol. I (London, 1977), p. 58.

3 CW4, p. 190.
4 Leonard Woolf, *The Autobiography of Leonard Woolf* (London, 1964), p. 204.
5 Anthea Trodd, *A Reader's Guide to Edwardian Literature* (London, 1991), p. 72.
6 Peter Childs, *Modernism* (London, 2002), p. 94.
7 A. R. Orage, 'Talks with Katherine Mansfield at Fontainebleau', *Century Magazine*, 87 (November 1924), pp. 36–40.
8 CW2, p. 401.
9 CL1, p. 344.
10 CL2, p. 340.
11 Ibid., pp. 324–5.
12 Frank Lea, *The Life of John Middleton Murry* (London, 1959), p. 113.
13 Jenny McDonnell, *Katherine Mansfield and the Modernist Marketplace: At the Mercy of the Public* (Basingstoke, 2010), p. 170.
14 Published by Edinburgh University Press, each one co-edited by me and other Mansfield scholars between 2010 and 2025, with all traces of Murry's editing finally excised and incorporating exciting new discoveries. For a detailed account of Mansfield's childhood, see Gerri Kimber, *Katherine Mansfield: The Early Years* (Edinburgh, 2016).

1 Childhood, 1888–1908

1 Terence Hodgson, *Colonial Capital: Wellington, 1865–1910* (Auckland, 1990), p. 11.
2 Sir Harold Beauchamp, *Reminiscences and Recollections* (New Plymouth, 1937), p. 82.
3 See Christine Dann, 'Sewage, Water and Waste', www.teara.govt.nz. See also Redmer Yska's account of infectious disease in Wellington at this time: *A Strange Beautiful Excitement: Katherine Mansfield's Wellington, 1888–1903* (Dunedin, 2017).
4 CW1, p. 3.
5 Ruth Elvish Mantz and John Middleton Murry, *The Life of Katherine Mansfield* (London, 1933), p. 137.
6 CW1, p. 6.
7 Kathleen M. Beauchamp, 'His Little Friend', *New Zealand Graphic and Ladies' Journal* (13 October 1900), pp. 710–11. See the introduction by Redmer Yska to 'Cousin Kate', the children's page editor of the *Graphic*, for a detailed account of Mansfield's youthful publication and letters to the paper, which he uncovered in 2015, in CL2, pp. 13–16.
8 This was not as modest as it sounds. Waterlow's was a major stationery and printing company, particularly for legal documentation, bank notes and stamps.
9 Vera Beauchamp, quoted in Antony Alpers, *The Life of Katherine Mansfield* (London, 1980), p. 27.
10 [Ida Baker], *Katherine Mansfield: The Memories of L. M.* (London, 1971), p. 19.
11 CW1, pp. 20–21.
12 Ibid., p. 21.
13 CL2, p. 429.

14 CW1, p. 59.
15 Ian Gordon, *Katherine Mansfield*, Writers and Their Work, no. 49 (London, 1954), p. 7.
16 Stephen Reynolds, 'Autobiografiction', *Speaker*, n.s. XV/366 (6 October 1906), pp. 28, 30.
17 Ibid., p. 28.
18 Max Saunders, *Self Impression: Life-Writing, Autobiografiction, and the Forms of Modern Literature* (Oxford, 2010), pp. 4, 5.
19 CL2, p. 155.
20 CW1, pp. 38–9.
21 Ibid., p. 40.
22 Ibid., p. 42.
23 Ibid., pp. 45 and 50.
24 Ibid.
25 Mantz and Murry, *Life*, p. 224.
26 CL1, p. 137.
27 CW4, pp. 47–8.
28 Ibid., p. 49.
29 Ibid., p. 51.
30 Ibid.
31 Ibid.
32 Ibid., pp. 51–2.
33 Baker, *Memories of L. M.*, p. 34.
34 CL1, p. 337.
35 Cited in Gerri Kimber, *Katherine Mansfield: The Early Years* (Edinburgh, 2016), p. 212.
36 CW1, pp. 78–84.
37 Ibid., p. 84.
38 Ibid., p. 87.
39 CW4, p. 78.
40 CL2, p. 469.
41 Anon., 'Personal Items', *New Zealand Herald*, XLV/13722 (11 April 1908), p. 8.
42 Beauchamp, *Reminiscences*, p. 90.
43 Anon., 'Social Gossip', *Free Lance*, VIII/417 (4 July 1908), p. 8.
44 Ruth Elvish Mantz, ed., *Katherine Mansfield: An Exhibition* (Austin, TX, 1975), p. 6.
45 HRC: Ruth Elvish Mantz Collection, Box 3. 'Unidentified research notes'.

2 London and Europe, 1908–9

1 ATL, MS-Papers-3981-141. Maude Morris, miscellaneous papers.
2 C. K. Stead, 'Men and Mansfield in *Mansfield*', in *Book Self: The Reader as Writer and the Writer as Critic*, ed. C. K. Stead (Auckland, 2008), p. 145.
3 See '"Notes re K. M." by Margaret Wishart (m. Woodhouse)', in *Katherine Mansfield and London*, ed. Aimée Gasston and Gerri Kimber (Edinburgh, 2024), pp. 153–64; Moira Taylor and Charles Woodhouse, 'Katherine Mansfield and Margaret Wishart in London during the Years 1908–09 and Beyond: Intimacy and Separation, Reconciliation and Forgiveness', in *Mansfield and London*, ed. Gasston and Kimber, pp. 61–84.

4 Wishart, 'Notes re K. M.', p. 154.
5 Ibid.
6 Ibid., pp. 156–7.
7 Ibid., p. 155.
8 Ibid., p. 156.
9 CW1, p. 525.
10 For a detailed account of the relationship between Mansfield and Bowden, see Gerri Kimber, '"An Intellectual Comradeship": A Reassessment of the Relationship Between George Bowden and Katherine Mansfield', in *Katherine Mansfield: New Directions*, ed. Aimée Gasston, Gerri Kimber and Janet Wilson (London, 2020), pp. 172–88.
11 Cited in Katherine Mansfield's will. ATL, John Middleton Murry Collection, MS-Papers-7224-06.
12 George Bowden, 'A Biographical Note on Katherine Mansfield', HRC, Katherine Mansfield Collection, container 2.6.
13 Ibid., p. 1.
14 Ibid., p. 3.
15 George Bowden to Lucy O'Brien, 21 November 1947. HRC, Katherine Mansfield collection, container 2.7.
16 Bowden, 'Biographical Note', p. 2.
17 Ibid., pp. 3–5.
18 [Ida Baker], *Katherine Mansfield: The Memories of L. M.* (London, 1971), pp. 45–6.
19 Bowden, 'Biographical Note', p. 6.
20 Ibid., p. 6.
21 Ibid., p. 10.
22 Ibid., pp. 10–11.
23 Ibid., p. 11. See the poem 'Loneliness', in CP, pp. 73–4.
24 Bowden, 'Biographical Note', p. 11.
25 Ibid., p. 12.
26 George Bowden to Lucy O'Brien, 21 November 1947. HRC, Katherine Mansfield collection, container 2.7.
27 Ibid.
28 CW1, pp. 538–44.
29 Antony Alpers, *The Life of Katherine Mansfield* (London, 1980), p. 89.
30 Ibid., p. 90.
31 CW1, p. 543.
32 Ibid.
33 Ibid., pp. 543–4.
34 Ibid., p. 544.
35 Baker, *Memories of L.M.*, p. 48.
36 Ibid., p. 47.
37 Jeffrey Meyers, *Katherine Mansfield: A Biography* (London, 1978), pp. 43–4.
38 CW4, p. 108.
39 Baker, *Memories of L. M.*, p. 48.
40 Bowden, 'Biographical Note', p. 12.
41 Taylor and Woodhouse, 'Mansfield and Wishart', p. 62.
42 CL2, pp. 683–4.
43 CW4, p. 298.

44 CL1, p. 186.
45 The name reappears in the story 'The Stranger', based on an incident in her parents' lives. See CW2, pp. 240–50.
46 ATL, qMS-0146.
47 Tom L. Mills, 'Katherine Mansfield: How Kathleen Beauchamp Came Into Her Own', *New Zealand Railways Magazine*, VIII/5 (1 September 1933), p. 7.
48 Ruth Elvish Mantz and John Middleton Murry, *The Life of Katherine Mansfield* (London, 1933), p. 322.
49 Ibid., p. 323.
50 Baker, *Memories of L. M.*, p. 52.
51 See Gerri Kimber, '"Always Trembling on the Brink of Poetry": Katherine Mansfield, Poet', *Modernist Women Poets: Generations, Geographies and Genders*, Special Issue of *Humanities*, VIII/4 (2009), www.mdpi.com.
52 CW1, p. 215.
53 Ibid., p. 218.
54 Ibid., p. 217.
55 Ibid., p. 219.
56 Martin Elste, *The High Priestess of the Harpsichord: Wanda Landowska and Early Music*. Catalogue for the temporary exhibition at the Berlin Musikinstrumenten-museum (13 November 2009 to 28 February 2010), trans. Oliver Dahin, SIMPK (Berlin, 2009).
57 Patricia Juliana Smith, 'Landowska, Wanda (1879–1959)', *GLBTQ Encyclopedia*, www.glbtqarchive.com.
58 Wanda Landowska, *Musique ancienne* (Paris, 1909).
59 Smith, 'Landowska, Wanda'.
60 Ibid.
61 Ibid.
62 Mantz and Murry, *Life*, p. 325.
63 CL1, pp. 259–60.
64 Alpers, *Life*, p. 101.

3 The *New Age*, 1910–11

1 ATL, letters relating to Katherine Mansfield collected by George Bowden, MS-Papers-3886.
2 Ibid. All translations from the German by Max Oettli.
3 Ibid.
4 Ibid.
5 Ibid.
6 John Wood, unpublished research notes, no page numbers.
7 ATL, MS-Papers-3886.
8 HRC, Ruth Elvish Mantz collection, 'Swing on the Garsington Gate', miscellaneous box.
9 Ibid.
10 ATL, MS-Papers-3886.
11 George Bowden, 'A Biographical Note on Katherine Mansfield', HRC, Katherine Mansfield Collection, container 2.6, p. 12.
12 Wood, unpublished notes.
13 Kathleen Jones, *Katherine Mansfield: The Storyteller* (Edinburgh, 2010), p. 125.

14 Bowden, 'Biographical Note', p. 13.
15 HRC, Katherine Mansfield Collection, container 2.6.
16 HRC, 'Swing on the Garsington Gate'.
17 Ibid.
18 Louise Welch, *Orage with Gurdjieff in America* (Boston, MA, 1982), p. 63.
19 Chris Mourant, *Katherine Mansfield and Periodical Culture* (Edinburgh, 2019), p. 92.
20 Welch, *Orage with Gurdjieff*, p. 15.
21 Philip Mairet, *A. R. Orage: A Memoir* (London, 1936), pp. 46–7.
22 Beatrice Hastings, *The Old 'New Age': Orage and Others* (London, 1936), pp. 3, 6.
23 John Carswell, *Lives and Letters: A. R. Orage, Beatrice Hastings, Katherine Mansfield, John Middleton Murry, S. S. Koteliansky: 1906–1957* (New York, 1978), p. 58.
24 Wood, unpublished notes. See CW4, p. 363.
25 Stephen Gray, *Beatrice Hastings: A Literary Life* (London, 2004), p. 191.
26 Quoted in CL2, p. 673.
27 William Orton, *The Last Romantic* (New York, 1937).
28 [Ida Baker], *Katherine Mansfield: The Memories of L.M.* (London, 1971), p. 61.
29 Antony Alpers, *The Life of Katherine Mansfield* (London, 1980), p. 117.
30 Letter from Shirley Weber to Margaret Scott, 22 June 1977. ATL, MS-Papers-9733-029.
31 Wood, unpublished notes.
32 Orton, *Last Romantic*, p. 275.
33 Ibid., pp. 282–3.
34 Ibid., p. 270.
35 Alpers, *Life*, p. 118.
36 Ibid., p. 119.
37 CL3, p. 109.
38 J. Lawrence Mitchell, 'Katherine Mansfield and the Aesthetic Object', *Journal of New Zealand Literature*, 22 (2004), p. 48.
39 Guy Morris, 'In Memory of . . . Katherine Mansfield', *New Zealand Railways Magazine*, XIII/7 (1 October 1938), p. 27; DVW2, p. 226.
40 Mitchell, 'Aesthetic Object', p. 50.
41 Amanda Herries, *Japanese Gardens in Britain* (Princes Risborough, 2001), p. 21.
42 Everett F. Bleiler, ed., *The Book of Tea by Kakuzo Okakura* (New York, 2010), p. xvii.
43 Arnold Bennett, *New Age*, VIII/6 (8 December 1910), p. 135.
44 *Morning Post* editorial, quoted in Angela Smith, *Katherine Mansfield: A Literary Life* (Basingstoke, 2000), p. 77.
45 CL1, p. 420.
46 CL2, p. 148.
47 CW3, p. 385.
48 Baker, *Memories of L. M.*, p. 62.
49 Alpers, *Life*, p. 123.
50 Ibid., p. 139n.
51 Ibid., p. 123.

52 Ibid.
53 Wood, unpublished notes.
54 Baker, *Memories of L. M.*, p. 63.
55 Ibid., p. 65.
56 For details of all the census information below, see Gerri Kimber, 'Katherine Mansfield and the Public Census of 1911', https://katherinemansfieldsociety.org, accessed 30 July 2023.
57 See J. Lawrence Mitchell, '"Not the Kind to Die": Katherine Mansfield and the Unquiet Ghost of "Little Brother"', in *Katherine Mansfield and Virginia Woolf*, ed. Christine Froula, Gerri Kimber and Todd Martin (Edinburgh, 2018), pp. 179–96.
58 Baker, *Memories of L. M.*, p. 65.
59 Hastings, *Old 'New Age'*, p. 10.
60 Welch, *Orage with Gurdjieff*, p. 63.
61 Orton, *Last Romantic*, p. 281.
62 CW4, pp. 120–21.
63 Baker, *Memories of L. M.*, p. 62.
64 Wood, unpublished notes.
65 Claire Tomalin, *Katherine Mansfield: A Secret Life* (London, 1987), p. 92.
66 Quoted ibid. Unpublished letter, Murry to Ida Baker, 29 May 1933: 'Murry places the reading and burning of the letters at Runcton Cottage, in the late summer of 1912', p. 249, n. 10.
67 Wood, unpublished notes.
68 Ibid.
69 Cited in James Laver, *Museum Piece or the Education of an Iconographer* (London, 1963), p. 118.
70 CL2, p. 502.
71 Mantz interview, quoted by Gray, *Beatrice Hastings*, p. 543.
72 CP, p. 100.
73 Baker, *Memories of L. M.*, p. 68.
74 Wood, unpublished notes.
75 Ibid.
76 Ibid.
77 '"Notes re K. M." by Margaret Wishart (m. Woodhouse)', in *Katherine Mansfield and London*, ed. Aimée Gasston and Gerri Kimber (Edinburgh, 2024), pp. 153–64 (p. 158).
78 Hastings, *Old 'New Age'*, p. 19.
79 See also Cynthia Crosse, 'Two Anzacs Meet in London', *Katherine Mansfield Society Newsletter*, 31 (December 2018), pp. 20–23.
80 Ibid., p. 20.
81 Ibid., p. 21.
82 Philip Hoare, *Oscar Wilde's Last Stand: Decadence, Conspiracy, and the Most Outrageous Trial of the Century* (New York, 1997), p. 34.
83 Wood, unpublished notes.
84 Letter from Rebecca West to Jeffrey Meyers, 4 February 1977, quoted in Jeffrey Meyers, *Katherine Mansfield: A Biography* (London, 1978), p. 37.
85 Wood, unpublished notes.
86 C. A. Hankin, ed., *The Letters of John Middleton Murry to Katherine Mansfield* (London, 1983), p. 53.

87 Laver, *Museum Piece*, p. 118.
88 Ibid., p. 118.
89 'Bernard Page: Two Songs', Radio New Zealand, 12 February 2021, www.rnz.co.nz.
90 Robert Sullivan, 'Bechhöfer (Roberts), Carl Erich (1894–1949)', https://modjourn.org, accessed 16 August 2024.
91 Paul Selver, *Orage and the New Age Circle* (London, 1959), pp. 29–30.
92 Sullivan, 'Bechhöfer'.
93 Ibid.
94 Gray, *Beatrice Hastings*, p. 206.
95 Ibid., p. 207.
96 Ibid., p. 218.
97 Ibid., p. 650.
98 Carl Bechhofer Roberts, *Let's Begin Again: A Novel* (London, 1940), p. 349.
99 CL3, p. 351.
100 Katherine Mansfield, 'Along the Gray's Inn Road', *New Age*, IX/23 (5 October 1911), p. 551.
101 Wood, unpublished notes.
102 John Middleton Murry, *Between Two Worlds: An Autobiography* (London, 1935), p. 204.
103 Publisher's blurb.
104 Dominic Head, 'Introduction', in *The Cambridge History of the English Short Story*, ed. Dominic Head (Cambridge, 2016), p. 13.
105 Quoted in Tomalin, *Katherine Mansfield*, p. 94.
106 Quoted in F. A. Lea, *The Life of John Middleton Murry* (London, 1959), p. 32.

4 *Rhythm* and the *Blue Review*, 1912–14

1 John Middleton Murry, 'Aims and Ideals', *Rhythm*, I/1 (1911), p. 36.
2 Peter Brooker, 'Harmony, Discord and Difference: *Rhythm* (1911–13), *The Blue Review* (1913) and *The Signature* (1915)', in *The Oxford Critical and Cultural History of Modernist Magazines*, vol. I: *Britain and Ireland, 1880–1955*, ed. Peter Brooker and Andrew Thacker (Oxford, 2009), pp. 334–5.
3 John Middleton Murry, 'Art and Philosophy', *Rhythm*, I/1 (1911), p. 12.
4 C. A. Hankin, ed., *The Letters of John Middleton Murry to Katherine Mansfield* (London, 1983), p. 16.
5 John Wood, unpublished research notes, no page numbers.
6 John Middleton Murry, *Between Two Worlds: An Autobiography* (London, 1935), p. 204.
7 Stephen Gray, *Beatrice Hastings: A Literary Life* (London, 2004), p. 232.
8 Murry, *Between Two Worlds*, p. 190; Wood, unpublished notes.
9 Wood, unpublished notes.
10 CW1, p. 268.
11 Ian A. Gordon, ed., *Katherine Mansfield: Undiscovered Country. The New Zealand Stories* (London, 1974), p. 28.
12 Quoted in Gerri Kimber, *Katherine Mansfield: The Early Years* (Edinburgh, 2016), p. 227.
13 CW1, p. 270.

14 Ibid., pp. 269, 272.
15 Francis Carco, *Montmartre à vingt ans* (Paris, 1938), p. 183. My translation.
16 [Ida Baker], *Katherine Mansfield: The Memories of L. M.* (London, 1971), p. 75.
17 CL1, p. 335.
18 Letter from George Bowden to Antony Alpers, 16 November 1949. ATL, qMS-0263.
19 Affidavit. Divorce Court File: 3888. Appellant: George Charles Bowden. Respondent: Kathleen Bowden. National Archives, https://discovery.nationalarchives.gov.uk.
20 Ibid.
21 Ibid.
22 HRC, Ruth Elvish Mantz collection, 'Swing on the Garsington Gate', miscellaneous box.
23 CW2, pp. 191–2.
24 CP, p. 129.
25 Murry, *Between Two Worlds*, p. 233.
26 Brooker, 'Harmony', p. 316.
27 Murry, *Between Two Worlds*, pp. 235–8.
28 Lady Beatrice Glenavy, *Today We Will Only Gossip* (London, 1964), p. 58.
29 Quoted in Gerri Kimber, '"That Pole Outside Our Door": Floryan Sobieniowski and Katherine Mansfield', in *Katherine Mansfield and Continental Europe: Connections and Influences*, ed. Janka Kascakova and Gerri Kimber (Basingstoke, 2015), pp. 75–6.
30 Jeffrey Meyers, *Katherine Mansfield: A Biography* (London, 1978), p. 339.
31 CP, p. 71.
32 CL3, p. 14.
33 Hankin, *Letters*, p. 24.
34 Gray, *Beatrice Hastings*, p. 253.
35 'Reviews: "The Blue Review"', *New Age*, XIII/9 (26 June 1913), p. 237.
36 Antony Alpers, *The Life of Katherine Mansfield* (London, 1980), p. 160.
37 See Gerri Kimber, '*Juliet* and *Maata*', in *The Bloomsbury Handbook to Katherine Mansfield*, ed. Todd Martin (London, 2020), pp. 37–54.
38 Sydney Janet Kaplan, *Katherine Mansfield and the Origins of Modernist Fiction* (New York, 1991), p. 97.
39 Claire Tomalin, *Katherine Mansfield: A Secret Life* (London, 1987), p. 120.
40 For more details on the relationship between the young Mansfield and the real Maata Mahupuku, see Kimber, *Early Years*.
41 See Kimber, '*Juliet* and *Maata*', p. 48.
42 Ibid.
43 Ibid., pp. 48–9.
44 CW1, p. 345.
45 Ibid., p. 347.
46 Ibid., p. 350.
47 Ibid., p. 351.
48 Ibid., p. 357.
49 Ibid., p. 355.
50 Ibid., p. 356.
51 Ibid., p. 364.

52 Ibid., p. 527.
53 Kaplan, *Modernist Fiction*, p. 99.
54 See Gerri Kimber, 'The Novella: Between the Novel and the Story', in *The Cambridge History of the English Short Story*, ed. Dominic Head (Cambridge, 2016), pp. 538–9.
55 Kaplan, *Modernist Fiction*, p. 89.
56 CLI, p. 202.
57 Carco, *Montmartre*, p. 188. My translation.
58 For a detailed examination of the genesis and development of the Katherine Mansfield legend in France, see Gerri Kimber, *Katherine Mansfield: The View from France* (Oxford, 2008).
59 John Middleton Murry, *Still Life* (London, 1916), p. 10.
60 CLI, p. 72.
61 Quoted in Sean Hignett, *Brett: From Bloomsbury to New Mexico: A Biography* (London, 1984), p. 75.
62 John Carswell, *Lives and Letters: A. R. Orage, Beatrice Hastings, Katherine Mansfield, John Middleton Murry, S. S. Koteliansky: 1906–1957* (New York, 1978), p. 131.
63 Darya Protopopova, 'Virginia Woolf's Versions of Russia', www.dur.ac.uk, accessed 9 September 2011.
64 Galya Diment, *A Russian Jew of Bloomsbury: The Life and Times of Samuel Koteliansky* (Montreal and Kingston, 2013), p. 4.
65 Claire Davison, 'Samuel Solomonovich Koteliansky and British Modernism', *Translation and Literature*, XX/3 (Autumn 2011), p. 336.
66 ATL, MS-Papers-4003-23.
67 Glenavy, *Today*, p. 193.
68 Anton Chekhov, *The Bet and Other Stories*, trans. S. S. Koteliansky and John Middleton Murry (London, 1915).
69 Catherine Carswell, *The Savage Pilgrimage: A Narrative of D. H. Lawrence* (London, 1932), p. 26.
70 Joanna Woods, *Katerina: The Russian World of Katherine Mansfield* (Auckland, 2001), pp. 112–13.
71 CW4, p. 144.
72 Carco, *Montmartre*, p. 189. My translation.
73 CW4, p. 144. My translations.

5 Death and Disillusionment, 1915–17

1 CW4, p. 149.
2 Lady Beatrice Glenavy, *Today We Will Only Gossip* (London, 1964), p. 81.
3 J. Lawrence Mitchell, 'Katie and Chummie: Death in the Family', in *Celebrating Katherine Mansfield: A Centenary Volume of Essays*, ed. Gerri Kimber and Janet Wilson (Basingstoke, 2011), p. 30; John Wood, unpublished research notes, no page numbers.
4 ATL, MS-Papers-2063-01.
5 Wood, unpublished notes.
6 Ibid.
7 CW4, pp. 161–2.

8 Ibid., p. 161.
9 Angela K. Smith, *The Second Battlefield: Women, Modernism and the First World War* (Manchester, 2000), p. 170.
10 CW1, p. 440.
11 Con Coroneos, 'Flies and Violets in Katherine Mansfield', in *Women's Fiction and the Great War*, ed. Suzanne Raitt and Trudi Tate (Oxford, 1997), pp. 197–218 (p. 203).
12 CW1, pp. 447–8.
13 J. Lawrence Mitchell, 'Katherine Mansfield's War', in *Katherine Mansfield and World War One*, ed. Gerri Kimber et al. (Edinburgh, 2014), pp. 30–31; John Middleton Murry, ed., *The Journal of Katherine Mansfield, 1904–1922: Definitive Edition* (London, 1954), p. 107.
14 John Middleton Murry, *Between Two Worlds: An Autobiography* (London, 1935), p. 340.
15 CW4, p. 202.
16 CL3, p. 65.
17 ATL, MS-Papers-4003-05.
18 Claire Tomalin, *Katherine Mansfield: A Secret Life* (London, 1987), p. 226n.
19 Francis Carco, *Montmartre à vingt ans* (Paris, 1938), p. 196. My translation.
20 Wood, unpublished notes.
21 CL3, p. 201.
22 Carco, *Montmartre*, pp. 177–8. My translation.
23 CL3, pp. 33–4.
24 Stephen Gray, *Beatrice Hastings: A Literary Life* (London, 2004), p. 333.
25 CL3, p. 41.
26 Ibid., p. 49.
27 C. A. Hankin, ed., *The Letters of John Middleton Murry to Katherine Mansfield* (London, 1983), p. 48.
28 CL3, p. 49.
29 Wood, unpublished notes.
30 CL3, p. 45.
31 Wood, unpublished notes.
32 CL3, p. 69.
33 CW4, p. 175.
34 See John Wood, 'Katherine Mansfield's Women: "Ninon de Longclothes"', in *Katherine Mansfield's Women*, ed. Aimée Gaston and Gerri Kimber (Edinburgh, 2025), pp. 9–24.
35 CL3, p. 51.
36 Murry, *Between Two Worlds*, p. 178.
37 J. Lawrence Mitchell, 'Katie and Chummie', p. 33.
38 Malcolm Bradbury, 'Modernism and the Magazines', http://malcolmbradbury.com, accessed 24 May 2024.
39 Ibid.
40 Quoted in Mitchell, 'Katie and Chummie', p. 33.
41 CL2, p. 51.
42 Mitchell, 'Katie and Chummie', p. 35.
43 ATL, MS-Papers-7224-05, James E. Hibbert to Mansfield, 13 November 1915.
44 Mitchell, 'Katie and Chummie', p. 36.
45 Murry, *Between Two Worlds*, p. 352.

46 CW1, p. 460; Wood, unpublished notes.
47 CL2, p. 51.
48 Ibid., p. 50.
49 Galya Diment, *A Russian Jew of Bloomsbury: The Life and Times of Samuel Koteliansky* (Montreal and Kingston, 2011), p. 112.
50 CL2, p. 53.
51 Hankin, *Letters*, p. 79.
52 Murry, *Between Two Worlds*, p. 387.
53 Frances Wilson, *Burning Man: The Ascent of D. H. Lawrence* (London, 2021), p. 67.
54 CL3, p. 199.
55 John Middleton Murry, *Katherine Mansfield and Other Literary Portraits* (London, 1949), p. 21.
56 Ruth E. Mantz, *Katherine Mansfield: An Exhibition* (Austin, TX, 1975), p. 5.
57 CL2, p. 165.
58 George J. Zytaruk and James T. Boulton, eds, *The Letters of D. H. Lawrence*, vol. II: *1913–1916* (Cambridge, 1981), p. 569.
59 Quoted in Antony Alpers, *The Life of Katherine Mansfield* (London, 1980), p. 202.
60 CL2, pp. 55–6.
61 Wilson, *Burning Man*, p. 74.
62 Ibid.
63 Ibid.
64 CL2, p. 171.
65 Quoted in Ray Monk, *Bertrand Russell: The Spirit of Solitude* (London, 1996), p. 485.
66 Alpers, *Life*, p. 209.
67 Miranda Seymour, *Ottoline Morrell: Life on a Grand Scale* (London, 1998), p. 365.
68 Leonard Woolf and James Strachey, eds, *Virginia Woolf and Lytton Strachey: Letters* (London, 1956), pp. 60–61.
69 CL3, pp. 127–8.
70 Quoted in Alpers, *Life*, pp. 225–6.
71 CW2, pp. 5–9.
72 Quoted in Alpers, *Life*, p. 227.
73 Grover Smith, ed., *Letters of Aldous Huxley* (London, 1969), p. 118.
74 HRC, Katherine Mansfield Collection, container 2.7.
75 Affidavit. Divorce Court File: 3888. Appellant: George Charles Bowden. Respondent: Kathleen Bowden. National Archives, https://discovery.nationalarchives.gov.uk.
76 Ibid.
77 Ibid.
78 HRC, Katherine Mansfield Collection, container 2.7.
79 John Carswell, *Lives and Letters: A. R. Orage, Beatrice Hastings, Katherine Mansfield, John Middleton Murry, S. S. Koteliansky: 1906–1957* (New York, 1978), p. 133n.
80 Wood, unpublished notes.
81 Tomalin, *Life*, p. 159.
82 Ibid.

83 Wood, unpublished notes.
84 R.H.C. [A. R. Orage,] 'Readers and Writers', *New Age*, XXI/2 (10 May 1917), p. 37.
85 R.H.C. [A. R. Orage], 'Readers and Writers', *New Age*, XXI/3 (17 May 1917), p. 61.
86 See Gerri Kimber, *Katherine Mansfield: The Early Years* (Edinburgh, 2016), pp. 144–5.
87 CW1, p. 233.
88 Wood, unpublished notes.
89 Carswell, *Lives and Letters*, p. 274.
90 Anne Olivier Bell, ed., *The Diary of Virginia Woolf*, vol. V: *1936–1941* (London, 1985), p. 353.
91 Anne Olivier Bell, ed., *The Diary of Virginia Woolf*, vol. I: *1915–1919* (London, 1977), p. 58.
92 Leonard Woolf, *The Autobiography of Leonard Woolf* (London, 1964), p. 204.
93 William Margrie, 'The House Hunters; or, Multum in Parvo', *New Age*, XXI/18 (30 August 1917), p. 389.
94 Wood, unpublished notes.

6 Marriage and Discontentment, 1918–20

1 CW4, p. 241.
2 CL3, pp. 228–9.
3 Frances Wilson, *Burning Man: The Ascent of D. H. Lawrence* (London, 2021), p. 140.
4 CW3, pp. 249–50.
5 Antony Alpers, *The Life of Katherine Mansfield* (London, 1980), p. 274.
6 Anne Olivier Bell, ed., *The Diary of Virginia Woolf*, vol. I: *1915–1919* (London, 1977), p. 125.
7 CW2, p. 146.
8 Ibid., p. 145.
9 Ibid., p. 152.
10 Nigel Nicolson and Joanna Trautmann, eds, *The Letters of Virginia Woolf*, vol. II: *1912–1922* (London, 1976), p. 243.
11 CL3, p. 343.
12 Ruth Mantz, 'K. M. – Fifty Years After', *Adam International Review*, XXXVIII/370–75 (1972–3), p. 119.
13 Bell, *Diary of Virginia Woolf*, vol. I, p. 179.
14 CL2, p. 230.
15 F. A. Lea, *The Life of John Middleton Murry* (London, 1959), p. 65.
16 [Ida Baker], *Katherine Mansfield: The Memories of L. M.* (London, 1971) p. 55.
17 CL2, p. 276.
18 CW2, p. 194.
19 Ibid., p. 196.
20 A. R. Orage, 'Talks with Katherine Mansfield at Fontainebleau', *Century Magazine*, 87 (November 1924), p. 40.
21 CW4, pp. 258–9.

22 CW2, p. 193.
23 John Wood, unpublished research notes, no page numbers.
24 Published in CW2, pp. 168–9.
25 Nicolson and Trautmann, *Letters of Virginia Woolf*, p. 293.
26 CL2, p. 242.
27 Ibid., p. 762.
28 CL4, pp. 155, 182.
29 Ibid., p. 236.
30 John Middleton Murry, ed., *Katherine Mansfield's Letters to John Middleton Murry, 1913–1922* (London, 1951), p. 309.
31 Alpers, *Life*, p. 291.
32 Ibid., p. 296.
33 CL4, p. 282.
34 Murry, *Katherine Mansfield's Letters*, p. 309.
35 Ibid., p. 310.
36 CL4, p. 38.
37 Ibid., p. 72.
38 C. A. Hankin, ed., *The Letters of John Middleton Murry to Katherine Mansfield* (London, 1983), pp. 201–2.
39 CL4, pp. 125–6.
40 Katherine Mansfield, 'A Ship Comes into the Harbour', *Athenaeum*, 4673 (21 November 1919), p. 1227. See CW3, pp. 532–5.
41 Bell, *Diary of Virginia Woolf*, vol. I, p. 314.
42 CL4, p. 155.
43 Hankin, *Letters*, p. 239.
44 CW4, pp. 288–90.
45 CL4, p. 224.
46 Sydney Janet Kaplan, *Katherine Mansfield and the Origins of Modernist Fiction* (New York, 1991), p. 128.
47 CL4, p. 249.
48 James T. Boulton and Andrew Robertson, eds, *The Letters of D. H. Lawrence*, vol. III: *1916–21* (Cambridge, 1985), p. 470.
49 Lea, *Life of Murry*, p. 83 and p. 362n4.
50 Alpers, *Life*, p. 310; Mark Kinkead-Weekes, *D. H. Lawrence: Triumph to Exile, 1912–1922* (Cambridge, 1996), p. 559.
51 A. R. Orage, *New Age*, XXVI/14 (5 February 1920), p. 221.
52 Stephen Gray, *Beatrice Hastings: A Literary Life* (London, 2004), p. 450.
53 CL4, pp. 292–3.
54 Hankin, *Letters*, p. 300.
55 CL2, pp. 618–19.
56 Bell, *Diary of Virginia Woolf*, vol. I, p. 52.
57 Quoted in Alpers, *Life*, p. 317.
58 CW4, p. 315.
59 Ibid.
60 Ibid., pp. 316–17.
61 CL4, p. 335.
62 Ibid., p. 363.
63 Ibid., p. 401.

64 Hankin, *Letters*, p. 317.
65 Gray, *Beatrice Hastings*, p. 456.
66 CL4, p. 344.
67 Ibid., p. 398.
68 Ibid., p. 422.
69 Gray, *Beatrice Hastings*, p. 451.
70 CW4, p. 405.
71 CL4, p. 427.
72 CL2, p. 340.
73 Nicolson and Trautmann, *Letters of Virginia Woolf*, p. 449.
74 CL2, p. 773.
75 CL4, p. 452.

7 Endgame, 1921–3

1 F. A. Lea, *The Life of John Middleton Murry* (London, 1959), p. 83.
2 Antony Alpers, *The Life of Katherine Mansfield* (London, 1980), p. 331.
3 Sydney Janet Kaplan, *Katherine Mansfield and the Origins of Modernist Fiction* (New York, 1991), p. 137.
4 CW2, p. 294.
5 Ibid., pp. 296–7.
6 CL2, pp. 399–400.
7 Alpers, *Life*, p. 325.
8 John Wood, 'The Social Modernism of Orage and the *New Age*', 2007, p. 27, available at https://modmags.dmu.ac.uk, accessed 29 March 2024.
9 John Wood, unpublished research notes, no page numbers.
10 James T. Boulton and Andrew Robertson, eds, *The Letters of D. H. Lawrence*, vol. III: *1916–21* (Cambridge, 1985), pp. 467, 470, 663.
11 CL1, pp. 94–5.
12 Ibid., pp. 100–101.
13 CL1, p. 326.
14 John Middleton Murry, ed., *Katherine Mansfield's Letters to John Middleton Murry, 1913–1922* (London, 1951), p. 625.
15 C. A. Hankin, ed., *The Letters of John Middleton Murry to Katherine Mansfield* (London, 1983), p. 233.
16 Murry, *Katherine Mansfield's Letters*, p. 643.
17 Lea, *Life of Murry*, p. 88.
18 William Atkinson, 'Mrs. Sheridan's Masterstroke: Liminality in Katherine Mansfield's "The Garden-Party"', *English Studies*, LXXXVII/1 (February 2006), pp. 53–61 (p. 54).
19 CW2, p. 409.
20 CL1, p. 580.
21 CW4, p. 399.
22 CL2, p. 606.
23 James Moore, *Gurdjieff and Mansfield* (London, 1980), p. 130.
24 CW4, p. 404.
25 Ruth Mantz, 'K. M. – Fifty Years After', *Adam International Review*, XXXVIII/370–75 (1972–3), p. 104.
26 Murry, *Katherine Mansfield's Letters*, p. 642.

27 ATL, MS-Papers-11326-005.
28 Wood, unpublished notes.
29 Colin Middleton Murry, ed., 'The Journals of J. Middleton Murry: "The Early Years" (1913–1923)', unpublished manuscript, ATL, MS-Papers-11327-001, p. 112.
30 Lea, *Life of Murry*, p. 89.
31 Colin Murry, 'Journals', pp. 114–15.
32 CL4, p. 495.
33 Colin Murry, 'Journals', p. 118.
34 CL4, p. 502.
35 ATL, MS-Papers-7224-06.
36 Mantz, 'Fifty Years After', p. 104.
37 [Ida Baker], *Katherine Mansfield: The Memories of L. M.* (London, 1971), p. 210.
38 Lea, *Life of Murry*, p. 90.
39 Colin Murry, 'Journals', pp. 121–2.
40 See Paul Beekman Taylor, *Gurdjieff and Orage: Brothers in Elysium* (York Beach, ME, 2001), p. 16.
41 Louise Welch, *Orage with Gurdjieff in America* (Boston, MA, 1982), p. 19.
42 Ibid., p. 23.
43 Ibid., p. 24.
44 Ibid., p. 25.
45 Taylor, *Gurdjieff and Orage*, p. 26.
46 A. R. Orage, 'Talks with Katherine Mansfield at Fontainebleau', *Century Magazine*, 109 (November 1994), pp. 36–7.
47 Ibid., p. 38.
48 Quoted in Lea, *Life of Murry*, pp. 90–91.
49 CL4, p. 517.
50 See Moore, *Gurdjieff and Mansfield*, p. 21.
51 James Moore, 'Gurdjieff: The Man and the Literature', *Gurdjieff International Review*, II/1 (Fall 1998), www.gurdjieff.org.
52 CW4, pp. 426–7.
53 Everett F. Bleiler, ed., *The Book of Tea by Kakuzo Okakura* (New York, 2010), p. 22.
54 CW4, p. 434.
55 Olgivanna, 'The Last Days of Katherine Mansfield', *The Bookman*, LXXIII (March 1931), p. 6.
56 James Moore, 'Katherine Mansfield and Gurdjieff's Sacred Dance', in *Katherine Mansfield: In from the Margin*, ed. Roger Robinson (Baton Rouge, LA, 1994), p. 191.
57 Michel de Salzmann and Serge Gautier d'Orier, eds, *Gurdjieff: A Master in Life: Recollections of Tcheslaw Tchekhovitch* (Toronto, 2006), p. 79.
58 P. D. Ouspensky, *In Search of the Miraculous* (London, 1950), pp. 385–6.
59 De Salzmann and d'Orier, *Gurdjieff*, p. 80.
60 Adele Kafian, 'Looking Back to the Last Days of Katherine Mansfield', trans. R. Bernstein, *Adelphi*, XXIII/1 (October–December 1946), p. 37.
61 See Taylor, *Gurdjieff and Orage*, p. 30.
62 CL4, p. 526.
63 Ibid., p. 536.

64 Orage, 'Talks with Katherine Mansfield', p. 37.
65 Quoted in Moore, *Gurdjieff and Mansfield*, p. 139.
66 Ibid., p. 152.
67 CL4, p. 542.
68 Jessmin and Dushka Howarth, *'It's Up to Ourselves': A Mother, a Daughter and Gurdjieff – A Shared Memoir and Family Photo Album* (New York, 2009), pp. 66–7.
69 Private recollection, private collection.
70 Baker, *Memories of L. M.*, p. 229.
71 Ibid., p. 230.
72 Moore, *Gurdjieff and Mansfield*, p. 159.
73 John Middleton Murry, ed., *Journal of Katherine Mansfield* (London, 1927), p. 252.
74 HRC, Dorothy Brett Collection.
75 HRC, Katherine Mansfield Collection, MS-2663, Box 5.
76 De Salzmann and d'Orier, *Gurdjieff*, p. 83.
77 Moore, 'Katherine Mansfield', p. 199.

8 Afterlife

1 With thanks to John Wood.
2 Cited in Paul Beekman Taylor, *Gurdjieff and Orage: Brothers in Elysium* (York Beach, ME, 2001), p. 26.
3 Cited in James Moore, *Gurdjieff and Mansfield* (London, 1980), p. 3.
4 Beatrice Hastings, *The Old 'New Age': Orage and Others* (London, 1936), p. 12.
5 Ian A. Gordon, *Katherine Mansfield*, Writers and Their Work, no. 49 (London, 1954), p. 29.
6 HRC, Katherine Mansfield, MS-2663, Box 5.
7 Roland Merlin, 'Le Drame de Katherine Mansfield', *France-Illustration*, XVI (19 January 1946), pp. 59–62. My translation.
8 HRC, Katherine Mansfield, MS-2663, Box 3.
9 Ibid.
10 Ibid.
11 Ibid.
12 Samuel Butler, *The Way of All Flesh* (Harmondsworth, 1947), p. 352.
13 Elizabeth Bennett, ed., *Idiots in Paris: Diaries of J. G. Bennett and Elizabeth Bennett, 1949* (Daglingworth, 1980), p. 43.
14 F. A. Lea, *The Life of John Middleton Murry* (London, 1959), p. 105.
15 John Wood, unpublished research notes, no page numbers.
16 Ibid.
17 A. R. Orage Memorial Number: *New English Weekly*, VI/5 (15 November 1934).
18 Wood, unpublished notes.
19 Stephen Gray, *Beatrice Hastings: A Literary Life* (London, 2004), p. 540.
20 Wood, unpublished notes.
21 Ibid.
22 Ibid.
23 Ibid.

24 A. R. Orage, 'On Love, Freely Adapted from the Tibetan', *New Republic*, (December 1924), pp. 36–8.
25 E. W. Tedlock Jr, ed., *Frieda Lawrence: The Memoirs and Correspondence* (New York, 1964), pp. 430–31.
26 Claire Tomalin, *Katherine Mansfield: A Secret Life* (London, 1987), pp. 103, 249.
27 Louise Welch, *Orage with Gurdjieff in America* (Boston, MA, 1982), p. 71.
28 Ibid.
29 Catherine Carswell, *The Savage Pilgrimage: A Narrative of D. H. Lawrence* (London, 1932), pp. 207–8.
30 Jenny McDonnell, *Katherine Mansfield and the Modernist Marketplace: At the Mercy of the Public* (Basingstoke, 2010), p. 170.
31 Aldous Huxley, *Point Counter Point* (London, 1928). Denis Burlap is a facetious and hypocritical individual who idolizes (and thinks himself like) St Francis. In his biography of Murry, Lea states, '[Murry] had been more outraged by Burlap than he cared to admit. His first impulse had been to challenge Huxley to a duel.' Lea, *Life of Murry*, p. 159.
32 Katherine Anne Porter, 'The Art of Katherine Mansfield', *Nation*, CXLV (23 October 1937), p. 435.
33 J. C. [D. H. Lawrence], *The Life of J. Middleton Murry* (privately printed, 1929).
34 Ibid.
35 Gray, *Beatrice Hastings*, p. 540.
36 Ibid., p. 541.
37 Ibid.
38 Ibid., p. 650.
39 Ibid.
40 Hastings, *Old 'New Age'*, p. 32.

SELECT BIBLIOGRAPHY

[Baker, Ida], *Katherine Mansfield: The Memories of L.M.* (London, 1971)

Beauchamp, Sir Harold, *Reminiscences and Recollections* (New Plymouth, 1937)

Bell, Anne Olivier, and Nigel Nicolson, eds, *The Diary of Virginia Woolf*, 5 vols (London, 1977–84)

Boulton, James T., et al., eds, *The Letters of D. H. Lawrence*, vols I–VIII (Cambridge, 1979–2001)

Brooker, Peter, and Andrew Thacker, eds, *The Oxford Critical and Cultural History of Modernist Magazines*, vol. I: *Britain and Ireland, 1880–1955* (Oxford, 2009)

Carco, Francis, *Montmartre à vingt ans* (Paris, 1938)

Carswell, John, *Lives and Letters: A. R. Orage, Beatrice Hastings, Katherine Mansfield, John Middleton Murry, S. S. Koteliansky: 1906–1957* (New York, 1978)

Davison, Claire, 'Samuel Solomonovich Koteliansky and British Modernism', *Translation and Literature*, XX/3 (Autumn 2011), pp. 334–47

—, and Gerri Kimber, eds, *The Edinburgh Edition of the Collected Letters of Katherine Mansfield*, vol. I: *Letters to Correspondents A–J* (Edinburgh, 2020)

—, and Gerri Kimber, eds, *The Edinburgh Edition of the Collected Letters of Katherine Mansfield*, vol. II: *Letters to Correspondents K–Z* (Edinburgh, 2022)

—, and Gerri Kimber, eds, *The Edinburgh Edition of the Collected Letters of Katherine Mansfield*, vol. III: *Letters to John Middleton Murry, 1912–1918* (Edinburgh, 2023)

—, and Gerri Kimber, eds, *The Edinburgh Edition of the Collected Letters of Katherine Mansfield*, vol. IV: *Letters to John Middleton Murry, 1918–1923* (Edinburgh, 2025)

Diment, Galya, *A Russian Jew of Bloomsbury: The Life and Times of Samuel Koteliansky* (Montreal and Kingston, 2013)

Glenavy, Lady Beatrice, *Today We Will Only Gossip* (London, 1964)

Gordon, Ian A., *Katherine Mansfield*, Writers and Their Work, no. 49 (London, 1954)

Gray, Stephen, *Beatrice Hastings: A Literary Life* (London, 2004)

Hankin, C. A., ed., *The Letters of John Middleton Murry to Katherine Mansfield* (London, 1983)

Hastings, Beatrice, *The Old 'New Age': Orage and Others* (London, 1936)

Hignett, Sean, *Brett: From Bloomsbury to New Mexico: A Biography* (London, 1984)

Hodgson, Terence, *Colonial Capital: Wellington, 1865–1910* (Auckland, 1990)

Jones, Kathleen, *Katherine Mansfield: The Storyteller* (Edinburgh, 2010)

Kaplan, Sydney Janet, *Katherine Mansfield and the Origins of Modernist Fiction* (New York, 1991)

Kimber, Gerri, *Katherine Mansfield: The View from France* (Oxford, 2008)

—, '"That Pole Outside Our Door": Floryan Sobieniowski and Katherine Mansfield', in *Katherine Mansfield and Continental Europe: Connections and Influences*, ed. Janka Kascakova and Gerri Kimber (Basingstoke, 2015), pp. 59–83

—, *Katherine Mansfield: The Early Years* (Edinburgh, 2016)

—, 'The Novella: Between the Novel and the Story', in *The Cambridge History of the English Short Story*, ed. Dominic Head (Cambridge, 2016), pp. 530–46

—, '"Always Trembling on the Brink of Poetry": Katherine Mansfield, Poet', in *Modernist Women Poets: Generations, Geographies and Genders*, Special Issue of *Humanities*, VIII/4 (2019), www.mdpi.com

—, '"An Intellectual Comradeship": A Reassessment of the Relationship Between George Bowden and Katherine Mansfield', in *Katherine Mansfield: New Directions*, ed. Aimée Gasston, Gerri Kimber and Janet Wilson (London, 2020), pp. 172–88

—, '*Juliet* and *Maata*', in *The Bloomsbury Handbook to Katherine Mansfield*, ed. Todd Martin (London, 2020), pp. 37–54

—, and Vincent O'Sullivan, eds, *The Edinburgh Edition of the Collected Works of Katherine Mansfield*, vols I and II: *The Collected Fiction* (Edinburgh, 2012)

—, and Angela Smith, eds, *The Edinburgh Edition of the Collected Works of Katherine Mansfield*, vol. III: *The Poetry and Critical Writings* (Edinburgh, 2014)

—, and Claire Davison, eds, *The Edinburgh Edition of the Collected Works of Katherine Mansfield*, vol. IV: *The Diaries of Katherine Mansfield, including Miscellaneous Works* (Edinburgh, 2016)

—, and Claire Davison, eds, *The Collected Poems of Katherine Mansfield* (Edinburgh, 2016)

Kinkead-Weekes, Mark, *D. H. Lawrence: Triumph to Exile, 1912–1922* (Cambridge, 1996)

Lea, F. A., *The Life of John Middleton Murry* (London, 1959)

McDonnell, Jenny, *Katherine Mansfield and the Modernist Marketplace: At the Mercy of the Public* (Basingstoke, 2010)

Mairet, Philip, *A. R. Orage: A Memoir* (London, 1936)

Mantz, Ruth, 'K. M. – Fifty Years After', *Adam International Review*, XXXVIII/370–75 (1972–73), pp. 117–27

—, ed., *Katherine Mansfield: An Exhibition* (Austin, TX, 1975)

—, and John Middleton Murry, *The Life of Katherine Mansfield* (London, 1933)

Meyers, Jeffrey, *Katherine Mansfield: A Biography* (London, 1978)

Mitchell, J. Lawrence, 'Katherine Mansfield and the Aesthetic Object', *Journal of New Zealand Literature*, XXII (2004), pp. 31–54

—, 'Katie and Chummie: Death in the Family', in *Celebrating Katherine Mansfield: A Centenary Volume of Essays*, ed. Gerri Kimber and Janet Wilson (Basingstoke, 2011), pp. 28–41

—, 'Katherine Mansfield's War', in *Katherine Mansfield and World War One*, ed. Gerri Kimber et al. (Edinburgh, 2014), pp. 27–41

—, "Not the Kind to Die": Katherine Mansfield and the Unquiet Ghost of "Little Brother"', in *Katherine Mansfield and Virginia Woolf*, ed. Christine Froula, Gerri Kimber and Todd Martin (Edinburgh, 2018), pp. 179–96
Monk, Ray, *Bertrand Russell: The Spirit of Solitude* (London, 1996)
Moore, James, *Gurdjieff and Mansfield* (London, 1980)
—, 'Katherine Mansfield and Gurdjieff's Sacred Dance', in *Katherine Mansfield: In from the Margin*, ed. Roger Robinson (Baton Rouge, LA, 1994), pp. 189–200
Mourant, Chris, *Katherine Mansfield and Periodical Culture* (Edinburgh, 2019)
Murry, John Middleton, *The Journal of Katherine Mansfield* (London, 1927)
—, *Between Two Worlds: An Autobiography* (London, 1935)
—, ed., *Katherine Mansfield's Letters to John Middleton Murry, 1913–1922* (London, 1951)
—, ed., *The Journal of Katherine Mansfield, 1904–1922: Definitive Edition* (London, 1954)
Nicolson, Nigel, and Joanna Trautmann, eds, *The Letters of Virginia Woolf*, 6 vols (London and New York, 1975–80)
Orage, A. R., 'Talks with Katherine Mansfield at Fontainebleau', *Century Magazine*, 87 (November 1924), pp. 36–40
Orton, William, *The Last Romantic* (New York, 1937)
de Salzmann, Michel, and Serge Gautier d'Orier, eds, *Gurdjieff: A Master in Life, Recollections of Tcheslaw Tchekhovitch* (Toronto, 2006)
Saunders, Max, *Self Impression: Life-Writing, Autobiografiction, and the Forms of Modern Literature* (Oxford, 2010)
Selver, Paul, *Orage and the New Age Circle* (London, 1959)
Seymour, Miranda, *Ottoline Morrell: Life on a Grand Scale* (London, 1998)
Smith, Angela, *Katherine Mansfield: A Literary Life* (Basingstoke, 2000)
Smith, Grover, ed., *Letters of Aldous Huxley* (London, 1969)
Taylor, Paul Beekman, *Gurdjieff and Orage: Brothers in Elysium* (York Beach, ME, 2001)
Taylor, Moira, and Charles Woodhouse, 'Katherine Mansfield and Margaret Wishart in London during the Years 1908–09 and Beyond: Intimacy and Separation, Reconciliation and Forgiveness', in *Katherine Mansfield and London*, ed. Aimée Gasston and Gerri Kimber (Edinburgh, 2024), pp. 153–64
Tomalin, Claire, *Katherine Mansfield: A Secret Life* (London, 1987)
Welch, Louise, *Orage with Gurdjieff in America* (Boston, MA, 1982)
Wilson, Frances, *Burning Man: The Ascent of D. H. Lawrence* (London, 2021)
Wishart, Margaret, 'Notes re K. M.', in *Katherine Mansfield and London*, ed. Aimée Gasston and Gerri Kimber (Edinburgh, 2024), pp. 153–64
Wood, John, 'Katherine Mansfield's Women: "Ninon de Longclothes"', in *Katherine Mansfield's Women*, ed. Aimée Gaston and Gerri Kimber (Edinburgh, 2025), pp. 9–24
Woods, Joanna, *Katerina: The Russian World of Katherine Mansfield* (Auckland, 2001)
Woolf, Leonard, *The Autobiography of Leonard Woolf* (London, 1964)
—, and James Strachey, eds, *Virginia Woolf and Lytton Strachey: Letters* (London, 1956)

ACKNOWLEDGEMENTS

First and foremost, my most heartfelt thanks go to John Wood. His generosity in sharing with me his unpublished research on A. R. Orage has been truly humbling. In fact, as the volume was being written he more or less became my unpaid researcher and a number of the important new discoveries in this biography are thanks to his diligence. This book is dedicated to John in honour of his immeasurable kindness.

I am so grateful to Vivian Constantinopoulos at Reaktion Books for commissioning this biography. She and her team have been wonderfully supportive, and my thanks also go to Amy Salter for her editorial management, the Design team, and especially Fran Roberts and Helen McCusker in the Publicity department.

Sincere thanks go to the Society of Authors as both the Literary Representative of the Estate of Katherine Mansfield and the Literary Representative of the Estate of John Middleton Murry, for granting permission to reproduce copyright material, and with special thanks to Sarah Baxter, who was so generous with her time. Thanks also to the following libraries, institutions and individuals for giving permission to use material in their possession: The Alexander Turnbull Library, Wellington, New Zealand and especially Dr Fiona Oliver and Kimberley Stephenson; The Harry Ransom Center, The University of Texas at Austin, USA, and especially Andi Gustavson and Cathy Henderson – research undertaken at the HRC during my Andrew W. Mellon Foundation Research Fellowship in 2014 informed my writing of this book; Roger Lipsey of the Gurdjieff Foundation of New York, for his unwavering support of my endeavours and for obtaining the permissions to reprint the images of George Gurdjieff and A. R. Orage; Edinburgh University Press and especially Dr Jackie Jones for her constant support and friendship; Bernard Bosque for permission to use his image of Mansfield's grave; Gilles Freyssinet for permission to use his image of Francis Carco; Martin Griffiths and Daniel Smith, for checking permissions regarding the image of Garnet Trowell; Miroslawa Kubasiewicz for checking permissions regarding the image of Floryan Sobieniowski; Barbara Sullivan for permission to use the image of S. S. Koteliansky; Jennifer Walker for permission to reprint the image of Elizabeth von Arnim. And thanks also go to Janine Renshaw-Beauchamp, who has been so generous in sharing precious Beauchamp family photos.

Susan and Beverley Price made their home in Wellington my own over a number of research trips to New Zealand; their never-ending kindness, immense generosity and, above all, friendship have come to mean a good deal to me.

Professor Claire Davison, with whom I have co-edited Mansfield's diaries, poems and letters, has influenced this volume with her superb erudition, for which I will always be grateful. Moira Taylor took on the (unpaid) task of being the book's first reader, after John Wood and myself. I am truly grateful to her for her generosity and perspicacity in finding overlooked errors. I have been on numerous physical Mansfield journeys with the delightful Bernard Bosque, his wife Coralie and daughter Ninon – I am so grateful for their friendship.

Ali Smith – aside from being one of the UK's foremost novelists – is a true Mansfield scholar; she never ceases to inspire me.

Finally, I wish to thank my daughter Bella Kimber and husband Ralph Kimber for their never-ending support and encouragement, and especially to Ralph for his compilation of the Index. They have never known a life with me that doesn't also include Katherine Mansfield. Somehow, as a family, we've found a way to make it work!

PHOTO ACKNOWLEDGEMENTS

The author and publishers wish to express their thanks to the sources listed below for illustrative material and/or permission to reproduce it:

Alexander Turnbull Library, Wellington: pp. 7, 18, 23, 26, 28, 31, 32, 33, 36, 103, 124, 139, 149, 168, 179, 180, 195, 217, 221; collection Bernard Bosque: p. 254; collection Gilles Freyssinet: p. 157; The Gurdjieff Foundation of New York, all rights reserved: p. 241; collection Gerri Kimber: p. 155; courtesy Ralph Kimber: pp. 24–5; Library of Congress, Prints and Photographs Division, Washington, DC: p. 229; collection Patty de Llosa, all rights reserved: p. 91; Narodowe Archiwum Cyfrowe, Warsaw: p. 81; private collection: pp. 58, 92, 146; collection Janine Renshaw-Beauchamp: pp. 21, 99; collection Barbara Sullivan: p. 147; The University of Texas at Austin: p. 62 (Harry Ransom Center, Katherine Mansfield Collection); from Jennifer Walker, *Elizabeth of the German Garden: A Literary Journey* (Brighton, 2013), reproduced with kind permission: p. 232.

INDEX

Page numbers in *italics* refer to illustrations